Framework-Based
Software Development in C++

**Prentice Hall Series
on Programming Tools and Methodologies**

P.J. Plauger   *Series Advisor*

Framework-Based Software Development in C++

Gregory F. Rogers

To join a Prentice Hall PTR Internet mailing list, point to
http://www.prenhall.com/register

Prentice Hall PTR
Upper Saddle River, New Jersey 07458
http://www.prenhall.com

Library of Congress Cataloging-in-Publication Data

Rogers, Gregory F.
    Framework-based software development in C++ / Gregory F. Rogers.
        p.   cm. — (Prentice Hall series on programming tools and
methodologies)
    Includes bibliographical references and index.
    ISBN 0-13-533365-2
    1. Computer software—Development. 2. C++ (Computer
program language) I. Title. II. Series.
QA76.76.D47R65 1997   96-39678
005.13'3--dc21   CIP

Editorial/production supervision: *Jane Bonnell*	Acquisitions editor: *Paul W. Becker*
Cover design director: *Jerry Votta*	Editorial assistant: *Maureen Diana*
Cover design: *Rod Hernandez*	Marketing manager: *Dan Rush*
Cover illustration: *James Yang courtesy of*	Manufacturing manager: *Alexis R. Heydt*
The Stock Illustration Source, Volume 4	

The publisher offers discounts on this book when ordered in bulk quantities. For more information, contact Corporate Sales Department, Prentice Hall PTR, One Lake Street, Upper Saddle River, NJ 07458. Phone: 800-382-3419; FAX: 201- 236-7141; E-mail: corpsales@prenhall.com

CORBA and ORB are trademarks and OMG is a registered trademark of Object Management Group. FrameMaker is a registered trademark of Adobe Systems Incorporated. Java is a trademark of Sun Microsystems, Inc. Motif is a registered trademark of Open Software Foundation. O_2 is a trademark of O_2 Technology, Inc. Orbix is a trademark of IONA Technologies Ltd. RiskMetrics is a trademark of JP Morgan. STL<Toolkit> is a trademark of ObjectSpace, Inc. UNIX is a registered trademark in the United States and other countries licensed exclusively through X/Open Company Ltd. Windows is a registered trademark and NT is a trademark of Microsoft Corporation. Other product names mentioned herein are trademarks or registered trademarks of their respective owners.

Printed in the United States of America
10 9 8 7 6 5 4 3 2

ISBN 0-13-533365-2

Prentice-Hall International (UK) Limited, *London*
Prentice-Hall of Australia Pty. Limited, *Sydney*
Prentice-Hall Canada Inc., *Toronto*
Prentice-Hall Hispanoamericana, S.A., *Mexico*
Prentice-Hall of India Private Limited, *New Delhi*
Prentice-Hall of Japan, Inc., *Tokyo*
Simon & Schuster Asia Pte. Ltd., *Singapore*
Editora Prentice-Hall do Brasil, Ltda., *Rio de Janeiro*

Contents

CHAPTER 3

Common Object Request Broker Architecture (CORBA)   *45*

CHAPTER 4

ODMG-93: An Object Database Standard   *87*

PART 2

Methodology

CHAPTER 5

Domain Analysis   *123*

PART 3

Example Frameworks

CHAPTER 10

A Horizontal Framework for Workflow   *281*

CHAPTER 11

A Framework for Monitoring Financial Risk   *325*

APPENDIX A

STL Lint Program   *361*

APPENDIX B

Notation   *371*

Bibliography   *377*

Index   *379*

Preface

This is a handbook for building the next generation of software commodities, called frameworks, on an object infrastructure consisting of CORBA™, ODMG-93 (a standard object database API), and ANSI C++ with STL. The development methodology focuses on domain analysis and a set of design patterns that are well suited to the development of frameworks that must operate in a distributed environment. Before I talk more about the book, I think it is important to give you a little history about the circumstances that compelled me to write it.

I've been a software developer for about fifteen years now, and it's just no fun lately. I'm so tired of having to rebuild proprietary software infrastructure for each new project. I'd rather be spending my time solving more complex problems. Luckily, there are credible standards bodies that have put a tremendous amount of effort into defining a software infrastructure based on the Object paradigm. As this infrastructure matures, it is becoming possible for skilled developers to finally take on more complex problems. Some of us will be able to do so in large development organizations. Many of us, however, will have the opportunity to become entrepreneurs.

I wasn't always optimistic about my future in software development. A few years ago I was almost embarrassed to say that I was an object-oriented designer. It all started when the OO companies began to emerge in the early 1990s. With them came the armies of sales and marketing geniuses promising all kinds of great things about OO technology and C++. Companies everywhere invested in OO/C++ tools, OO/C++ consultants, and OO/C++ training, so that they wouldn't miss out on achieving the tremendous levels of software reuse promised. This would help them "gain the competitive edge," "increase profit margins," and stuff like that. Well, by the mid 1990s none of this had really materialized and corporate America was growing increasingly impatient. It was just about then that I started to hear people condemning C++ for its complexity.

The root cause of all the disappointment was the widely held belief that OO would allow people of all skill levels to approach hard problems from an easier angle. It doesn't. On the contrary, using the paradigm to its full advantage demands that a hard problem be approached from an even harder angle. Many people didn't understand this. Those who did were often not given the time to use the paradigm correctly.

All this nonsense didn't discourage people in standards organizations like ANSI, the OMG®, and the ODMG that used the period of OO-mania to create standards that are so essential to the case for C++ and OO. As a result of their efforts, there is now a tidal wave of object standards approaching. Because of the standards efforts, developers can now buy an industry-standard "object infrastructure" for less than the cost of a good PC, and it's only going to get cheaper. This is really exciting because it makes possible, and even encourages, a new OO-related industry to emerge. This new industry would thrive on a mixture of highly skilled software entrepreneurs that specialize in solving complex problems using OO, and corporate customers who have complex problems to solve, but have not had the resources to solve them. The entrepreneurs would focus on building software that captures reusable abstractions like business models, analytical models, industrial processes, and scientific phenomenon. These software "frameworks" could become commodities designed to work on the object infrastructure.

The challenging development work in the years ahead will be done, in large part, by two types of software developers: those who develop applications using frameworks and those who actually develop the frameworks. The framework users will be average programmers with an in-depth knowledge of specific problems. The framework developers will be extraordinary programmers, with tremendous breadth of domain knowledge and an uncanny ability to generalize a situation. You need to start to decide what you want your role to be in this new order. If you have ambitions to be a framework developer, you need to start to cultivate the appropriate skills. And now I arrive at the reason for writing this book, and the reason you may want to read it. To my knowledge, there is no publicly documented methodology that explains how to develop software frameworks in C++. Reading this book is a good first step toward becoming a framework developer.

Overview of Contents

The book has three parts: Part 1 — *Introduction*, Part 2 — *Methodology,* and Part 3 — *Example Frameworks*. Part 1 starts by giving an overview of the methodology, which I call "Framework-Based Software Development." In order to understand the details of the methodology, it is necessary to have a basic knowledge of the new standards comprising the object infrastructure that the methodology depends on: ANSI C++ with STL, CORBA, and ODMG-93. I, therefore, include a chapter for each of the new standards. I should mention that I am not going to explain any features of the core C++ language; only STL, because it is so new. If you aren't up on some of the newer language features, like `namespace`, for instance, you may have to do some homework. But, wait until you encounter the unfamiliar features before you run out and buy another book. You may be able to understand the feature just by seeing the way I use it.

The infrastructure offers tremendous productivity increases over the proprietary ones we've had to use in the past. As you will see, however, using such an infrastructure to build frameworks requires skills that are more sophisticated than has traditionally been required. Framework developers will also be data modelers, DBAs, analysts, and system architects.

Part 2 of the book presents the actual methodology. The methodology includes:

- Procedures for creating framework requirements
- The framework design standard
- Framework design metrics
- Procedures that show you how to design and implement a conforming framework
- Recommendations for documenting and testing frameworks
- Recommended strategies for managing a software development organization

In Part 3 of the book, I use the methodology to develop two frameworks. I will walk through the analysis, design, and some of the implementation of each of these frameworks and illustrate how they would be used to develop applications.

Acknowledgments

I am grateful to Paul Becker, my publisher, for making this project possible. I would like to thank Frank Gielen, Chak Kolli, John Peterson, Michael Connick, Sal Ricci, David Spuler, John McEnroe, and P. J. Plauger for their comments on the manuscript. Paul Hickey and John Petri from IONA Technologies have been very supportive. Mike Florence and Sophie Gamerman from O2 Technologies were also very helpful.

This book exists because my good friend and former colleague Joe DiBiase convinced me to write it and encouraged me all the way through it. Thanks, Joe.

I need to apologize to my kids—Megan, Lauren, Kierstin, and Glenn—for all the time I missed with them over the past year. And finally, I must thank my wife, Kim, for doing her best to keep the kids occupied as I wrote the manuscript in the corner of my living room.

Greg Rogers
Point Pleasant, New Jersey
grogers@monmouth.com

Framework-Based Software Development in C++

PART 1
Introduction

CHAPTER 1
Overview of Methodology

1.1 What Is a Framework?

Let's ease into the methodology with an informal illustration of what a framework is. You've got to participate, however, by answering the following question. What do an insurance company, a fixed-income derivatives trading operation, a cable-television company, a mail order catalog company, and a mortgage company have in common? Nothing real specific, that's for sure. But, we do know that people in these organizations each have a role to play in a human assembly line, often called a *workflow*.

Take the mail order catalog company, for example. Someone prepares the catalog and then someone else has to distribute it. Before the catalog reaches the customers, someone must make sure that the items in the catalog are stocked and in the computer system. Then, of course, sales people will have to take orders which must be packaged. Someone must then ship the items and someone will take returns.

If you study an insurance company, you will see well-defined workflow for claims processing. In fixed-income derivatives trading, a trader starts the workflow when a deal is struck and then a sequence of people act on that deal, each with a role to play in completing a legal transaction. New cable TV subscribers call their cable company, someone asks for service, which is then scheduled. Eventually a technician installs the necessary hardware, someone activates the service, and billing is notified. Lastly, anyone who has gotten a mortgage knows that a sequence of people must be dealt with before you actually have a closing.

A piece of software should be able to capture workflow behavior in such a way that it is not biased toward any one of these types of businesses. Such a piece of software is called a *framework*. We will actually develop such a framework later in this book.

Now consider just mail order catalog companies. What do they all have in common? They all have workflow requirements similar to those we described a few paragraphs ago. In addition, they all have catalogs, inventory, shipping departments, and phone sales departments. And yet, each will have some unique aspects to the way that they are run. First of all, the products are different. A seed catalog company has a different set of problems than a clothing catalog company. But even two companies with a similar product line will be different simply because of the personal preferences of the owners. Regardless of the differences, it should certainly be possible to define those things that distinguish a mail order operation from any other kind of business. If that is possible, it should also be possible to write a partially completed software application that can be used by any mail order operation. This partially completed application will be more specific than the workflow framework and not so specific that it is biased towards one particular mail order company. A mail order framework is a partial application built on top of a workflow framework. It can be completed to suit the exact specifications of any mail order operation.

Now you sort of know what a framework is: a partially completed software application that is intended to be customized to completion. You also know that some frameworks are more specific than others and, in fact, the more specific ones may depend on the more general ones. A more technical definition follows:

> A *framework* is a class library that captures patterns of interaction between objects. A framework consists of a suite of concrete and abstract classes, explicitly designed to be used together. Applications are developed from a framework by completion of the implementations of the abstract classes.
>
> A framework can also include additional utilities to aid in the completion of end-user applications. A utility can be a code generator or algorithm, for example.

In C++, we generally use the term *abstract class* to refer to any class that can't be instantiated because it has at least one pure virtual function. This is, indeed, one technique for designing an abstract class, but in the context of this methodology, the term *abstract class* is much more liberal, meaning any class that does not have its implementation completely resolved. In Chapter 8 we will discuss the various techniques for implementing abstract classes.

The different types of objects in a framework each play a role in the overall workings of that framework, in much the same way that organs each play a role in the workings of the human body. They interact and depend on each other, which is what distinguishes a framework from a component library.

1.2 What Are the Benefits of Using Frameworks?

We've already said that frameworks are partially completed applications. When someone gives you a framework to start from, your job is to provide only those pieces that are specific to your problem. You no longer have to worry about developing those pieces that are common to similar applications. This application infrastructure comes built into the framework and traditionally has consumed most of the development effort associated with new applications.

Up until now, the primary reuse vehicle associated with C++ has been component libraries. As mentioned in the last section, a framework is different from a component library. Objects instantiated from classes in a component library have little, if any, interaction with each other (e.g., `string`, `date`, `list`). Each class in a component library can be used by itself to add value to an application.

There are advantages to using a framework to build complex applications, as opposed to components. Components are important, but they should not be viewed as the cornerstone of a development paradigm. I'll draw an analogy to illustrate why.

Suppose you are a master carpenter and were asked to build a custom-made, intricately carved piece of furniture. If the only thing you were given to build this with was raw materials (i.e., lumber, hardware, glue, finish) and hand tools, you would have to do a significant amount of up-front work before you could concentrate on the carving and finish of the piece. What you really need to do the job well and quickly is a kit of unfinished parts to start from, that can be customized with a good set of chisels and a finish of your own choosing.

Building a complex application is like building the intricately carved piece of furniture. The skills involved in building such a piece are patience, craftsmanship, and a fair amount of artistic talent. Also, like the person who wanted the piece of furniture customized, users of software tend to want systems that are built exactly to their liking.

The raw materials are like a component library and the hand tools are like a programming language. With hard work the components can be used to build just about anything if integrated in the right combination using a programming language.

Frameworks are like kits of unfinished parts. When developing an application by using a framework, less effort must be expended before you can concentrate on the details of the problem you are solving. Inheritance allows the developer using a framework to customize its behavior, just as the chisels and finish can be used by the carpenter to finish the piece to an exact specification.

Developing an application by first developing a framework, upon which details are to be added, will take longer to implement than simply developing code that solves one specific problem, because separating generalities from specifics is difficult. If, however, it is foreseen that the application will have many new features added after the first release, developing a framework first will make it easier to add these features, because behavior that is common to all features is factored out of application code and put into a framework.

Lastly, frameworks that are domain-specific give developers a jump-start on understanding the problem they are solving, because such frameworks embody the general nature of that problem. In other words, they can be great educational material.

1.3 What Is the Difference Between a Horizontal and Vertical Framework?

There are two broad categories of frameworks: *horizontal* and *vertical*. A horizontal framework is more general than a vertical one and therefore can be used by more types of applications. GUI toolkits are examples of horizontal frameworks. Such frameworks can be used to build the user interfaces for applications in a wide variety of industries. Vertical frameworks are specific to a particular application domain, and therefore will not be as widely used. For example, a framework for performing statistical analysis of economic data is specific to financial applications.

There are actually three variables that can be used to distinguish a vertical framework from a horizontal one:

1. The level of generality
2. The average portion of the framework that is used per application
3. The average portion of code in an application that is built from the framework

The level of generality is a measure of how many applications can potentially use features in a framework. The second variable is a measure of the average utilization of a framework. This could mean the amount of framework code that is used or the amount of its interface that is used. An example of the latter is, 25 percent of the classes in a framework are used in a typical application, and of them usually 50 percent of the member functions are used.

In Figure 1-1, the point furthest from the origin in each graph shows the relative values of these variables for each type of framework. A tension is revealed between each of the variables. The more vertical a framework is, the less general it tends to be, but it is usually better utilized and provides a more complete solution. In contrast, the more horizontal a framework is, the more general it tends to be, but its developer has to be concerned about introducing too much overhead and unwanted features for the average user. In summary, the developer of a horizontal framework has a different set of concerns than the developer of a vertical one.

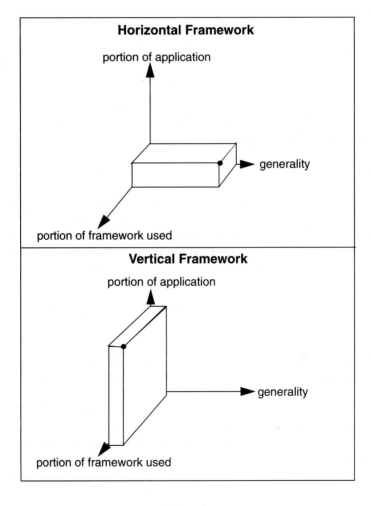

FIGURE 1-1.

The distinction between horizontal and vertical is not black and white. In fact, there is a huge gray area. I suggest that frameworks falling squarely in the middle of this gray area are *not* ones that you want to purchase or develop. These are what I'll call the "all things to all people" frameworks and are generally the ones with the thickest reference manuals. They have trouble becoming successful because they seem to possess the worst qualities of each type of framework, with a dilution of the benefits of each. Mixing and matching a "best in class" set of horizontal and vertical frameworks may provide a better solution for most applications.

1.4 What Is Framework-Based Software Development?

Now that you know a little about what frameworks are and what they can do for you, we'll start to talk about *Framework-Based Software Development*, which is a methodology that relies on interconnected frameworks as the underpinning of applications. This requires a different approach to solving problems. It's not really top-down or bottom-up, it's sort of inside-out. You start by studying your current problem. Then you compare it to other problems and determine those aspects of your problem that are not unique. Those aspects that are not unique are built into frameworks. The frameworks are then tied together and extended for a specific problem.

The key to increases in productivity comes from the by-products of this approach: a growing repository of frameworks. This repository will enable its users to produce new applications faster and of higher quality. By higher quality I mean two things. First, the applications won't break as often because a large part of each has been tested already. Second, framework users get to focus more on the details that please their customers. This gives the customers a higher opinion of their work.

I think we need a hypothetical example to demonstrate how you would approach a problem using this methodology. Let's suppose that you just went out on your own as an independent software contractor and were asked to develop a completely integrated system for a specific car dealership: "Honest Joe's Autos." Joe hasn't been able to find a turnkey system that satisfies him, and he doesn't want you to piecemeal a bunch of off-the-shelf packages together. So you sit down and discuss Joe's operation in great detail, listening to his vision of how things should work. You also visit all of his departments and interview workers about how they do their job. After this, you organize your notes into a more formal requirements specification. You go back to Joe and say, "OK, Joe, is this about what you want?"—knowing full well that Joe will change his mind as time goes on. You get the OK from Joe and then go off on your own, not to start building the application, but to think. By the way, don't ever tell your customer, or boss, that you are thinking because they will never understand why this is necessary. They want to see your fingers immediately pounding the keys or they'll suspect that you're goofing off. So what are you thinking about? You are mentally sucking things out of the specification that are not unique to Joe's situation and writing them down. You do this based on your experiences developing systems prior to this one and conducting independent research.

When you are done, you conclude that the data processing needs of the payroll, accounting, and inventory management departments are not only run the same way in other auto dealerships, but any retail operation for that matter. You, therefore, deem the operation of each of these departments to be worthy of an independent horizontal framework. To tie them all together in a fashion that makes them uniquely "auto dealerish," you conclude that there should be a general auto dealership framework, which is more vertical than the others. You also determine that you need a GUI framework to build the application. The GUI framework is the only one that you can buy off-the-shelf, so you've got to build the rest.

Next, you go off and build the necessary frameworks. The frameworks that are the most general need to be built first, since others depend on them. Finally, you write Joe's application, using the frameworks.

The block diagram shown in Figure 1-2 illustrates how the frameworks and the application "snap" together. After you are done building this application for Joe, you should be one leg up on the competition when you bid on your next contract. Much of your next auto dealership or retail application is already built. Perhaps you decide to market your frameworks and go for high-volume sales instead of the custom jobs!

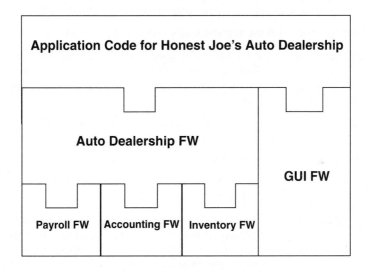

FIGURE 1-2.

In this example, we engaged in the following tasks to develop an application:

Tasks involved in development of an application:

1. Collect application requirements.
2. Specify frameworks by generalizing requirements (called *domain analysis*).
3. Design and implement framework(s).
4. Design and implement application.

Although each of these tasks is started in the order shown, none are fully completed until the application is delivered. In fact, at the peak of development you usually end up doing some of them simultaneously. This example roughly illustrates the approach taken when applying Framework-Based Software Development. The methodology, however, only addresses tasks 2 and 3, as well as management strategies that are not illustrated in the example. Now I'll introduce the pieces of the methodology that enable you to accomplish these tasks. Before I do, however, I want to briefly discuss common software engineering terms that are integral to understanding the methodology.

Several closely related terms are defined below, in the context in which they are used in this book. Because they are so closely related, they are easily confused and often misused. Since they are important to understanding the methodology, I suggest that you study their definitions.

Glossary of terms used to define the methodology:

convention - not required, but generally agreed upon, rules.

design (noun) - includes the precisely specified public interfaces of C++ classes comprising a framework (i.e., public section of class declarations). The design also includes descriptions of the relationships and interactions between these classes.

design pattern - an abstract model or loosely defined procedure that can be applied to a specific design problem (defined in detail in Chapter 6).

design rule - a rigid procedure for solving a design problem.

design standard - a set of design patterns and design rules that must be applied. Also referred to as design guidelines.

idiom - "a speech (C++) form or expression of a given language that is peculiar to itself grammatically or that cannot be understood from the individual meanings of its elements." [DICTIONARY85] An idiom can be specified as part of a design pattern or rule. This term was popularized in the context of C++ by Jim Coplien [COPLIEN92].

implementation - complete C++ class declarations and implementations.

The methodology, which will be formally presented in Part 2 of this book, consists of the following:

The Methodology:

Domain Analysis **(Chapter 5) - the procedure used to identify the need for frameworks and to produce framework requirements specifications.**

Framework Design Standard **(Chapter 6) - contains A) a catalog of *design patterns* that must be used when situations where they are applicable are encountered and B) a catalog of *design rules* that must be followed when situations are encountered where they are applicable.**

Framework Design Metrics **(Chapter 7) - metrics that provide an objective measure of framework quality.**

Framework Development Procedures **(Chapter 8) - procedures that help you conform with the *Framework Design Standard*, supplemented with additional requirements for documenting and testing frameworks.**

Framework Development Strategies **(Chapter 9) - strategies for managing Framework-Based Software Development. This includes how to set up a development organization to most efficiently develop and use frameworks.**

I should also mention that Part 2 of this book can get you a long way towards being ISO 9001 compliant, if you choose to use a framework-based approach to software development. It documents procedures, organizational structure, and roles for engaging in such an approach, which are required for certification.

1.5 What Is the Object Infrastructure?

The methodology is very dependent on a set of emerging standards that, when used together, comprise what I call an *object infrastructure*. In this section, I want to briefly introduce you to each of them. In the chapters that follow, I will cover each in far greater detail.

Until recently, it was very difficult to engage in pure object-oriented software development, because older paradigms drove the commercial software market. Even if you came up with an object-oriented design for an application, when you went to build it you had to resort to cobbling together classes with relational data, socket-level communications, and a vendor-specific component library consisting of a string class and various types of container classes.

Now, however, things are a little less clumsy thanks to three emerging standards:

1. ANSI C++ with the *Standard Template Library* (*STL*).
2. The *Common Object Request Broker Architecture* (*CORBA*) from the *Object Management Group* (*OMG*).
3. *ODMG-93* from the *Object Database Management Group* (*ODMG*).

Growing acceptance of these standards has led to the availability of off-the-shelf products that conform to them. When you use an ANSI-compliant C++ compiler together with a CORBA-compliant Object Request Broker (ORB) and an ODMG-93-compliant object database, you are building applications on a vendor-independent, platform-independent infrastructure designed specifically for object-oriented software development. Although these standards have not reached maturity, when you use them you no longer have to contend with legacy technologies like relational databases and message passing IPCs, which are tedious to deal with and dilute the object-oriented character of an application.

STL includes templatized container classes like vector, set, list, and map, which can be instantiated to contain built-in types as well as user-defined types. Also integral to the library is the notion of iterator classes, which will allow you to navigate through objects kept in a container. There is a string class, of course. There are also many generalized algorithms for doing things like sorting the contents of containers. It is really quite nice, but its greatest benefit is the fact that it is now part of the C++ language. You're guaranteed platform and vendor independence when you use it. We discuss STL in much greater detail in Chapter 2.

CORBA enables you to call a member function of an object, regardless of its physical location, using standard C++ syntax. In other words, the code will look the same whether you are calling a member function of an object in same process space, in a different process space on the same machine, or on a different machine. If the object is on a different machine, it doesn't matter what kind of hardware it is or what operating system it is running. The object could even be implemented in a different programming language! There is no longer a need to have an inter-process communication mechanism that is syntactically different from the intra-process communication mechanism. Wow, what a productivity enhancer. We discuss this more in Chapter 3.

ODMG-93 is an industry-standard API to object databases, developed by the Object Database Management Group (ODMG). When you use this API, your C++ class declarations *are* your database schema. Your code will also be portable to essentially all commercially available object databases. You can forget about the horrors of making your C++ code work with a relational database. We discuss ODMG-93 further in Chapter 4.

All is not perfect with this new object infrastructure. You have more to think about when designing your framework, because distribution and persistence are now an integral part of the design. You have to decide whether a class needs to be a CORBA server, ODMG-93 persistent, a regular C++ class, or some combination of these. Server classes can have persistent parts, use regular classes in their implementations, and can themselves be clients of other server classes. Persistent classes can also employ objects of server classes, but there are restrictions on the types of objects that they can be comprised of. Regular C++ classes can use servers and contain persistent parts. I know that this is a mouthful. Don't worry; this will be discussed at great length as we progress through the book.

As of this writing, it is also a bit complicated to combine these standards because the products that enable us to implement them have evolved from different lineages. Although they are starting to come together, they are not there yet. There are currently overlapping features. For example, each standard defines its own string and list types.

In the following three chapters, we discuss the standards comprising the object infrastructure. If you are already comfortable with the basic concepts of each and are familiar with the associated syntax, skip over these chapters and start reading Part 2 of the book. If you aren't, then read the following three chapters. I pack a lot of information on the infrastructure into these chapters, and they will probably leave you with more questions than answers. You will need to assemble the infrastructure in your own environment and do a lot of prototyping before you really start to understand how to use it.

CHAPTER 2
The Standard Template Library (STL)

A few years ago I went to a conference and attended a talk on designing class libraries. The speaker was fairly well known and drew a large crowd of interested developers. The talk started out to be quite entertaining, as the speaker was used to lecturing in front of large groups of students as a professor. Not too long into the talk, however, he made a statement that instantly brought his credibility into question. Someone in the audience asked him about libraries of general components (i.e., those that have containers, strings, date, etc.). He answered in a fairly arrogant tone: "If I need a component, I just build it myself." The audience was dead silent, until one guy couldn't restrain himself and challenged the wisdom of the statement. The speaker became very indignant and insisted that there was no real benefit to using libraries that consisted of general components, since they never do exactly what you want. I think it was about at that point when I left. As I walked out, I asked myself, "Don't they screen these people before they put them in front of a crowd that paid good money to hear experts?" It was obvious that this person had not developed code in the real world, because anyone who has and has used a component library knows how much time they can save you. Oh, by the way, I haven't heard much about this person since that talk.

To be honest, I don't know what I would do these days without the use of a library of general components. I cringe at the thought of being without a string class and having to go back to battling core dumps (I know, I'm showing my UNIX® roots) because I accidentally copied a big character string into a little array.

2.1 Getting Started with STL

As much as I have grown accustomed to relying on a component class library, I've had to learn a new one every time I move on to a new project. This is a problem. Lack of portability and vendor dependence were also problems with the libraries that I've had to use in the past. But, all that is changing with the new ANSI C++ standard. Now we can all learn a standard API for component classes that are, or will be, provided with the compiler: the Standard Template Library (STL). Once you know STL, on every project you move to, you'll be able to wield it like a weapon against the evils of lengthy, unreadable, and unreliable code.

To get comfortable with STL, you need to understand the design philosophy and be given some good examples, none of which you will find in the ANSI standard itself. In fact, I found trying to learn from the standard itself to be nearly impossible. Don't get me wrong, the formal specification style that they use is essential for understanding very specific behavioral detail but not for learning how to use the library. That's why I wrote this chapter: to supplement, not replace, other sources of information that you can find on STL. I am first going to talk about the design of STL, and then I will present a series of examples. After reading this chapter, I suggest that you go out and buy yourself a good implementation of STL (I use STL<ToolKit>™ from ObjectSpace [OBJECTSPACE95]), read the programmer's guide, and go through the examples provided with it.

The examples that I'm going to present go beyond the simple ones typically provided with a programmer's guide, which are usually intended to show you how to use the syntax of one class at a time. I want to show you some practical examples of how to combine the features of the various component classes to build compact applications. I think you'll find it very satisfying to see 20 lines of code do what used to take hundreds of lines of C.

I assume the reader is already comfortable with the core C++ language and iostreams. STL, however, is new, and the usage idioms are just beginning to emerge. I am not going to discuss STL in a reference-like manner. Instead, I'll use a storybook format to step through typical "micro" design scenarios. This will help demonstrate usage idioms.

One last thought before we move on; I've found that memorizing a little syntax goes a long way toward helping me become proficient in using a component library. You can realize significant productivity gains, even if you only use a subset of the public interfaces, because there are generally a lot of ways to accomplish the same thing. Whenever I have to learn a new library, I study it but once, pick my favorite set of member functions and coding idioms, and then just use them most of the time. After that, only when I want to do something out of the ordinary will I need to pick up the reference manual. This not only makes coding easier, it gives your code a consistent "look and feel" which will be most appreciated by someone who ends up maintaining it.

2.2 The Design of STL

To be a truly effective with STL, you need to understand the underlying design philosophy. I'm not going to talk much about implementation or performance. Performance, in particular, is too subjective for me to be comfortable saying anything about. Most of the applications that I've used with containers have not required blinding speed, and it has never been an issue. What I can tell you is that the designers of STL— Alex Stepanov and Meng Lee— had good performance as a major objective when they designed STL. In the rest of this section, I'm going to talk mostly about the patterns and rules evident in Stepanov and Lee's design. The design patterns and rules are important because some of them are used in the Framework Design Standard (Chapter 6).

One aspect of the library that makes it real easy to learn, relative to others that I've used, is that its designers don't overwhelm you with an enormous number of member functions. One of my biggest complaints about other component libraries is that there are often what I'll call "no-value-added second order" member functions; this means that you can accomplish the same thing with a combination of other functions.

In STL, you'll also notice that similar types of classes have interfaces that look very much alike, even though they share no inheritance relationships. This reflects a changing attitude toward the use of inheritance, which many feel has been overused. The latest philosophy is more one of placing the burden on the designer, instead of the compiler, to provide consistent interfaces when designing a library of classes sharing similar semantics.

Templatized container classes are at the heart of STL. A container is simply an object that contains other objects, built in or user defined. If an object to be stored in a container is user defined, there are certain requirements placed upon it. Very strange compiler errors will be encountered when you try to instantiate a template to contain a type that doesn't meet these requirements. Appendix A presents a tool that you can used to detect such errors in your code before you compile it.

STL has the following container classes: `vector`, `bit_vector`, `deque`, `list`, `multiset`, `set`, `multimap`, and `map`. There is also a `string` class, which looks and behaves like a vector of characters. The class declaration of each container looks similar to the one shown in Listing 2-1. The word "*CNTR*" is just a placeholder for a container class name (e.g., `vector`, `bit_vector`, etc.).

```
        // the following shows common aspects of the class declarations
        // of vector,bit_vector,deque,list,multiset,set,multimap,map,string.

 1   namespace std {
 2       template <class T,..class Allocator = allocator>
        class CTNR {
        public:
 3       // types:
           typedef ..  reference;
           typedef ..  const_reference;
           typedef ..  iterator;
           typedef ..  const_iterator;
           typedef ..  size_type;
           typedef T   value_type;

         // construct/copy/destroy:
 4         CTNR(Allocator& = Allocator());
 5         CTNR(const CTNR<T,.. Allocator>&, Allocator& = Allocator());
 6         ~CTNR();
 7         CTNR & operator=(CTNR<T,.. Allocator>&);

 8       // iterators:
           iterator        begin();
           const_iterator  begin() const;
           iterator        end();
           const_iterator  end() const;

         // capacity:
 9         bool          empty() const;
10         size_type     size() const;
11         size_type     max_size() const;

         // element access:
         // modifiers:
         };

12       template<class T,.. class Allocator>
         bool operator==(const CTNR<T,..Allocator>&,
                         const CTNR<T,..Allocator>&) const;
13       template<class T,.. class Allocator>
         bool operator< (const CTNR<T,..Allocator>&,
                         const CTNR<T,..Allocator>&) const;
     }
```

LISTING 2-1.

Let's briefly go through this "boilerplate" container class declaration. After you understand the common syntax and semantics, you will already know a good percentage of the features of each.

First, notice that each class declaration is in the std namespace[1] **1** . This applies to all classes in the library, so you don't have to worry about STL class names clashing with any older code you may have that uses list or string types, for example. Also notice that each class is a template with at least two type arguments, T and Allocator **2** . T is the type of object kept in the container, and Allocator is a type of object that is used to allocate and deallocate memory for objects of type T. All containers use the allocate and deallocate member functions of the Allocator object passed to their constructors (instead of directly calling new and delete), when they need to get or give back memory for objects that they are responsible for keeping. If you have your own memory allocation mechanism that you want the library to use instead of the standard new and delete operators, you can put it in a class that you derive from allocator (see pg 20-11 of [ANSIC++96]). If you don't, then don't worry about Allocator. It defaults to use the standard new and delete operators.[2]

The allocator design feature shows foresight, because it creates a "hook" for object databases. In fact, I was recently talking to a technical guy from a major object database vendor about it. He told me that his company actually worked closely with Stepanov and Lee to make sure that there was a feature like this. I suspect, based on what he told me, that it won't be long before object databases will come with their own allocator class that you can simply pass to container constructors and voila! the objects you put in the container will automatically be stored persistently for you. Well, as you will see in Chapter 4, it's not quite that easy, but you get the general intent.

As we move down the declaration, you'll notice that there are a bunch of typedefs **3** . Some are used to make class interfaces portable across hardware architectures. Others are to simplify syntax. We discuss each as it becomes relevant.

We can see that container classes are in what Jim Coplien calls "Orthodox Canonical Form,"[3] which means that they were designed to be used like built-in types, except that they don't necessarily have mathematical operations. Orthodox Canonical Form means that the following are provided in a class declaration:

- default constructor **4**

- copy constructor **5**

- destructor **6**

- assignment operator **7**

- equivalence operator **12**

---

1. If you are not familiar with namespaces, refer to [ANSIC++96].

2. At the time of this writing, I did not have access to a compiler that implemented default template arguments. This is a really new feature of the language.

3. See [COPLIEN92], pg 94.

Every container class also has functions that enable you to determine if the container is empty **9**,[4] how many elements are in the container **10**, and the maximum number of elements that you are allowed to put in the container **11**. Notice that `size()` and `max_size()` return a `size_type`, which is a `typedef` defined at the top of the class declaration. This is one of those `typedef`s introduced to make the syntax of application code using STL portable across hardware platforms.

Let's spend a little time talking about a very important concept in STL: *iterators*. For those of you not familiar with the concept, an iterator is an object that has one purpose: to help you access each object kept in a specific container, one at a time. The goal of an STL iterator, in particular, is to help you do so in a manner that is similar to iterating through a C array.

STL has the following types of iterators:

- Forward iterator – to navigate from the beginning of a container to the end of it
- Reverse iterator – to navigate from the end to the beginning
- Bidirectional iterator – to navigate back and forth
- Random access iterator – to navigate back and forth and to jump to any element in the container

I'm only going to discuss the forward iterator, since it is the only one that is common to all container types.[5]

Every container class has a `typedef` called `iterator` and one called `const_iterator` **3**, each representing a forward iterator for that class. An `iterator` will allow you to modify the container and its elements. A `const_iterator` will not allow you to modify the container or its elements. The declaration of a forward iterator object named s that would help you navigate through a `vector` of `string`s and allow you to modify its contents would look like this:

```
vector<string>::iterator s;
```

You don't even have to worry about instantiating `iterator` objects. The containers do it for you. That is the purpose of the `begin` and `end` functions **8**, which return iterators either pointing at the *begin*ning or *end* of the container. You can get an iterator that will allow you to modify the container and its elements (i.e., `iterator`) or one where you cannot modify the container or its elements (i.e., `const_iterator`). The `iterator` and `const_iterator` classes are both forward iterators, because they only allow you to go forward from the first element to the last. So what's the point in having the end

---

4. This seems like one of those "no-value-added second-order" member functions since you can accomplish the same thing by checking to see if the `size() == 0`.

5. See [OBJECTSPACE95] pg 29-36 for tutorial coverage of the other types of iterators.

member function, which returns an `iterator` that points *one past* the last element? That's how we decide when to stop iterating; when the begin `iterator` has morphed itself to be equal to the end `iterator` as a result of the ++ operator being applied to it. Applying the ++ operator to an iterator makes it point at the next element in the container.

The interface design of STL classes gives programmers a nice comfortable feeling when they use it. This is readily apparent with iterators, which were designed to be used with the same coding idioms (i.e., group of C++ statements) used to iterate through C arrays. Consider the following C code fragment:

```
char* str   = "Hello World!";
char* begin = str;
char* end   = str + strlen(str);
while(begin != end)  // start of iteration coding idiom
{
        cout << *begin++;
}
```

This will print "Hello World!", one character at a time. All STL iterator classes have `operator*()` and `operator++()` defined, so you can use a similar syntax. For example:

```
string str = "Hello World!";
string::iterator begin = str.begin();
string::iterator end   = str.end();
while(begin != end)  // start of iteration coding idiom
{
        cout << *begin++;
}
```

This will also print "Hello World!" one character at a time. Remember, a `string` is basically a container of characters, so everything we've said about containers in general applies to a `string` object as well. `str.begin()` returns an `iterator`, which can be viewed as a pointer to the beginning of the string. `str.end()` returns an iterator that is semantically equivalent to a pointer *one past* the end of the string, which in the case of a C string, would be the `NULL` terminator.

Iterators are particularly important in STL, because they are the mechanism that is used by a large number of generic algorithms provided with STL. In fact, the idiom that I just showed you in the above code fragment is at the heart of most of these algorithms. Because the idiom applies to C arrays and STL containers and the algorithms are templates, the algorithms can be applied to both C arrays and STL container classes. For example, the following is the source code for the STL `copy` algorithm.

```
template <class InputIterator, class OutputIterator>
OutputIterator copy(InputIterator first, InputIterator last,
                    OutputIterator result)
{
    while (first != last)
        *result++ = *first++;
    return result;
}
```

As you can see, the only requirement placed upon the template argument types is that they have pointer semantics, which both STL iterators and C array pointers have.[6] The designers of STL have created a set of template functions that perform the algorithms in such a way that they can be applied to any type meeting certain requirements, built in or otherwise. This is what makes them "generic."

Generic algorithms are integral to the philosophy of STL: reuse through delegation, not inheritance. Instead of copying the code from one class to another and modifying it a little to suit each class, you capture algorithms in free functions. This is how you squeeze every last bit of common code into one place to get what I'll call fine-grained reuse.

There is one other design technique that makes STL unique: function objects.[7] A function object is an instance of a template class that has one member function—operator()— so you can use regular function call syntax to get it to do its assigned task for you. For example, a function object class, called less, is declared as follows:

```
template<class T> struct less : binary_function<T,T,bool> {
    bool operator()(const T&, const T&) const;
}
```

The following code fragment instantiates a less function object and then uses it to see if 1 is less than 2:

```
less<int> x;
if(x(1,2) == true)
{
    cout << "1 is less than 2!" << endl;
}
```

Function objects are categorized by the type of signature that their operator() has. STL comes with a number of them, like less, for example. Many of them do some kind

---

6.　There is a danger of specifying illogical arguments to algorithms. For further discussion on these potential errors and how to prevent them, see Appendix A.

7.　Function objects are often referred to as "functors." I believe that the term was introduced by Andrew Koenig. Function objects are covered in section 20.3 of [ANSIC++96].

of comparison between objects and are used for things like ordering objects in a container. STL uses them instead of function pointers when a user-provided function is necessary.

2.3 Using the `string` Class

The ANSI `string` is actually a `typedef` of the ANSI `basic_string` template class, with the parameterized type being `char`. There is also a `typedef` called `wstring` that allows you to have strings of wide characters (`wchar_t`) for international applications. The rules and syntax discussed for `string` in the rest of this section apply to `wstring` also. Remember they are both just different instances of the same template class, `basic_string`, and they behave like other STL containers.

One of the benefits of using `string` instead of `char[]` is that you avoid having to worry about memory management (i.e., carefully picking the maximum size of the string in advance). It also allows you to work with sequences of characters, using a syntax that is more consistent with that of a built-in type (i.e., `strcmp` is replaced by `==` and `strcpy` by `=`). Since this is not intended to be an STL reference manual, I'm not going to go through all of the syntax associated with `string` usage. What I am going to discuss, however, are the most commonly used features (i.e., those that will address your situation, let's say, 75 percent of the time).

As I hinted at before, the beauty of `string` is that you have enhanced behavior but can still treat the `string` like a built-in type. Well, almost. For example, with a built-in `const char*` you can do this:

```
const char* s = "hello world";
cout << s << endl;
```

With a `string` you can sort of do the same thing:

```
string s = "hello world";
cout << s.c_str() << endl;
```

The `string(const char*)` constructor is invoked on the first line. On the second line, the `string::c_str()` function returns a `const char*` pointing to "hello world", which is inserted onto the `cout` stream. When I first used `string`, I was a little bit surprised that I had to explicitly call a member function to get a character pointer. From using other libraries, I was used to automatically having the promotion done for me by an `operator const char*()` member provided with `string` classes. But, when I thought about it a little, I realized that the ANSI committee was probably trying to prevent mistakes by requiring an explicit function call. I asked Andrew Koenig via email, and he confirmed that this was, in fact, the reason.

In many applications you want to do things like append to a character string, compare one with another, and copy from one to another. Here's an example of where using `string` becomes easier than using `char[]` because overloaded operators allow you to use a more intuitive syntax. In the olden days if you wanted to safely build up a string and compare it with a string literal you would have to do the following:

```
char s[50];        // hardcoded size is always a dangerous policy.
s[0] = '\0';       // automatics are uninitialized.
strncat(s,"first Part ",50);
int len = strlen(s);
strncat(s,"second Part",50-len);
if(strcmp(s,"first Part second Part") == 0)
{
    cout << "They match" << endl;
}
```

With the `string` class, you can do the equivalent as follows:

```
string s;
s += "first Part ";
s += "second Part";
if(s == "first Part second Part")
{
    cout << "They match" << endl;
}
```

This is much more readable. Operator overloading makes `string` look like a built-in type.

Now I'll demonstrate some additional features of `string` that make it very powerful. Suppose you were asked to write an application that filled in a form letter, consisting of the ASCII text shown in Box A of Figure 2-1, to look like Box B. The variables to be filled in are shown in capital letters (DATE, ADDRESS, RECEIVER, PRODUCT, PRICE, DAYS, SENDER, TITLE). The code shown in Listing 2-2 would do this for you. First, the contents of the form letter file are read into a `string` **4**. Then, a sequence of calls is made to the `replace` function **1**, which is where all the magic occurs. `string::find()` **2** locates the variable, and `string::replace()` **3** replaces it with the character sequence to be substituted. The code is not as bulletproof as it could be, and obviously quite specific, but it is functionally correct. I'll leave it as an exercise for you to figure out how to generalize it, which should be fairly simple for you to do after reading this chapter.

There are a couple significant points to be made about this example. First, all of the code shown in this example is ANSI C++, which means it is portable to any platform that has an ANSI C++ compiler. Second, think about what you would have to do to write this entirely in C. After doing so, it should start to become apparent how powerful C++ has become with the addition of the STL `string` class.

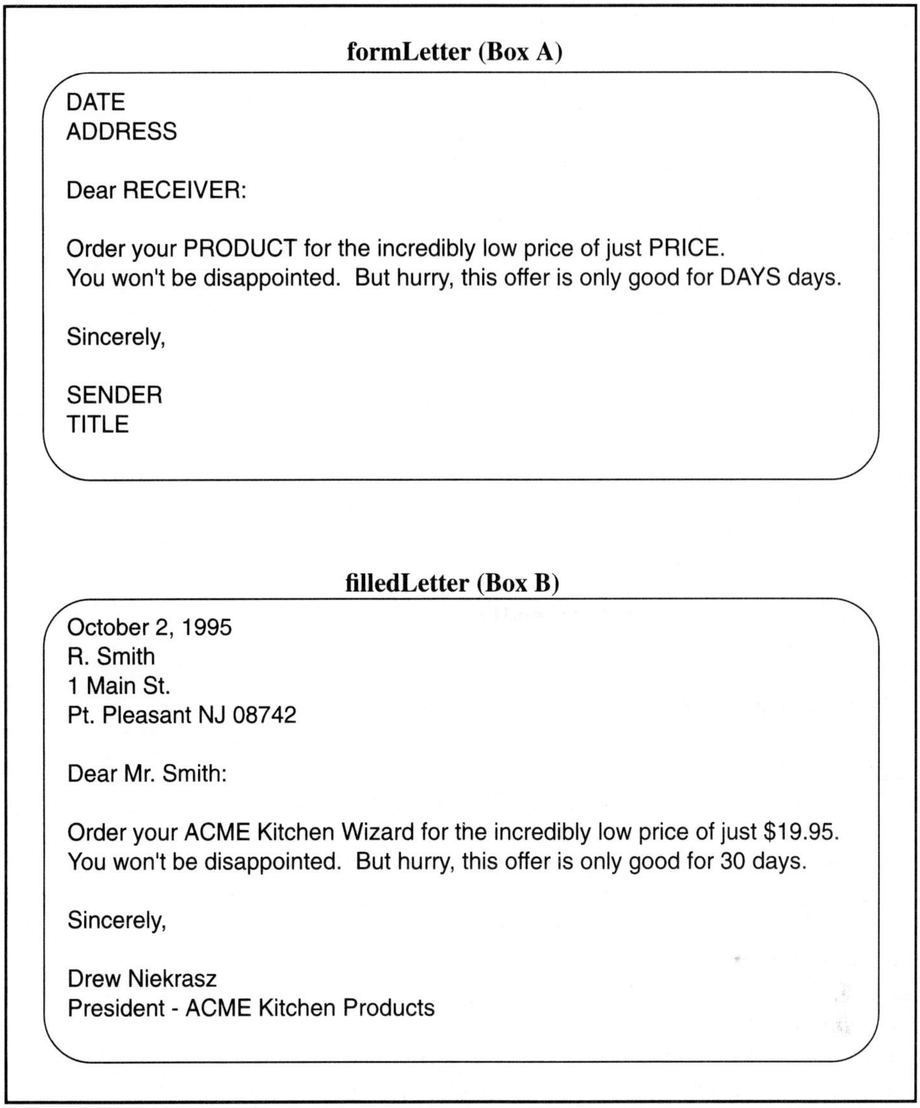

formLetter (Box A)

```
DATE
ADDRESS

Dear RECEIVER:

Order your PRODUCT for the incredibly low price of just PRICE.
You won't be disappointed.  But hurry, this offer is only good for DAYS days.

Sincerely,

SENDER
TITLE
```

filledLetter (Box B)

```
October 2, 1995
R. Smith
1 Main St.
Pt. Pleasant NJ 08742

Dear Mr. Smith:

Order your ACME Kitchen Wizard for the incredibly low price of just $19.95.
You won't be disappointed.  But hurry, this offer is only good for 30 days.

Sincerely,

Drew Niekrasz
President - ACME Kitchen Products
```

FIGURE 2-1.

```
    #include <fstream.h>
    #include <ostring.h>

    void
①  replace(string& s, const char* before, const char* after)
    {
        int i;
②      if((i = s.find(before)) != npos)
        {
③          s.replace(i,strlen(before),after);
        }
    }

    main()
    {
        ifstream in("formLetter");
        const int bufLen = 256;
        char buf[bufLen];
        strings;

④      while(in.getline(buf,bufLen))
        {
            s += buf;
            s += '\n';
        }
        replace(s,"DATE","October 2, 1995");
        replace(s,"ADDRESS",
                "R. Smith\n1 Main St.\nPt. Pleasant NJ 08742");
        replace(s,"RECEIVER","Mr. Smith");
        replace(s,"PRODUCT","ACME Kitchen Wizard");
        replace(s,"PRICE","$19.95");
        replace(s,"DAYS","30");
        replace(s,"SENDER","Drew Niekrasz");
        replace(s,"TITLE","President - ACME Kitchen Products");
        ofstream out("filledLetter");
        out << s.c_str();
    }
```

LISTING 2-2.

2.4 Using STL Container Classes

2.4.1 Example 1

Now let's discuss how to use some of the STL container classes, starting with a simple example. Suppose that you worked for a brokerage house and were asked to write an application that:

1. Takes an ASCII file containing today's stock trades[8] and converts them into objects of a class called `StockTrade`. The header file for `StockTrade` is shown in Listing 2-3.
2. Prints the trades in alphabetical order by company name.
3. Prints the net dollar amount of today's trades.

Assume that today's trades are in a file called `todaysTrades`, the contents of which are shown below:

```
AT&T            ATT    Buy    1000   61
MacDonalds      MCD    Buy    5000   53.50
IBM             IBM    Sell   2500   82.25
Intel           INTC   Sell   1200   90
```

The first thing you need to consider in approaching this problem is where you are going to store all these new `StockTrade` objects. The answer, of course, is in some kind of container. It's easy to get a little confused at this point, because STL gives you so many different types to choose from. Whenever you're faced with this situation, first ask yourself, "When I put these objects in the container, do they need to be in a particular order?" In this case the answer is definitely yes: by company name. Most problems requiring simple ordering can be solved with the `vector` or `list` class. So let's focus on these as the two most likely alternatives for this application.

If you know the order in advance, you can use a `vector`, which is very similar to using a C array. The difference is that a `vector` can vary in size, and the memory management is not a concern of the programmer.[9] If you don't know order in advance, which is the case for this problem, the `list` class is probably sufficient. It is distinguished from a `vector` by the fact that items can be inserted anywhere in the container, and there are some fancy member functions for doing things like sorting elements.

---

8. The trades could just as easily have been retrieved by using an SQL query, and in fact, this is likely how it would be done in brokerage houses today, since most are still using relational databases to store their stock transactions.

9. You might also want to consider a `deque`, which is a suped-up version of a vector.

```
#ifndef STOCKTRADE_H
#define STOCKTRADE_H
#include <string>
#include <strstream.h>
#include <iomanip.h>
const int bufLen = 81;
class StockTrade {
  public:

    StockTrade(string companyName, string stockSymbol,
         string buyOrSell, unsigned shares, double pricePerShare);
    const char* c_str() const;
    operator double() const;
    bool  operator<(const StockTrade&) const;
  private:
    string     companyName;
    string     stockSymbol;
    string     buyOrSell;
    unsigned   shares;
    double     pricePerShare;
    char       buf[bufLen];
};

StockTrade::StockTrade(string c, string s, string b,
    unsigned shrs, double p): companyName(c), stockSymbol(s),
    buyOrSell(b), shares(shrs), pricePerShare(p)
{
    ostrstream ostrm(buf,bufLen);
    ostrm << setw(20) << companyName << "\t" <<
    stockSymbol << "\t" << buyOrSell <<
    "\t" << shares << "\t" << pricePerShare << ends;
}

inline const char* StockTrade::c_str() const {return buf;}

inline StockTrade::operator double() const
{
    double sign;
    (buyOrSell == "Buy")?(sign = 1):(sign = -1);
    return sign*shares*pricePerShare;
}

inline bool StockTrade::operator<(const StockTrade& other) const
{ return (companyName < other.companyName); }
#endif // STOCKTRADE_H
```

LISTING 2-3.

Unlike a `vector`, the convenient indexing (i.e., `[]`) syntax cannot be used to iterate through elements in a `list`. This means there must be some other way to iterate through a `list`, and, in fact, there are many. In our case, we know that after the elements have been sorted internally, we will want to iterate from the beginning to the end to print the trades in alphabetical order, so we could use the `iterator` class, which was designed to be used exclusively for forward iteration. This same type of `iterator` can be used to tally the day's trades, since it is irrelevant how we iterate through all the trades as long as we don't miss any. You have to call `list::begin()` to get an `iterator` pointing to the first element in the `list`.

Listing 2-4 shows the application. First, the file containing the trades is opened and attached to a file stream **3** . Then, each line is extracted from the stream and parsed into local variables **4** . The local variables are then used to instantiate a `StockTrade` object **5** , which is put on the end of the `list` by `list<>::push_back()` **6** . After all the trades have been converted to objects and put on the `list`, they are sorted alphabetically by company name. The `list<>::sort()` function does this **7** , using the < operator, so `StockTrade` was required to provide:

```
bool StockTrade::operator<(const StockTrade&) const.
```

Next, I take advantage of STL's `for_each` algorithm **8** , which simply calls the function whose pointer is passed in the third argument, for each object in the range specified by the first two arguments. As you can see, I pass the pointer to a function **1** that prints a representation of each `StockTrade` object using `StockTrade::c_str()` **2** . This could have been any function with the signature `void function(T)`, where `T` is the type of object in the container or C array, being iterated through. Finally, I use STL's `accumulate` algorithm **9** to tally the dollar amount of the day's trades. All it does is apply the + operator to add up the values associated with each object. In this case, the compiler automatically promotes each object to a `double` by using `StockTrade::operator double()`, which is the dollar amount of each trade.

The following is the output of this program:

```
            AT&T       ATT     Buy     1000     61
             IBM       IBM     Sell    2500     82.25
           Intel       INTL    Sell    1200     90
      MacDonalds       MCDN    Buy     5000     53.5
Net: 14875
```

```
    #include <list.h>
    #include <algo.h>
    #include "StockTrade.H"

①  void print(StockTrade t)
    {
②      cout << t.c_str() << endl;
    }

    main()
    {
        list<StockTrade> todaysTrades;
③      ifstream f("todaysTrades");
        while(1)
        {
            string    companyName;
            string    stockSymbol;
            string    buyOrSell;
            unsigned shares;
            double    pricePerShare;

            // Assumes that each line has all five fields.
④          if(f>> companyName>> stockSymbol>> buyOrSell>>
                shares>> pricePerShare)
            {
⑤              StockTrade t(companyName,stockSymbol,
                            buyOrSell,shares,pricePerShare);
⑥              todaysTrades.push_back(t);
            }
            else
            {
                break;   // EOF
            }
        }
⑦      todaysTrades.sort();
⑧      for_each(todaysTrades.begin(),todaysTrades.end(),print);
        cout << "\nNet: " <<
⑨      accumulate(todaysTrades.begin(),todaysTrades.end(),0) << endl;
    }
```

LISTING 2-4.

There's something a little fishy about the design of the StockTrade class: the < operator. Is it a good idea to build semantics into StockTrade that forever say that the order of the elements is based on the alphabetical order of the company names? What if someone came along tomorrow and asked for an application similar to this one, but the objects were to be printed in order of decreasing dollar amount of the trade? We can't go back and rewrite the < operator. STL accommodates us with a suite of algorithm functions, one of which is sort, which will order the elements, using a function of our choosing. So StockTrade::operator<() should simply be viewed as the default ordering relationship.

We will talk a lot more about algorithms later. I just wanted to mention the sort function here so you were not left with a nagging question about why it was okay to tightly couple the design of what should be a generic StockTrade class with this one little application. If it wasn't nagging you, it should be. You have to internalize what is good design and what may not be.

2.4.2 Example 2

Let's move on to another example that uses more than one type of container. I will base the next example on a problem with the previous one: the whole approach to parsing ASCII text. In the previous example, the parsing logic is hardcoded and far too fragile. If just one token is missing in one line of the file, everything else will get screwed up. Let's try to use containers to develop a more general parsing mechanism.

A task that is pervasive in applications these days is converting ASCII files into data that can be stored in a database or operated on by C++ code. The reason is simple: there are all kinds of data feeds, database dumps, generated reports, and spreadsheet dumps that are spit out by one application that must be used by another. It's a fact of life that there is no standard way that all different types of applications can communicate data. This is particularly ugly up on Wall Street, where many generations of systems have to talk to each other. The newer ones accept whatever junk the older ones produce and turn it into something they can use. The StockTrade example dealt with such a conversion. We could simplify a lot of people's lives by creating a helper class that parses an ASCII file and creates a set of attribute-value pairs based on a specification. STL containers are quite useful for simplifying this task. This is also a rich example of how you can use containers and iterators together with the string class and iostreams. It utilizes many of the functions that you'll often need. Again, I encourage you to imagine how you would have to do this without these components, to gain an appreciation for how powerful they are.

We will start by considering the various ways that values can be embedded in the text. The simplest case is the one we gave for the StockTrade class: for each line, all values are always present and appear in the same order.

Another common format is where some values may be absent, but the ones that are present will always start at a given column. For example:

```
Resort          Rooms   Tennis   Sailing   Golf
Ocean Breeze    125     X        X
Paradise Cove   500     X        X         X
Joe's Hotel     35               X
```

Another way that data can be received is already formatted as attribute-value pairs. In this case, we must know what delimiter separates the attribute from the value, and one pair from another. For example:

```
COMPANY = AT&T, SYMBOL = ATT, ORDER = Buy, SHARES = 1000, PRICE = 61
```

Let's design something that can pull data values out of an ASCII text file in any combination of the formats shown. Ultimately, we want to capture all the attribute-value pairs that are extracted from all lines in a given file. This can be represented by: `vector<map<string,string>>`, where each element of the `vector` is an STL map (i.e., associative array) containing the attribute-value pairs for one line of a file. Containers of containers can be a little tricky to visualize, so consider what this would look like for the `Resort` file I just showed you:

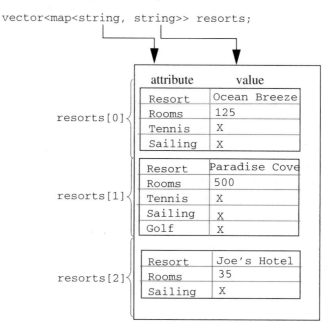

A class called `ValueExtractor`, shown in Listing 2-5.a and 2-5b,[10] will parse an ASCII file according to a specification and put the results in a `vector` of maps.

Let's walk through the declaration of the `ValueExtractor` class (shown in Listing 2-5.a.). To make it a little simpler to use, a couple of `typedefs` are defined: `AVmap` ❶ and `AVvector` ❷ . `AVmap` stands for "Attribute-Value" map and `AVvector` stands for "Attribute-Value" vector. An `AVmap` will hold all the attribute-value pairs for one line in a data file. An `AVvector` will contain all `AVmaps`.

When a `ValueExtractor` object is instantiated, it will pull values from an ASCII file in accordance with the `ValueExtractor::Spec` ❸ object passed to its constructor ⓬ . Let's go through the declaration of `ValueExtractor::Spec`. First there is the `tokenValues` map ❺ , which is used to accommodate the format used in the `StockTrade` example. If you recall, in that example a line in a data file looked like this:

```
AT&T      ATT      Buy      1000      61
```

This format is based on token order and can be specified something like this:

```
ValueExtractor::Spec s;
s.tokenValues["CompanyName"]    = 0;
s.tokenValues["CompanySymbol"]  = 1;
s.tokenValues["Order"]          = 2;
s.tokenValues["Shares"]         = 3;
s.tokenValues["Price"]          = 4;
```

This attribute is assigned this token number.

The `columnValues` map ❻ is used to accommodate a format like that shown in the resorts example. It is similar in concept to `tokenValues`, only now you associate a column number with an attribute name, so the resorts file format could be specified as follows:

```
ValueExtractor::Spec s;
s.columnValues["ResortName"]  = 0;
s.columnValues["Rooms"]       = 16;
s.columnValues["Tennis"]      = 23;
s.columnValues["Sailing"]     = 31;
s.columnValues["Golf"]        = 40;
```

This attribute starts at this column number.

---

10. I deviated from my normal coding style to fit code on one page. My apologies if it is hard on your eyes. I normally put { and } on lines by themselves. Also, I usually never put constructors in a header file.

The next three elements ❼ ❽ ❾ are used to specify data that is already in an attribute-value pair format in the text file. The `attributes` vector ❼ should be populated with the names of all attributes whose values should be extracted if encountered. `delimiter1` ❽ should be set to the character sequence that separates an attribute name from its value. `delimiter2` ❾ should be set to the character sequence that separates the pairs themselves.

The last element of `Spec` is `inputFile` ❿, which is the name of the data file from which values are to be extracted. If it is not set to the name of a readable file, `ValueExtractor` will throw a `BadDataFile` ⓫ exception when it is instantiated. I designed `ValueExtractor` to pull out data from one file (`inputFile`) when it is instantiated (i.e., ⓬ is called). The only thing you can do with a `ValueExtractor` object after you construct it is get a reference to the data values it extracted from the `inputFile`. You use the `ValueExtractor::operator()()` ⓭ to get the values.

The extraction process is captured in the `ValueExtractor` constructor ⓬, which is defined in Listing 2-5.b. The constructor first attempts to attach to an `ifstream` ⓮. If it can't, a `BadDataFile` exception is thrown. If the file attaches successfully, a `while` loop is entered where the values are pulled out of the file one line per loop iteration ⓯.

Here's how the values are extracted from a line. First, each token specified in `spec.tokenValues` is retrieved ⓱. Each token is retrieved by first creating an `istrstream` out of the current line ⓲. Repeated extractions then occur until the desired token is extracted ⓴. This token then becomes the value of an attribute-value pair which is added ㉑ to a temporary `AVmap` ⓰ for the current line. Notice that as you iterate through a `map`, you get a `pair` returned when you dereference an `iterator` ⓳, as opposed to one value. `pair::first` contains the key and `pair::second` contains the value (i.e., `map[key] = value`) of the current `map` element.

Next, each value starting at column specified in `spec.columnValues` is retrieved ㉒. The value is assumed to consist of all characters from that column up to whitespace or the end of the line ㉓. As you can see, this requires a character by character extraction. After extracting all characters comprising the value, an attribute-value pair is added ㉔ to the temporary `AVmap` ⓰.

The last thing we look for on each line is the data that is already formatted as attribute-value pairs ㉕, as specified in `spec.attributes`, `spec.delimiter1`, and `spec.delimiter2` ❼ ❽ ❾. Here we take advantage of some of the slicker `string` features. For each attribute name in the attributes `vector`, we use `string::find()` to locate its index into the line ㉖. Then we find the index of the delimiter, separating the attribute name from its value ㉗ (i.e., `delimiter1`), and the index of the delimiter designating the end of the value ㉘ (i.e., `delimiter2`). The value is the `substring` of the line located between these two indexes ㉙.

```
// ValueExtractor.H
#ifndef VALUEEXTRACTOR_H
#define VALUEEXTRACTOR_H

#include <functional>
#include <map>
#include <string>
#include <vector>

class ValueExtractor {
  public:

①    typedef map<string,string,less<string> > AVmap;
②    typedef vector<AVmap> AVvector;

③    struct Spec {
④      Spec();
⑤      map<string,unsigned,less<string> > tokenValues;
⑥      map<string,unsigned,less<string> > columnValues;
⑦      vector<string> attributes;
⑧      string delimiter1;      // separates attribute from value.
⑨      string delimiter2;      // separates pairs.
⑩      string inputFile;
    };

⑪    class BadDataFile {};     // exception class

⑫    ValueExtractor(const Spec&);
⑬    const AVvector& operator()();

  private:
    AVvector attrValues;
};

ValueExtractor::Spec::Spec() : delimiter1(""), delimiter2("") {}

inline
const AVvector& ValueExtractor::operator()() {return attrValues;}

#endif  // VALUEEXTRACTOR_H
```

LISTING 2-5.a.

```
     // ValueExtractor.C
     #include "ValueExtractor.H"
     #include <iostream.h>
     #include <fstream.h>
     ValueExtractor::ValueExtractor(const Spec& spec)
     {
(14)     ifstream ifstrm(spec.inputFile.c_str());
         if(!ifstrm) { throw BadDataFile(); }
         const int bufSize = 1024;
         char buf[bufSize];
(15)     while(ifstrm.getline(buf,bufSize))
         {
(16)         AVmap avmap;
             map<string,unsigned, less<string> >::const_iterator i;
(17)         for(i=spec.tokenValues.begin();i!=spec.tokenValues.end(); i++)
             {
(18)             istrstream isstrm(buf);
(19)             const pair<const string,unsigned> p = *i;
                 char tmp[bufSize];
(20)             for(int y = 0; y <= p.second; y++) { isstrm >> tmp; }
                 string value(tmp);
(21)             if(value.size() > 0) { avmap[p.first] = value; }
             }
(22)         for(i = spec.columnValues.begin();
                 i!= spec.columnValues.end(); i++)
             {
                 string line(buf);
                 string value;
                 const pair<const string,unsigned> p = *i;
(23)             for(int y = p.second; y <= line.size(); y++)
                 {
                     if(line[y] == ' ' || line[y] == '\t' ||
                         line[y] == '\n'|| line[y] == '\0') { break;}
                     else { value += line[y]; }
                 }
(24)             if(value.size() > 0) { avmap[p.first] = value; }
             }
(25)         for(int j= 0; j < spec.attributes.size(); j++)
             {
                 string line(buf);
                 int index;
(26)             if((index = line.find(spec.attributes[j])) != npos)
                 {
(27)                 if((index = line.find(spec.delimiter1,index)) != npos)
                     {
                         index++;
(28)                     int index1 = line.find(spec.delimiter2,index);
(29)                     avmap[spec.attributes[j]] =
                                     line.substr(index,index1-index);
                     }
                 }
             }
(30)     if(avmap.size() > 0) { attrValues.push_back(avmap); }
         }
     }
```

LISTING 2-5.b.

The last thing we do for every line in the file is add the temporary map (i.e., `avmap`) that we just populated, to `ValueExtractor::attrValues` which is the official repository of all data extracted from the file **30** .

Now, suppose that you want to use the `ValueExtractor` class to parse a file called `stock.data` that has the following contents:

blank line
```
GPU   31.0   X   11/8/95   Description:General Public Utilities Corp.
ABC   50     X   11/7/95   Description:American Broadcasting Company.
CBS   35     X   11/8/95   Description:Central Broadcasting Company.
IBM   92     X   11/8/95   Description:International Business Machines.
```

You could use the little program shown in Listing 2-6 to do the parsing. The output of the program looks like this:

```
Date=11/8/95
Description=General Public Utilities Corp
Price=31.0
Symbol=GPU
----------------------------------

Date=11/7/95
Description=American Broadcasting Company
Price=50
Symbol=ABC
----------------------------------

Date=11/8/95
Description=Central Broadcasting Company
Price=35
Symbol=CBS
----------------------------------

Date=11/8/95
Description=International Business Machines
Price=92
Symbol=IBM
----------------------------------
```

```
#include "ValueExtractor.H"
#include <iostream.h>

main()
{
    ValueExtractor::Spec s;
    s.tokenValues["Price"]   = 1;
    s.tokenValues["Date"]    = 3;
    s.columnValues["Symbol"] = 0;
    s.delimiter1 = ":";
    s.delimiter2 = ".";
    s.attributes.push_back("Description");
    s.inputFile = "stock.data";

    try
    {
        ValueExtractor e(s);
        AVvector v = e();
        vector<AVmap>::const_iterator ix = v.begin();
        while(ix != v.end())
        {
          AVmap m = *ix++;
          map<string,string,less<string> >::const_iterator iy
                 = m.begin();
          while(iy != m.end())
          {
              const pair<const string,string> p = *iy++;
              cout << p.first << "=" << p.second << endl;
          }
           cout << "----------------------------------" << endl;
        }
    }
    catch(ValueExtractor::BadDataFile)
    {
        cerr << "Bad Data File" << endl;
    }
}
```

LISTING 2-6.

2.5 Adding Your Own Generic Algorithms

We have already discussed the notion of generic algorithms and how they fit into the overall design of STL. There are a bunch of these algorithms provided with STL. We saw a couple of them being used in the `StockTrade` example: `for_each` and `sort`.

You can, and should, add your own generic algorithms. It could be argued that you are not developing in the spirit of STL if you don't. Generic algorithms are potentially of enormous value to analytical applications, where different statistical models are to be applied to a sampling of data. For example, analyzing a stream of data being collected from an unmanned spacecraft exploring a distant planet, monitoring network traffic patterns in a communication network, or analyzing time-series financial data. Let's continue with the financial theme to get a more detailed appreciation of the value of generic algorithms.

Let's take an example, following the financial theme that started with the `StockTrade` class. Assume that before a trader makes a trade resulting in a `StockTrade` object being instantiated, he wants to do some research on that stock. One commonly looked at measure of the risk of buying a particular stock is its volatility. Volatility can often be estimated by the standard deviation of the stock's price over some period of time. There may be some other analytical algorithms that this trader's quantitative analyst whipped up for him that will also take this time-series data as input. The right combination of output from all of these algorithms independently run against the time series will indicate whether or not this trader should buy the stock. This is a situation where we want to apply a number of algorithms to a container filled with time-series data, but we don't know exactly what form that data is in: user-defined object or built in. What we want to do is write code that doesn't care what type of container or array this data is in, or even what its exact form is. In order to accomplish this, the data shall be convertible to a `double`.

Please refer now to Listing 2-7, which shows algorithms that I wrote for mean, variance, and standard deviation. Notice that none of the algorithms depend on STL. They were simply designed in the spirit of STL and can be used with STL containers or built in C arrays, as long as they contain elements that can be promoted to an arithmetic value through a conversion operator (e.g., `operator double()`). Anyone else who has some kind of time-series data (e.g., geological, intelligence) can use these algorithms without having to write the "glue code" usually required to make data fit the function call input requirements. I'll show you how flexible and reusable these little routines are.

```
#ifndef STDDEV_H
#define STDDEV_H
#include <math.h>
template <class InputIterator>
double mean(InputIterator first, InputIterator last, unsigned& cnt)
{
    double total = 0;
    cnt = 0;
    while(first != last)
    {
        total = total + *first++;
        cnt++;
    }
    return total/cnt;
}

template <class InputIterator>
double variance(InputIterator first, InputIterator last,
                unsigned historical=1)
{
    unsigned cnt = 0;
    double    total = 0;
    double m = mean(first, last, cnt);
    for(int i = 1; i <= cnt; i++)
    {
        total = total + (*first - m)*(*first - m);
        first++;
    }
    return total/(cnt - historical);
}

template <class InputIterator>
double standard_deviation(InputIterator first, InputIterator last)
{
    return sqrt(variance(first, last));
}
#endif // STDDEV_H
```

LISTING 2-7.

First, consider the simple case where a stock's rate of return for five consecutive years is in a C array:

```
double r1[] = {-10.5, 40.3, -5, 35.9, 15};
unsigned cnt = 0;
cout << "historical return: " << mean(r1,r1+5,cnt) << "%" << endl;
cout << "standard deviation: " << standard_deviation(r1,r1+5) << endl;
```

The results printed are as follows:

```
historical return: 15.14%
standard deviation: 23.06
```

If you want to keep these returns in an STL container, you can still use the algorithms:

```
vector<float> r2;
r2.push_back(-10.5);
r2.push_back(40.3);
r2.push_back(-5);
r2.push_back(35.9);
r2.push_back(15);

cnt = 0;
cout << "historical return: " << mean(r2.begin(),r2.end(),cnt)<< "%"
     << endl;
cout << "standard deviation: " << standard_deviation(r2.begin(),r2.end())
     << endl;
```

The results are the same:

```
historical return: 15.14%
standard deviation: 23.06
```

This is just the beginning. Suppose we have the following class:

```
class YearlyReturn {
  public:
    YearlyReturn(const char* n,unsigned y,double r) :
                 name(n),year(y),ret(r) {}
    operator double() { return ret; }
  private:
    const char*   name;
    unsigned year;
    double   ret;
};
```

And suppose that you put `YearlyReturn` objects in a container:

```
vector<YearlyReturn> r3;
r3.push_back(YearlyReturn("ABC Corp.",1992,-10.5));
r3.push_back(YearlyReturn("ABC Corp.",1993,40.3));
r3.push_back(YearlyReturn("ABC Corp.",1994,-5));
r3.push_back(YearlyReturn("ABC Corp.",1995,35.9));
r3.push_back(YearlyReturn("ABC Corp.",1996,15));
```

You can still use these algorithms on a container of `YearlyReturn` objects, because the `YearlyReturn` class meets the algorithm requirement of being able to convert its objects to `double` values:

```
cnt = 0;
cout << "historical return: " << mean(r3.begin(),r3.end(),cnt) << "%"
     << endl;
cout << "standard deviation: " << standard_deviation(r3.begin(),r3.end())
     << endl;
```

Yes, the results are the same:

```
historical return: 15.14%
standard deviation: 23.06
```

One more: Suppose a trader has a shorter-term focus and wants to look at the daily volatility of a stock, based on a series of daily closing prices. Assume that these closing prices are kept in an array of `doubles` and, for simplification, that only trading days are kept in the array. Now I've got a little problem; I've got to translate the array of prices into a container, or array, of daily returns before I can apply the `mean` and `standard_deviation` algorithms. Mmmmm, well, I looked through the STL algorithms catalog and found a `transform` algorithm that transforms one sequence into another, which is just what I want to do. The `transform` algorithm expects you to provide a function that takes an object of the first container/array as input and returns a transformed object to be put in another container/array. So we can do what I show in Listing 2-8 and get the following output:

```
daily return: 0.25%
daily return: -0.2%
daily return: -0.25%
daily return: 0.333333%
daily return: 0.0625%
daily return: 0.0635294%
daily return: 0.106195%
daily return: 0%
daily return: -0.2%
historical return: 0.0183953%
standard deviation: 0.203803
```

```
#include "stddev.H"
#include <string>
#include <algorithm>
#include <vector>
#include <iostream.h>

main()
{
    double dailyPrices[] = {1,1.25,1,.75,1,1.0625,1.13,1.25,1.25,1};
    double dailyReturns[10];

    double dailyReturn(double p);  // defined below
    transform(dailyPrices,dailyPrices+10,dailyReturns,dailyReturn);
    cnt = 0;
                        // Start at second, because first is bogus.
    cout << "historical return: " <<
        mean(dailyReturns+1,dailyReturns+10,cnt) << "%" << endl;
    cout << "standard deviation: "
        << standard_deviation(dailyReturns+1,dailyReturns+10) << endl;
}

double dailyReturn(double p)
{
    static double yesterdaysPrice=0;
    double dret = 0;
    if(yesterdaysPrice != 0)
    {
        dret = (p - yesterdaysPrice)/yesterdaysPrice;
        cout << "daily return: " << dret << "%" << endl;
    }
    yesterdaysPrice = p;
    return dret;
}
```

LISTING 2-8.

This section has demonstrated a few things:

- The notion of generic programming
- How STL iterators help us take advantage of generic algorithms
- How when you design, it may be beneficial to separate out new algorithms that you identify, following the same "design pattern" employed in the design of STL algorithms

CHAPTER 3
Common Object Request Broker Architecture (CORBA)

CORBA is a standard developed under the auspices of the Object Management Group (OMG), a consortium of more than 500 companies. It has been said that CORBA will provide a "software backplane" that will finally allow software vendors to build products that can live in harmony and communicate with each other. This is certainly not the first time that a software backplane standard has been proposed. But this time, there are three factors that imply it is the one that is finally going to take root. First, it is the first time that one has been proposed that supports the current development paradigm of choice: Object-Oriented Development. Second, industry participation in defining the standard is overwhelming. And third, the CORBA vendors are providing gateways to competing technologies, nullifying any perceived risk in choosing CORBA.

In this chapter, I introduce you to those aspects of CORBA that are employed in the methodology. The focus is more on designing with CORBA and less on nitty-gritty implementation issues. There are excellent references available for that. Stay away from the CORBA Specification [CORBA95] itself, unless you enjoy mentally torturing yourself. It's just too abstract to be the first thing you read on the subject. Instead, read the programmer's guide of a CORBA-based product. It was only after I read [ORBIX95] that I truly appreciated what CORBA offered me as a C++ developer. Before you try to get your hands on that, however, I'd suggest you read this chapter. It will provide you with a little more focus.

3.1 High-Level Overview

So, what exactly is CORBA? I offer the following definition:

> *CORBA,* which stands for *Common Object Request Broker Architecture,* is an industry-standard model for communication between objects. The model specifies how objects invoke each other's member functions, regardless of their physical proximity to each other. Objects communicating as per this model can be on different machines, as long as there is network connectivity between these machines. Communicating objects need not have the same implementation language, hardware platform, or be executing under the same operating system.

CORBA is nothing without software to implement it. The software that makes the magic of CORBA come to life is called an *Object Request Broker.* The following is a detailed definition:

> An Object Request Broker (*ORB*) is a software package that implements the CORBA standard, enabling objects to invoke each other's member functions, regardless of their proximity to each other. A C++ language binding, specified as part of CORBA, must be supported by an ORB. This binding specifies the C++ syntax that can be used by C++ programmers to take advantage of the features provided by the ORB.

The features that I describe in the rest of this chapter and the ORB that I use, are compliant with CORBA 2.0. Although ORBs often provide many nice features that go beyond the standard, like multithreading and fault-tolerance, this book is only interested in those that pertain directly to CORBA. In particular, the CORBA binding to C++ is of primary concern to us, and that will be the focus of the rest of this chapter.

3.2 The Marriage Between the WWW and CORBA

While many have been caught up in the euphoria of the World Wide Web and Java™, those of us who develop complex applications for a living have looked on with reserved curiosity, not too impressed by the fact that we will now be able to do cute little things like download a Java calculator applet with our checkbook Web page. The reason that we have not been too impressed is because the applets would have very limited power. They were basically stand-alone programs. Until now, a gaping hole has existed that has made it very difficult for these applets to act as clients that communicated directly with compute servers. Yes, I'm sure that with enough patience, you could rig up something using HTML and CGI, but it would be very ugly and inefficient.

All this reserved curiosity about Java and the Web is now bursting into immense anticipation with recent announcements by several ORB vendors that they are providing a Java language binding with their ORBs. This means that a Java object will be able to directly invoke member functions of C++ objects on some other machine. This marriage is, perhaps, the single most significant software innovation of the late 1990s. And it is one that is already blessed by the OMG, which has sent out a Request For Proposals for a standard Java binding.

The fact that CORBA will enable a Java object to become a client of a C++ object is a wonderful thing. It means that C++ frameworks built using the methodology presented in this book can be directly used to build complex Web applications , where Java applets are clients to industrial-strength compute servers.

There is one group of vendors that have great cause for concern: those who sell GUI toolkits. Just as STL has rendered much of the commercially available component libraries obsolete, so too will this marriage. The Java/HTML GUI capabilities just may provide a much needed industry standard GUI interface. In the next edition of this book, I hope that HTML, Java, and a CORBA Java Language binding have reached stability and are widely available, so that I can include a GUI into the object infrastructure employed by the methodology.

3.3 Using an ORB—An Informal Description

I'm not going to mislead you; using an ORB requires a little getting used to. First of all, your design needs to be modeled a little differently. You may find memory management conventions a bit confusing. The development procedure that you are used to following must also be altered.

Those are some of the things that negatively impact you, the C++ developer. But, what are the positive effects on the person who has to use an ORB daily? The most basic is that objects appear to be stand-alone executable entities. The public member functions of such objects can be called by any program using regular C++ syntax, regardless of the physical location of the executing object. CORBA defines an architecture that is sort of like RPCs[1] for objects. Let me illustrate by starting with a regular C++ program. Consider the little C++ main() and header file shown in Figure 3-1.

---

1. Remote Procedure Calls

```
                main.C                              Server.h
  #include "Server.h"                    class Server {
                                             public:
  main()                                          Server() {}
  {                                               void fcn() {}
     Server* s = new Server;             };
     s->fcn();
  }
```

FIGURE 3-1.

This syntax tells a C++ compiler to create an executable program that instantiates a new
Server object in the process space of the program, then invoke the fcn() member
function of that object. Wouldn't it be nice to have the flexibility to allow that Server
object to be executing anywhere and be able to use syntax as simple as this? You can do
this with an ORB, except the code might look more like that shown in Figure 3-2.

```
                main.C                              Server.h
  #include "Server.h"                    class Server {
                                             public:
  main()                                          Server() {}
  {                                               void fcn() {}
     Server_var s=Server::_bind();       };
     s->fcn();
  }
```

FIGURE 3-2.

Notice that you don't directly instantiate the Server class. Instead, access to a Server
object is via an *object reference*, which is used like a pointer to invoke functions of a
remote object. An object reference type has the same name as the class whose object is
being referenced, suffixed with "_var". This type is generated for you by tools provided
with your ORB.[2] You must ask the ORB for an object reference. In the case of this
example, the Server::_bind() function[3] does this for you. Once you have a
reference to a Server object, you can call its member function by using the dereference

---

2. There is also a type generated having the same name as the class suffixed with "_ptr". This is a more
    primitive type of object reference.

3. _bind() is specific to Orbix™. The exact syntax for retrieving an object reference (i.e., Server_var)
    will vary from ORB to ORB, unless the standard Naming Service specified in [COSS94] is used.
    Implementations of the Naming Service are just starting to hit the market as of this writing.

operator (->). You may be wondering about function arguments and return values. Yes, the ORB is responsible for marshalling[4] arguments, passing them over the network, and then unmarshalling them for you. And yes, it does the same thing for return values.

All this magic doesn't just happen. In fact, C++ programmers who want to use an ORB must program differently, as I alluded to before. First, the programmer writes interfaces in an *Interface Definition Language (IDL)*, not C++. An IDL compiler generates a C++ class that implements the location transparency. I will refer to such a class as a *CORBA class*.

Take the `Server` class shown in Figure 3-2 as an example. First, the IDL compiler generates a complete class declaration and definition for `Server` that gets linked into the client program (i.e., `main.C` in Figure 3-2). This satisfies the linking requirements of the C++ compiler. The body of the `fcn()` member function, however, simply fakes out the program by issuing a remote call to the real object, which lives on another machine. The real object that gets called on the remote machine will have the implementation of `fcn()` provided by the programmer in a class that has a member function with the same signature but that is not necessarily related to `Server` in any other way. In other words, the function call can be delegated to any object of the implementor's choosing. This will become clearer a little later. I know it all sounds a little foreign, and perhaps scary. I assure you that it is easy for a good developer to get used to. The newfound ability to quickly build distributed applications is well worth leaving your comfort zone.

3.4 Using an ORB—The Detailed Steps

Six steps must be taken to use an ORB. This section goes through each in detail. Bear in mind that, in the context of the overall methodology, these steps are low-level implementation details. A considerable amount of design work must be accomplished before performing these steps.

Step 1. Describe interfaces, using IDL.

When you are ready to start developing a CORBA class, you must first describe its public interface. A C++ programmer has traditionally done this by writing a C++ header file. CORBA requires you to take sort of the same approach, but instead of writing a header file in C++, you write an interface specification file using an Interface Definition Language (IDL). This IDL is included in the CORBA Specification.

It's hard enough just remembering C++. Now we have to learn yet another language? You are probably grumbling something like, "Why should I have to go through this nonsense if all my objects are going to be implemented in C++?" Well, IDL is almost C++. Not a good enough answer? OK. There are two other things you should bear in mind. First, as I

---

4. *Marshalling* means translating argument values into a form that is platform independent (e.g., XDR).

alluded to earlier, I anticipate that many of the client programs communicating with C++ frameworks in the future will be written in Java. Even though Java is, to a large extent, just C++, there are some differences. So, a language-neutral IDL is necessary. The second reason is that you have no choice. To use an ORB, you must first pass your IDL Specification through an IDL compiler, which generates the C++ code that implements the location transparency for you. The IDL compiler may also be required to convert that same IDL into a Smalltalk implementation. So an ORB product can't use the complete C++ language as its IDL. Some C++ features just don't exist in Smalltalk, and vice versa. Consequently, IDL must be a language that provides the least common denominator if all popular OO programming languages are to be able to talk via an ORB.

Since I have the luxury of knowing that my target readers are C++ programmers, I think the best way to teach you a little IDL is through analogy. Table 3-1 shows IDL code fragments and the C++ code with equivalent semantics. In other words, it shows the CORBA C++ language binding. Any text that is shown in italics is arbitrary and irrelevant to the actual mapping.

Because there is no standard memory size associated with C++ built-in types, it was necessary to provide the mappings shown in **1** to provide platform independence. As you can see, there is a CORBA namespace that harbors the typedefs that resolve this for you.

A very useful IDL type, is sequence **2** . When you specify a typedef for a sequence, the IDL compiler you are using actually generates a class with semantics that are similar to the STL vector class. I suspect that someday soon the C++ language binding will be upgraded to actually use the STL vector class. We will see how to use a sequence in the example presented a little later.

The standard CORBA IDL to C++ binding requires that all attributes declared in IDL be converted by the IDL compiler to public member functions of the CORBA class **3** . The actual storage of those attributes will be defined in the implementation class.

An interface maps to one CORBA class, which is derived from CORBA::Object **4** . Arguments passed to member functions can be specified as in, out, or inout, which means read-only, output only, and read-write, respectively. For built-in types (e.g., CORBA::Short), argument passing modes determine whether the generated C++ code should pass the associated argument by value or reference. When a CORBA object is passed, there is an automatic conversion to an object reference.

An interface can inherit operations and attributes from another interface **5** . The implementation classes do not necessarily exhibit the same inheritance relationships, as will be demonstrated in an example a little later.

TABLE 3-1.

IDL	C++
/* comment */	/* comment */
// comment	// comment
module	namespace
short	CORBA::Short
long	CORBA::Long
unsigned short	CORBA::UShort
unsigned long	CORBA::ULong
float	CORBA::Float
double	CORBA::Double
char	CORBA::Char
boolean	CORBA::Boolean
void	void
string	char*
const string *s* = "Hi!";	static const char* const s = "Hi!";
typedef *X Y*;	typedef *X Y*;
typedef sequence<string> *Sq*;	class *Sq* {};
enum *X* {*A*,*B*,*C*};	enum X {*A*,*B*,*C*};
struct {};	struct {};
union {};	union {};
exception *Bad* {};	class *Bad* : public UserException {};

interface *X* {
  readonly attribute short *x*;
}
	class *X* : public virtual CORBA::Object{
	  public:
	    virtual CORBA:Short *x*(CORBA::Environment&);
	};

interface X {
  Func1(in *BuiltIn* x);
  Func2(out *BuiltIn* x);
  Func3(inout *BuiltIn* x);
  Func4(in *ServerType* x);
};
	class X : public virtual CORBA::Object{
	  public:
	    Func1(BuiltIn x,CORBA::Environment&);
	    Func2(BuiltIn& x,CORBA::Environment&);
	    Func3(BuiltIn& x,CORBA::Environment&);
	    Func4(ServerType_ptr x,CORBA::Environment&);
	};

interface *Derived* : *Base* {};	class *Derived* : public *Base* {};

It is appropriate at this point to introduce the notion of *widening*. In general C++ terms, *widening* means converting an object pointer (or reference) from an object of a derived class to an object of a base class. Using the term *widening* to describe this may sound a bit counterintuitive. But, I think the logic is that you are widening the applicability of the reference to more general situations.

Widening a reference to an object of a derived CORBA class requires a call to the _duplicate function. This is a static member function of the derived CORBA class. The following illustrates the rule:

```
// IDL
interface Derived : Base {};

// C++ code
Derived_var d; Base_var b;
b = Derived::_duplicate(d);

b = d; // Compiler Error
```

Widening is the basic mechanism used for polymorphism. Let's use a little C++ example to demonstrate widening in terms that we are more comfortable with, and then I'll show you what needs to be done when you are using an ORB. Consider the following overused example:

```
class Shape {
  public:
    virtual void draw() = 0;
};

class Circle : public Shape {
  public:
    void draw();
};
```

Given the abstract base class Shape, you can write code that knows how to draw any type of Shape object, without knowing specifically what that Shape is:

```
foo(Shape* s) { s->draw(); }
:
Circle* c;
:
foo(c);
:
```

So, a pointer to a `Circle` was automatically cast to a base class Shape object. With the C++ mapping of CORBA, there is no implicit cast. You must do the following:

```
// IDL
interface Shape {
  void draw();
};

interface Circle : Shape {
  void draw();
};
```

The following is the associated C++:

```
foo(Shape_var s) { s->draw(); }

Circle_var c;
:
foo(Circle::_duplicate(c));
:
```

So there's a little IDL; not all of it! You will pick up more as we go through the examples later in this chapter. But remember, the emphasis of the book is design methodology, not code mechanics. As a homework assignment, I expect you to read the IDL C++ Language Binding in [CORBA95].

Step 2.   Develop the implementations of CORBA classes.

Now you have to develop the implementations of CORBA classes, starting with the output of the IDL compiler, which includes:

- The C++ header file declaring the CORBA classes that correspond to the interfaces in the IDL file
- The code that must be linked into the client program
- The code that must be linked into the server program (i.e., the one that will execute the implementation)

Two techniques are specified in the IDL C++ Language binding for providing the implementation of a CORBA class. There is no need to endorse both in the methodology. It will only lead to more confusion and inconsistency in framework designs.

One technique is called the *Basic Object Adapter* (*BOA*) approach; it relies heavily on deep inheritance hierarchies. This approach is also very limiting, unless you resort to using multiple inheritance. The other technique is called the *tie* approach; it doesn't require you to use any inheritance, multiple or otherwise.[5] Instead, it employs delegation. This is far more flexible and is consistent with the STL design philosophy we discussed in Chapter 1. I also find it less confusing.The only disadvantage of the tie approach is that an extra object will be instantiated to perform the delegation. This requires that an additional function call be made that would not be required with the BOA approach.

It could be argued that neither approach has an overwhelming advantage over the other. But, the tie approach is more consistent with the standard rules and patterns of this methodology. The fact that you don't have to go down a minimum of three levels of inheritance is significant. I also think the fact that you don't have to resort to multiple inheritance to make a legacy class into a CORBA class implementation is significant. For these reasons, the methodology will endorse only the tie approach.

Step 3. Write server program.

After you implement the classes in C++, you need to write a little program to instantiate an object (or objects) of that class. The program waits for any objects running in another program to invoke its member functions. We'll refer to this as a *server program*.

A reality that cannot be removed from our sight is the fact that we all use operating systems. None in the mainstream (e.g., UNIX and Windows® NT™) allow objects to "live" on their own. They must exist inside running programs. As a consequence, objects are not truly autonomous entities. An object still needs to be instantiated in a program, running as a process on a prespecified machine.

Step 4. Write client programs.

Client application code needs to include the header file, generated by the IDL compiler, for a CORBA class that the client is interested in using. To create an executable client program, you will also be required to compile the code generated by the IDL compiler that provides access to the remotely executing server program harboring the implementation of a CORBA class.

Step 5. Register CORBA objects with the ORB.

There are a number of ways to register a CORBA object. You can have a server program run persistently, just waiting for a client to call member functions on CORBA objects that it contains. Or, you can set it up such that the server program is only invoked when a client

---

5. This is assuming that you are not inheriting from existing classes that already use multiple inheritance.

needs to call a member function of an object contained in the server program. The CORBA Specification talks about the various modes that server programs can run in.

Step 6. Run the client programs.

Start the programs that invoke member functions of CORBA objects.

3.5 CORBA and Frameworks

Now you know a little bit about what CORBA is and how to use an ORB. How does CORBA support framework design? To answer this, consider the fact that CORBA C++ client software works with IDL compiler-generated CORBA classes, and the delegate classes that implement the interfaces are unknown to the client software. Client C++ code sees the CORBA class as a regular C++ class with the same name as the IDL interface. A CORBA class, however, is actually just a conduit to the delegate class that implements the member functions. A CORBA class is useless without the delegate class to provide an implementation. So, a CORBA class is abstract.

This is significant to framework developers because, if you recall the definition that was presented in Chapter 1, abstract base classes are the major constituents of a framework. A C++ class library that supports one or more CORBA IDL interfaces can be considered a framework if there are potentially many different implementations of those interfaces.

3.6 The Impact of CORBA on Modeling Notation

Graphical notation is important for quickly conveying high-level concepts. To be honest, I think that people have gone way overboard trying to present very detailed designs graphically. When they try to do this, the diagrams end up being more difficult to produce and read than the code that implements it, and are always more ambiguous. Instead of going to the trouble of learning what is inevitably an unstable notation, why not just learn C++ and use that to express design details?

I'm not sure what the latest representation of a class is: a rectangle, a hexagon, a cloud; oh, wait, I think clouds are out. Let's not worry about that too much. The notation that will be employed in this book is quite similar to that employed in [PATTERNS95], which is OMT based. It is simple and fairly easy to remember. Appendix B covers the notation in its entirety, but at this point, I think it is appropriate to point out that using an ORB does demand that OMT notation be augmented. It just doesn't capture everything that you need to truly depict what's going on in a CORBA environment. I'm not talking about inventing any more fancy geometric shapes or squiggly lines that you will never remember—just a couple of extra keywords and conventions.

The notational deficiency stems from the fact that when you use an ORB, client objects work with CORBA classes and the actual classes that implement their interfaces are unknown to these clients. The member functions are the same as those declared in the IDL interface, but the CORBA class that has the same name as the interface actually dispatches the invocation to a delegate object. Delegation can be represented with regular OMT notation, but the delegating CORBA class is really just an extension of the ORB and is not worthy of the same stature that other classes in the model have. With this in mind, I employed the following conventions in the notation used throughout this book.

First, consider class diagrams. A CORBA class will be represented as a box with the string "(interface)" appearing under the class name, indicating that it serves only as an interface to the actual class providing the implementation. The border of the box will be a lighter shade than that of a normal class to designate that objects of this class simply provide a conduit between the client and the implementation object. Also, an arrow will be drawn from an interface box to each class that provides an implementation of that interface. The arrow will be labeled with the word "tie" to indicate that it is possible for a tie object (not shown) to delegate calls received by a CORBA object to an object of the class pointed to. Please note that the only arrows that will ever leave an interface box will be those labeled as "tie." Figure 3-3 demonstrates these conventions.

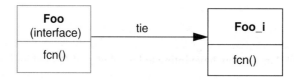

FIGURE 3-3.

There is also an effect on Object Interaction Diagrams (OIDs). CORBA objects will appear with "(interface)" under their names, just as on a class diagram. In addition, the vertical line representing a CORBA object will be a lighter shade than that of a regular object. Last, because the CORBA objects are simply a conduit, there is never any activation time indicated for a CORBA object (i.e., you will never see a rectangle on a vertical line representing an interface object). Figure 3-4 demonstrates these conventions.[6]

---

6. In the implementation of this scenario, there will actually be a "tie" object that dispatches the call to aFoo_i, but I do not feel that it is pertinent to our modeling, and its appearance on the diagram would only be distracting.

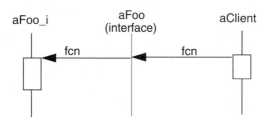

FIGURE 3-4.

3.7 An Example: Event Notification

In this section, we investigate an example of how to use an ORB. Our example will center around a general pattern of object interaction that is pervasive in many types of applications.

Very often, the state of a particular object (A) impacts the behavior exhibited by another object (B), but it is inefficient for B to have to poll the state of A. It is more efficient for A to simply notify B when its state changes. However, this not an optimal arrangement from a design standpoint if A must now have intimate knowledge of B's public interface. This would create "tight coupling" between the two class implementations, which we all know from our structured design days is generally not a good thing.

In this example, we will implement a tiny framework that captures this type of object interaction, using event notification. We would also like the design to be such that the notifying object has minimal knowledge about the objects it is notifying (i.e., there is loose coupling between them). After implementing such a framework, we will extend it into the telecommunications domain. More specifically, we will build a little C++ class library that can be used by network management software for disseminating security alarms.

3.7.1 Background for Example

Creating mechanisms of event notification, where a notifying object knows little about the object, or objects, it is notifying, has become a very hot topic over the past few years. And for good reason. This model is well suited to many types of applications and has assumed different names, depending on the application domain.

For example, modern GUI toolkits rely heavily on this model. The term *Model-View-Controller* is usually used in this context. GUI toolkits usually enable an application programmer to present screens as an arrangement of widget objects (e.g., text fields, scrolling lists). This arrangement represents a *View* of some *Model*, which is a completely separate set of objects that encapsulate business logic. The *Controller* associates user interaction with a corresponding update in the View (e.g., how mouse clicks and keyboard input change the video screen contents). Glue logic will associate the Model, the View, and the Controller by instructing which member functions (i.e., often called callback functions) in the Model classes should be called when the Controller indicates that a certain part of the View has been modified.

On Wall Street, the term *Publish-Subscribe* is most often used to describe systems that give traders real-time updates on financial information. In such systems, a *Publisher* is a source of reams of financial information that is constantly changing. Traders are only interested in a small portion of this information, depending on what is currently in their portfolio, or what they are looking to purchase for their portfolio. In other words, they want to be notified when certain financial events occur, so they *Subscribe* to specific categories of information.

Another domain where this event notification model is very significant is telecommunications, where network management systems must be notified when events such as equipment failures, spikes in network traffic, and security alarms occur.

There have been at least two very public attempts at defining a standard event notification model. The OMG has standardized on an "Event Services Specification" as part of its Common Object Services Specification [COSS94], and the OSI has defined an Event-Report-Management Function (X.734/ISO 10164-5) as part of its Systems-Management Standards. This is confusing, not only because of the differences in terminology, but because of the different levels of detail and slightly different semantics associated with each model. Instead of struggling to understand one of these standards, we will approach this problem by starting with a simple design pattern, called *OBSERVER*, that cuts to the essence of each.

In an OBSERVER pattern, there is a *Subject* object and usually a bunch of *Observer* objects that are interested in the state of that Subject. When an Observer object is interested in knowing when the state of a given Subject changes, it *attaches* to that Subject. When the Subject is told to *notify* Observers of a change in its state, it *updates* all the Observer objects that are currently attached to it. The Subject doesn't need to know anything about the Observer object, other than it has an `update()` function. This supports our design goal of maintaining loose coupling. The OBSERVER pattern structure is documented in

[PATTERNS95] with a class diagram similar to the one shown in Figure 3-5.[7] I generalized the behavior somewhat by allowing an Observer to be attached to more than one Subject.

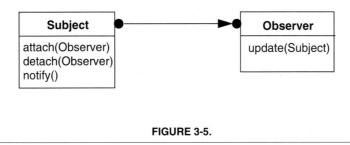

FIGURE 3-5.

If you look at our definition of a framework in Chapter 1, the combination of a `Subject` class and an `Observer` class technically qualifies as a very tiny framework. Both of these classes are intended to be abstract classes, and there is a distinct type of object interaction that they capture. In the next subsection, I will design and build an OBSERVER framework.

Now let's discuss this pattern in the context of network management, so we have something real to use the framework for. The OSI Systems-Management Standards for communication between systems are based on a seven-layer protocol stack. The highest layer is the application layer. In the case of network management, this application layer is run on network equipment, as well as adjunct systems that coordinate and manage the equipment. This application layer is also decomposed into various components, each described by a standard, as shown in Figure 3-6.[8]

---

7. This notation is not adequate to reflect the relationships that exist when an Object Request Broker is used. When we start to develop the example, I will modify this diagram accordingly.

8. This figure is based on information from [STALLINGS93].

OSI System Management: Application Layer Components

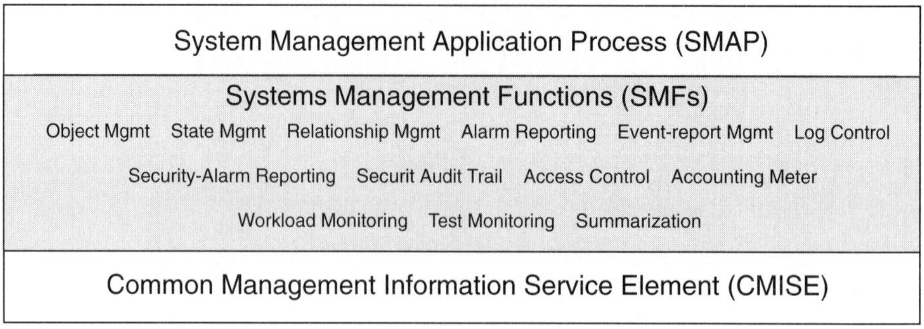

System Management Application Process (SMAP)
Systems Management Functions (SMFs) Object Mgmt   State Mgmt   Relationship Mgmt   Alarm Reporting   Event-report Mgmt   Log Control Security-Alarm Reporting   Securit Audit Trail   Access Control   Accounting Meter Workload Monitoring   Test Monitoring   Summarization
Common Management Information Service Element (CMISE)

FIGURE 3-6.

A component[9] of the Common Management Information Service Element (CMISE) provides a means of executing the operations of objects located on a different physical device. That's exactly what an ORB does for you, so we can consider an ORB to be the logical equivalent of that component of CMISE. This being the case, we can implement the CMISE-dependent models described in the OSI standards, using an ORB instead of CMISE (see Figure 3-7). If you study the differences between CMISE and an ORB, you will find that an ORB is far less clumsy for C++ programmers and much more flexible.

System Management, Using an Object Request Broker

System Management Application Process (SMAP)
Systems Management Functions (SMFs) Object Mgmt   State Mgmt   Relationship Mgmt   Alarm Reporting   Event-report Mgmt   Log Control Security-Alarm Reporting   Security Audit Trail   Access Control   Accounting Meter Workload Monitoring   Test Monitoring   Summarization
Object Request Broker (ORB)

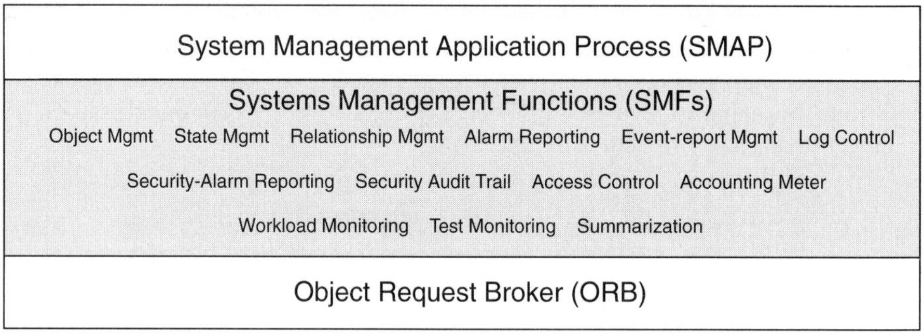

FIGURE 3-7.

In section 3.7.2, I will implement the OBSERVER framework. In section 3.7.3, I will extend the framework to create a small, distributed, class library that implements the ISO

---

9. The Remote Operations Service Element (ROSE), not shown.

Security Alarm Reporting Function (i.e., ISO 10164-7) that you see in the middle of Figure 3-7.

Most of the code that you will see in this example is CORBA compliant and therefore easily ported. Some of the details, however, are beyond the scope of CORBA. When I use syntax that is not part of CORBA, I will be sure to point it out. I'm also going to use a little STL in this example, to show you that it is compatible with CORBA as long as you know where to use it. Because I won't put any code in the book that I haven't tested myself, I need to use a real ORB. The one that I'm using is Orbix 2.0 from IONA Technologies (www.iona.ie).

3.7.2 Phase 1: Developing an OBSERVER Framework

The design of the OBSERVER framework is shown in Figure 3-8. You can see that the `Subject-Observer` class relationships introduced in Figure 3-5 are now replaced by equivalent interface relationships. There are also concrete implementation classes for both the `Subject` and `Observer` interfaces: `Subject_i` and `Observer_i`, respectively. The diagram shows that whenever a member function of `Subject` is invoked by a client, the call can be delegated to a `Subject_i` object by using the tie approach. Likewise, whenever a member function of `Observer` is invoked, the call can be delegated to an `Observer_i` object by using the tie approach. The diagram also indicates that a `Subject_i` object maintains references to `Observers`: more specifically, those that have attached to its `Subject`.

Structure of OBSERVER Framework with CORBA

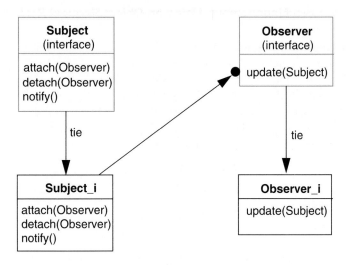

FIGURE 3-8.

The dynamic nature of the interaction between instances of the classes and interfaces shown in Figure 3-8 is depicted in Figure 3-9. At some point after an `Observer_i` object `attaches` to a `Subject`, the `Subject_i` object generally notifies itself to update all `attached Observers`. The reason the `Subject_i` usually notifies itself is because application-specific logic is what changes the state of the `Subject_i` object, based on an application-specific stimulus. This application-specific logic should remain separate from the general-purpose logic provided by `notify`.

Collaborations in the OBSERVER Framework with CORBA

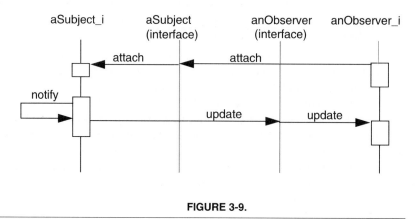

FIGURE 3-9.

Step 1. Describe interfaces, using IDL.

Listing 3-1 shows the IDL file for `Subject`. Since a `Subject` must be able to accept references to an `Observer`, a forward declaration of `Observer` **1** is necessary, just as it would be with C code. The `attach` function **2** is called by an `Observer` that wants to be notified of any change in the state of the `Subject`. The calling `Observer` will pass a reference to itself to the `attach` function, so that the `Subject` knows how to get in touch with the `Observer`. Notice that the argument is named "o" to satisfy the IDL requirement that function signatures have a name for all arguments. The second `Subject` function is `detach` **3**. When an `Observer` calls `detach`, it will no longer be notified when the state of the `Subject` changes.

```
    // Subject.idl

 1  interface Observer;

    interface Subject {
 2      void attach(in Observer o);
 3      void detach(in Observer o);
        void notify();
    };
```

LISTING 3-1.

Listing 3-2 shows the IDL file for Observer. A forward declaration of Subject ❶ is necessary, since a reference to Subject is used in the interface declaration. There's not a whole lot to an Observer: just the update function ❷ that will be called by a Subject that the Observer is attached to, when the state of that Subject has changed. Notice that this is a oneway operation, which means that it is nonblocking. In other words, when a Subject calls update, it will not have to wait until the Observer finishes the processing of update before the call returns. This is crucial for two reasons. First, there may be a lot of Observers waiting to be notified. If update blocked until each Observer was finished, you have no idea how long it will take to update all of them. There is an even more basic reason why you don't want update to block. When it is called, the first thing that an Observer may do is make a call back to the Subject to find out what has changed—so you would have a deadlock.

```
    // Observer.idl

 1  interface Subject;

    interface Observer {
 2      oneway void update(in Subject s);
    };
```

LISTING 3-2.

Step 2. Develop the implementations of CORBA classes.

In an OBSERVER pattern, both Subject and Observer are CORBA classes. First, the Subject acts as a server for Observers, by allowing them to attach. Then, an attached Observer will act as a server when a Subject has to call the Observer's update function. If you recall from Figure 3-8, the implementation classes of Subject and `Observer` are `Subject_i` and `Observer_i`, respectively. Each will be implemented in a module consisting of one header file and one source file. This is consistent with the methodology. The methodology also insists that header and source file name prefixes be the same as the name of the class that is implemented in them. This will hold true for this example, as well. Also, please note that in the interest of conserving printing costs, I will not be protecting against multiple includes of the same header file in this example.

Listing 3-3 contains the declaration of `Subject_i`, the implementation "tied" to the `Subject` interface. First, you need to include the header file containing the declaration of the CORBA C++ class generated from the `Subject` interface by the IDL compiler ❶. If you look in that file, you will find a class called `Subject` (i.e., the same name as the interface itself), whose declaration conforms to the C++ language binding specified by CORBA. All that interests us in `Subject.hh` is a macro ❼ and the signatures of the two functions that `Subject_i` will be delegated: `attach` and `detach`. `Subject_i` must have the exact same signatures for each of these functions, because the macro ❼ that expands into the code that actually does the delegation expects them to have this signature. If they don't, the compile will fail. I'm obliged to point out, at this point, that the exact C++ mechanism for implementing the tie approach is not specified in the CORBA C++ binding. The macro name, therefore, is specific to Orbix. The easiest thing to do is just copy and paste the `attach` ❸ and `detach` ❹ signatures from `Subject.hh` into `Subject_i.h`. The second argument passed to these functions provides an interface to the ORB, should you need it. We don't for this implementation, but the macro assumes that it is present.

```
// Subject_i.h

❶ #include "Subject.hh"
❷ #include "vector.h"

class Subject_i {
  public:
    Subject_i();
    virtual ~Subject_i();
❸    virtual void attach(Observer_var, CORBA::Environment&);
❹    virtual void detach(Observer_var, CORBA::Environment&);
    virtual void notify() const;
  private:
❺    vector<Observer_var> observers;
❻    Subject_var myRef;
};

// The following is ORBIX-specific
❼ DEF_TIE_Subject(Subject_i)
```

LISTING 3-3.

There are a couple of other things to note about `Subject_i.h`. First, you can see that we take advantage of the STL `vector` class **2** , demonstrating that CORBA and STL can coexist. We use a `vector` to store references to all `Observers` that are currently attached to the `Subject` **5** . You'll also note that a `Subject` keeps a reference to itself **6** . This reference will be passed to all `Observer::update` function calls.

Listing 3-4 shows the `Subject_i` member function definitions. The default constructor does something that looks a bit strange. It instantiates the object that will actually delegate the `Subject` member function calls to the `Subject_i` object **1** . Notice that the `Subject_i` object passes a pointer to itself to the `TIE_Subject` constructor, so that it knows where to delegate to. The pointer to the newly constructed `TIE_Subject` object is then assigned to the `Subject_i myRef` data member.

The syntax used for setting up the tie is specific to Orbix, but the concepts behind the syntax are defined in the CORBA C++ Language binding. This nonportable code, albeit small, may make you uncomfortable. I wouldn't worry about it too much. This code could be used, as is, with another ORB. We know that all CORBA-compliant ORBs would provide support for the tie approach, so all I would have to do is `typedef DEF_TIE_Subject` and `TIE_Subject` to correspond to the new ORB's tie macro and tie class, respectively.

Let's have a look at the `attach` function next **3** . The first thing we do in `attach` is call a static member function of `Observer`, called `_duplicate`. This bumps the reference count on `o`, to let the ORB know that we are not done using the reference when the `attach` function returns. If we didn't call `_duplicate`, the ORB would think we were done with `o` and would delete it when `attach` returns. After calling `_duplicate()`, a reference to the `Observer` that just attached is added to `observers`, and the function returns. The `detach` function **4** basically undoes what `attach` did. It removes the specified `Observer` from the `observers` vector and decrements its reference count with `CORBA::release()`.

The `notify` member function **5** iterates through the `observers` vector and calls the `update` member function of all `Observers` referenced. `Subject_i` passes a reference to itself, so the `Observers` know how to access it to query for more information.

When a `Subject_i` is deleted, its destructor **2** releases all the `Observers` that are still attached to it. This lets the ORB know that those references can now be deleted as well.

```
    // Subject_i.CC
    #include "Subject_i.h"
    #include "Observer.hh"

    Subject_i::Subject_i()
    {
1       myRef = new TIE_Subject(Subject_i)(this); // Orbix
    }

2   Subject_i::~Subject_i()
    {
        for(int i= 0; i<observers.size(); i++)
        {
            CORBA::release(observers[i]);
        }
    }

    void
3   Subject_i::attach(Observer_var o, CORBA::Environment&)
    {
        Observer::_duplicate(o);
        observers.push_back(o);
    }

    void
4   Subject_i::detach(Observer_var o, CORBA::Environment&)
    {
        for(int i= 0; i<observers.size(); i++)
        {
            if(observers[i] == o) {observers.erase(i);}
            CORBA::release(o);
        }
    }

    void
5   Subject_i::notify() const
    {
        for(int i= 0; i<observers.size(); i++)
        {
            Observer_var o = observers[i];
            o->update(myRef);
        }
    }
```

LISTING 3-4.

Moving right along, let's now turn our attention to the Observer. Observer_i is basically a skeleton Observer implementation class from which anyone wishing to develop an application-specific Observer can start. Listing 3-5 contains the boilerplate Observer implementation declaration. First, you need to include the header file generated by the IDL compiler ❶ .You will also need to provide a constructor ❷ that binds the Observer to the appropriate Subject and attaches to it. And, of course, you need to provide the update function ❸ that will be called by this Subject when its state changes. Last, but not least, you can't forget the macro that expands into the code for the class that delegates the update to an Observer_i object ❹ .

```
    // Observer_i.h

❶  #include "Observer.hh"

    class Observer_i {
      public:
❷      Observer_i();
❸      virtual void update(Subject_var, CORBA::Environment &);
    };

❹  DEF_TIE_Observer(Observer_i)
```

LISTING 3-5.

Listing 3-6 contains the boilerplate Observer implementation. The first thing that an Observer must do is get a reference to its Subject ❶ . It does this by calling a function (i.e., _bind(), for Orbix) that asks the ORB to go find out where an object of that type resides and return a reference to it. It is prudent to watch for both CORBA-specified exceptions ❷ and other exceptions ❸ that are specific to your ORB. The argument to _bind() is the name of the Server that you are interested in, as it was registered with the ORB.

After obtaining a reference to a Subject, an Observer_i must attach to that Subject ❹ , passing a reference so that the Subject knows where to find it when a state change occurs. As you can see, it is necessary to actually create a tie object and pass the reference to it, instead of the Observer_i object itself. There is no way that an ORB could navigate directly to an Observer_i object because it wasn't created with the necessary hooks. I know programmers are not very good at taking things on faith, but it is beyond the scope of this chapter to go into what those hooks are. Besides, you really don't need to know.

The update function of Observer_i ❺ is completely uninteresting, but would be the most exciting function in a real Observer implementation.

Suppose we instantiate a `Subject` object. After we do this, the following drama starts to unfold. The `Subject` is sitting somewhere saying, "Okay, anybody out there who wants to know when I have some news to report, just let me know by calling my `attach` function. I don't care where you are or what kind of hardware you are running on. I don't care if you are implemented in Java or OO Cobol. If you are a C++ object, I don't care about your heritage. All I care about is that you are an `Observer` with an `update` operation. Don't you worry, I'll let you know when I have news by calling your `update` operation. I'll even pass you a reference to myself when I do."

Now, in comes a newly instantiated `Observer`: "Hello, I know you are out there somewhere `Subject`. I'm going to attach to you even though I don't have a clue exactly where or what you are, only that you behave like a `Subject` object. Okay, thanks for letting me attach, I'll be waiting for news from you." Yes, with those few simple lines of code and the power of an ORB beneath it, you have accomplished all this.

```
// Observer_i.C
#include "Observer_i.h"
#include "Subject.hh"
#include <iostream.h>
#include <stdlib.h>

Observer_i::Observer_i()
{
  Subject_var subjectVar;
  try {
    subjectVar = Subject::_bind(":SubjectSrv");
  }
  catch (CORBA::SystemException &sysEx) {
    cerr << "Unexpected system exception" << endl;
    cerr << &sysEx;
    exit(1);
  }
  catch(...) {
    cerr << "Bind to Subject object failed" << endl;
    cerr << "Unexpected exception " << endl;
    exit(1);
  }
  try {
      subjectVar->attach(new TIE_Observer(Observer_i)(this));
  }
  catch (CORBA::SystemException &sysEx) {
    cerr << "Unexpected system exception" << endl;
    cerr << &sysEx;
    exit(1);
  }
  catch(...) {
    cerr << "call to attach failed" << endl;
    cerr << "Unexpected exception " << endl;
    exit(1);
  }
  cout << "Observer now attached to Subject " << endl;
}

void
Observer_i::update(Subject_var, CORBA::Environment &)
{
  cout << "Observer notified by Subject" << endl;
}
```

LISTING 3-6.

Step 3.   Write server program.

Listing 3-7 is the server program in which the implementation of the `Subject` interface will be a `Subject_i` object ❶ . The call to `impl_is_ready()` ❷ will tell the ORB that we have completed the server's initialization and that a `Subject` server named "SubjectSrv" is now ready to start fielding function call invocations. Obviously the call, as specified is specific to Orbix, but the C++ binding requires that all ORBs provide a function called `impl_is_ready` for implementing server programs. `impl_is_ready()` returns only when there is some sort of error or the ORB times out waiting for a client to call a `Subject` member function in the SubjectSrv server program.

```
// Subject_Main.C

#include <iostream.h>
#include <stdlib.h>
#include "Subject_i.h"

int main()
{
    Subject_i s;

    try {
        CORBA::Orbix.impl_is_ready("SubjectSrv");
    }
    catch (CORBA::SystemException &sysEx)
    {
        cerr << "Unexpected system exception" << endl;
        cerr << &sysEx;
        exit(1);
    }
    catch(...)
    {
        cout << "Unexpected exception" << endl;
        exit(1);
    }
    return 0;
}
```

LISTING 3-7.

Step 4.   Write client programs.

In this example and in all applications that employ the OBSERVER pattern, the client is also a server, because the `Observer` must provide an `update` function for a `Subject` to call. The program in which an `Observer_i` object will live, will look like the one shown in Listing 3-8. It looks just like the one shown in Listing 3-7, except that now an `Observer_i` object is instantiated. Recall that the tie object will automatically be instantiated as well, in the `Observer_i` constructor. One other thing to note is that even though this program, when run, registers itself as an `Observer` server named "ObserverSrv," this name is really irrelevant. The `Subject` will never need to ask the ORB for a reference to the `Observer`, as the `Observer` was required to do to find its `Subject`. `Subjects` are passed `Observer` references as they `attach` themselves.

```
// Observer_Main.C

#include <iostream.h>
#include <stdlib.h>
#include "Observer_i.h"

int main() {
  Observer_i o;

  try {
     CORBA::Orbix.impl_is_ready("ObserverSrv");
  }
  catch (CORBA::SystemException &sysEx)
  {
    cerr << "Unexpected system exception" << endl;
    cerr << &sysEx;
    exit(1);
  }
  catch(...)
  {
    cout << "Unexpected exception" << endl;
    exit(1);
  }
  return 0;
}
```

LISTING 3-8.

Step 5. Register CORBA objects with the ORB.

This step will vary with the ORB you are using. There are different modes of server operation. You may opt to start up `Subject_main` and then register it as a persistent server. CORBA also allows servers to be started only when a member function is called that is implemented in that server. Refer to the CORBA Specification for more details.

Step 6. Run the client programs.

When you run `Observer_main`, the `Observer` will attach itself to the `Subject_i` instance running in `Subject_main`, and that's about it. I haven't invoked `notify()` as shown in the interaction diagram in Figure 3-9, so we haven't really tested all `Observer-Subject` collaborations.

3.7.3 Phase 2: Security Alarm Reporting (ISO 10164-7) with CORBA

Now we can extend the basic OBSERVER pattern depicted in Figure 3-8 to address
Security Alarm Reporting (see Figure 3-10).

Security Alarm Reporting—Class Structure with CORBA

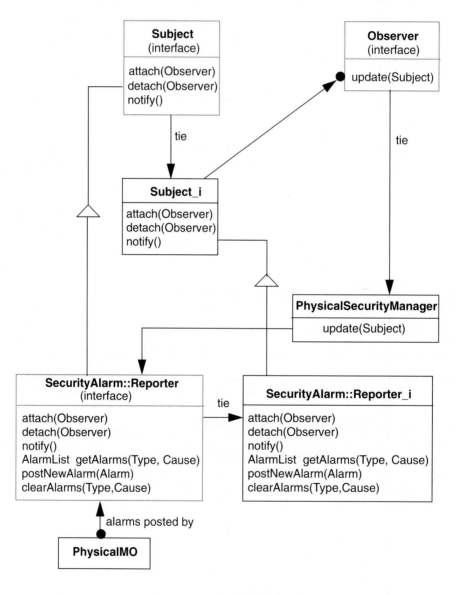

FIGURE 3-10.

You can see that the basic `Subject-Observer` interface relationships remain intact, but now there is a more specific type of `Subject` interface in the picture, named `SecurityAlarm::Reporter`. This type of interface adds member functions supporting the notion of alarms. There is no need to derive a more specific interface on the Observer side. The plain old vanilla `Observer` interface will work just fine with this new type of `Subject` interface.

There are more specific types of implementation classes for `Subject` and `Observer`, named `SecurityAlarm::Reporter_i` and a `PhysicalSecurityManager`,[10] respectively. Notice in the case of `SecurityAlarm::Reporter_i`, we derive from the more basic `Subject_i` implementation to reuse the `attach`, `detach`, and `notify` functions that it provides. In the case of `PhysicalSecurityManager`, however, there is no point in deriving from `Observer_i`, because it really doesn't add any logic worth reusing. This is one of the newfound freedoms that you, as a C++ developer, now experience when you use an ORB with the tie approach. You don't have to extend a framework by using inheritance if there is no benefit in doing so. You can tie any object to the interface, as long as it provides member functions with the same signatures as the interface it supports.

So, in summary, the design model employs a combination of inheritance and delegation, using each where it makes the most sense. And although `PhysicalMO` (Managed Object) is also represented as a class, it can be implemented as any software running as a client of the `SecurityAlarm::Reporter`.

Turning now to the dynamic side of the design: Figure 3-11 depicts the typical scenario that will be played out time and time again in a real system. First, the `PhysicalSecurityManager` attaches to a `SecurityAlarm::Reporter` that is keeping track of all security violations reported by the Managed Objects it is responsible for. Then both just wait for something to happen. All of a sudden, some sort of physical violation occurs and is sensed by `aPhysicalMO`, which dutifully reports the violation by calling `postNewAlarm()`, a function of the `SecurityAlarm::Reporter` that it is bound to. The `SecurityAlarm::Reporter` then records the alarm internally and calls its own `notify` function to `update` all `Observers` that have `attached` and are awaiting news of violations. The `PhysicalSecurityManager`, having `attached` previously, has its `update` function called and promptly requests information on any physical violations. The `AlarmList` returned by this call will contain one `Alarm`, the one just reported by `aPhysicalMO`. The `aPhysicalSecurityManager` takes actions necessary to address the violation and then clears this alarm from the `SecurityAlarm::Reporter`.

---

10. In a real system, there could be a variety of Security Manager classes, each specializing in a different type of security problem. In the interest of brevity, I will address only one such manager, namely, the one that would be responsible for physical security violations like cable tampering and unauthorized intrusions.

Object Interaction in Security Alarm Reporting with CORBA

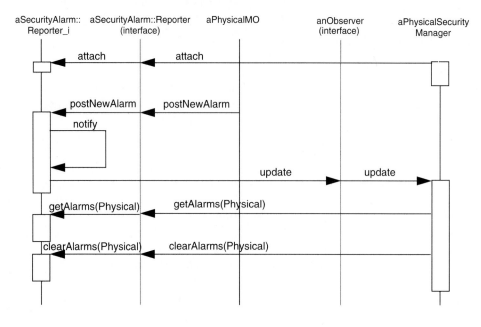

FIGURE 3-11.

Step 1. Describe interfaces, using IDL.

The `interface` for the more sophisticated type of `Subject` required now is, of course, more complex than we saw in the last section. In fact, we declare a new `module` for Security Alarms, because quite a few new types are now required to support the interface. Listing 3-9 shows `SecurityAlarm.idl`, which declares the `SecurityAlarm` module ❶. If you recall, this translates into a C++ `namespace` with the same name.[11] Moving down the `interface` declaration, you can see that there are enumerated data types for an alarm's `Type` ❷, its `Cause` ❸, and its `Severity` ❹. These are all defined in ISO 10164-7. There is also an `Alarm` data structure ❺, also defined in ISO 10164-7. This is followed by a `typedef` for a `sequence` of `Alarms` ❻. I haven't mentioned it yet, but in order to use an IDL `sequence`, you must `typedef` it. Finally, the interface for `Reporter` is declared.[12] You can see that it is derived from the `Subject interface` ❼. The three new functions added by this derived `interface`

---

11. At the time of this writing, Orbix did not support the generation of namespaces for the Visual C++ 4.0 environment, which is what I was using. But, I wanted to reflect the C++ binding that uses the latest C++ language features. So, After testing the code and importing it into the book, I manually substituted the namespace syntax for the pre-namespace syntax that Orbix generated.

12. Appears as a fully qualified `SecurityAlarm::Reporter` on Figure 3-10 and Figure 3-11.

work as follows. The getAlarms function ⑧ is called with a Type and Cause. A list of all Alarms matching the Type and Cause that have been posted with the nonblocking postNewAlarm function ⑨ and have not been cleared with the nonblocking clearAlarms function ⑩ will be returned in a sequence typedefed as AlarmList. Notice that all types and all causes can be specified.

```
    // SecurityAlarm.idl

    #include "Subject.idl"
①  module SecurityAlarm {
②    enum Type{IntegrityViolation,OperationalViolation,
              PhysicalViolation, SecurityService,
              TimeDomainViolation, AllViolationTypes};

③    enum Cause{DuplicateInfo, InfoMissing, InfoModDetected,
              InfoOutOfSequence, UnexpectedInfo, DenialOfService,
              OutOfService, ProceduralError, OtherOperational,
              OtherPhysical,OtherSecurity, CableTamper,
              IntrusionDetection, AuthenticationFailure,
              BreachOfConfidentiality, UnauthorizedAccessAttempt,
              DelayInformation, KeyExpired, OutOfHoursActivity,
              AllCauses};

④    enum Severity {Critical, Major, Minor, Warning, Cleared,
              Indeterminate};

      typedef string NotificationId;

⑤    struct Alarm {
          string MOClass;// not to be confused with STL string
          string MOInstance;
          Type type;
          Cause cause;
          stringeventTime;
          Severity severity;
          string serviceUser;
          string serviceProvider;
          NotificationId notificationId;
          sequence<NotificationId> correlatedIds;
          string text;
          string data;
      };

⑥    typedef sequence<Alarm> AlarmList;
⑦    interface Reporter : Subject {
⑧      AlarmList getAlarms(in Type t,in Cause c);
⑨      oneway void postNewAlarm(in Alarm a);
⑩      oneway void clearAlarms(in Type t, in Cause c);
      };
    };
```

LISTING 3-9.

Step 2. Develop the implementations for CORBA classes.

If you compare the implementations presented in this section with those shown in the last section, you will see the same basic idioms being applied. The only difference is that now we are using some inheritance, a namespace, a little more STL, and a lot more application logic. I'm not going to go into a lot of code commentary at this point, I will let most of it speak for itself.

There are a few key things to remember as you read through the code. In Listing 3-10, we declare the more sophisticated Subject implementation for security alarms. You can see that we extend the SecurityAlarm namespace ❶ introduced when we generated the SecurityAlarm module in SecurityAlarm.idl. Notice the usage of map ❷ to provide an association that groups alarm causes by type. Also notice that we can't forget to include the macro ❸ that generates the tie delegation code.

```
    // Reporter_i.H

    #include "SecurityAlarm.hh"
    #include "Subject_i.h"
    #include "vector.h"
    #include "map.h"

❶  namespace SecurityAlarm {

    class Reporter_i : public Subject_i {
      public:
        Reporter_i();
        virtual AlarmList* getAlarms (Type, Cause, CORBA::Environment &);
        virtual void postNewAlarm (const Alarm&,CORBA::Environment &);
        virtual void clearAlarms (Type t, Cause, CORBA::Environment &);
      protected:
        vector<Alarm*> alarms;
❷      map<Cause,Type, less<Cause> > legalFor;
        Reporter_var myRealRef;
    };

❸  DEF_TIE_Reporter(Reporter_i)
    }
```

LISTING 3-10.

The implementation of SecurityAlarm::Reporter_i is shown in Listing 3-11.a and Listing 3-11.b. In the constructor, we first instantiate the object that will delegate the member function calls to a SecurityAlarm::Reporter_i object ❶ . The rest of the constructor initializes the legalFor map ❷ , which is used in postNewAlarm to validate the combination of Cause and Type associated with a given alarm ❸ . In postNewAlarm, if values are legitimate, the Alarm is put on the list. If not, it isn't. There is a trade-off here. Ideally, we would like to throw an exception if the alarm is not legal. But if we do that, the call cannot be oneway (i.e., nonblocking). We will opt for speed and instead just print an error on cerr if the alarm is not legal.

```
// Reporter_i.CC
#include "Reporter_i.h"
#include "Observer.hh"
#include <iostream.h>

using namespace SecurityAlarm;
Reporter_i::Reporter_i()
{
    myRealRef = new TIE_Reporter(Reporter_i)(this);

    legalFor[DuplicateInfo]= IntegrityViolation;
    legalFor[InfoMissing]= IntegrityViolation;
    legalFor[InfoModDetected]= IntegrityViolation;
    legalFor[InfoOutOfSequence]= IntegrityViolation;
    legalFor[UnexpectedInfo]= IntegrityViolation;
    legalFor[DenialOfService]= OperationalViolation;
    legalFor[OutOfService]= OperationalViolation;
    legalFor[ProceduralError]= OperationalViolation;
    legalFor[OtherOperational]= OperationalViolation;
    legalFor[CableTamper]= PhysicalViolation;
    legalFor[IntrusionDetection]= PhysicalViolation;
    legalFor[OtherPhysical]= PhysicalViolation;
    legalFor[AuthenticationFailure]= SecurityService;
    legalFor[BreachOfConfidentiality]= SecurityService;
    legalFor[UnauthorizedAccessAttempt] = SecurityService;
    legalFor[OtherSecurity]= SecurityService;
    legalFor[DelayInformation]= TimeDomainViolation;
    legalFor[KeyExpired]= TimeDomainViolation;
    legalFor[OutOfHoursActivity]= TimeDomainViolation;
}
```

LISTING 3-11.a.

```
AlarmList*
Reporter_i::getAlarms (Type t, Cause c, CORBA::Environment &)
{
    AlarmList* aListPtr = new AlarmList;
    aListPtr->length(alarms.size());
    CORBA::ULong i;
    for(i = 0; i < alarms.size(); i++)
    {
        if((alarms[i]->type == t  || t == AllViolationTypes) &&
           (alarms[i]->cause == c || c == AllCauses))
        {
            (*aListPtr)[i] = Alarm(*(alarms[i]));
        }
    }
    return aListPtr;
}

void
Reporter_i::postNewAlarm (const Alarm& a, CORBA::Environment&)
{
    cout << "new alarm posted" << endl;
    if(legalFor[a.cause] != a.type)
    {
        cerr << "attempt to post illegal alarm" << endl;
    }
    else
    {
        alarms.push_back(new Alarm(a));
    }
    notify();// let all Observers know about new alarm.
}
void
Reporter_i::clearAlarms (Type t, Cause c, CORBA::Environment&)
{
    vector<Alarm*>::iterator i;
    for(i = alarms.begin(); i != alarms.end(); i++)
    {
        Alarm* a = *i;
        if((a->type==t  || a->type == AllViolationTypes) &&
           (a->cause==c || a->cause == AllCauses))
        {
            alarms.erase(i);
        }
    }
}
```

③

LISTING 3-11.b.

Next, we need to implement the `Observer`, alias `PhysicalSecurityManager`
(Listing 3-12). To develop this implementation, I started with a copy of the `Observer_i`
implementation and supplemented/modified it with physical security stuff. For example, I
made it easier to print alarm messages by initializing a couple of `maps` (see Listing 3-12
and Listing 3-13.a **1**) that associate data that will be received in an alarm with ASCII
representations. In fact, all the `PhysicalSecurityManager` does when it gets
updated is `getAlarms`, check to see if any are physical, and then print out those that are
(see Listing 3-13.b **2**).

```
// PhysicalSecurityManager.h

#include "SecurityAlarm.hh"
#include "Observer.hh"
#include <map.h>

class PhysicalSecurityManager {
  public:
    PhysicalSecurityManager();
    virtual void update(Subject_var, CORBA::Environment&);
  protected:
    SecurityAlarm::Reporter_var reporterVar;
    map<SecurityAlarm::Cause,
        const char*, less<SecurityAlarm::Cause> > causeStrings;
    map<SecurityAlarm::Severity,const char*,
        less<SecurityAlarm::Severity> > severityStrings;
};

DEF_TIE_Observer(PhysicalSecurityManager)
```

1 (margin marker beside the map declarations)

LISTING 3-12.

```
// PhysicalSecurityManager.cc
#include "Observer_i.h"
#include "SecurityAlarm.hh"
#include "PSManager.h"
#include <iostream.h>
#include <stdlib.h>


PhysicalSecurityManager::PhysicalSecurityManager()
{
  using namespace SecurityAlarm;
  causeStrings[CableTamper]= "Cabling Tampering";
  causeStrings[IntrusionDetection]= "Intrusion Detected";
  causeStrings[OtherPhysical]= "Other Physical Violation";
  severityStrings[Critical]= "Critical";
  severityStrings[Major]= "Major";
  severityStrings[Minor]= "Minor";
  severityStrings[Warning]= "Warning";
  severityStrings[Cleared]= "Cleared";
  severityStrings[Indeterminate]= "Indeterminate";
  try {
    reporterVar = Reporter::_bind(":SecurityAlarmReporterSrv");
  }
  catch (CORBA::SystemException &sysEx) {
    cerr << "Unexpected system exception during bind" << endl;
    cerr << &sysEx;
    exit(1);
  }
  catch(...) {
    cerr << "Bind to SecurityAlarm::Reporter object failed" << endl;
    exit(1);
  }
  try {
    reporterVar->attach(new
                TIE_Observer(PhysicalSecurityManager)(this));
  }
  catch (CORBA::SystemException &sysEx) {
    cerr << "Unexpected system exception" << endl;
    cerr << &sysEx;
    exit(1);
  }
  catch(...) {
    cerr << "call to attach failed" << endl;
    exit(1);
  }
}
```

(1)

LISTING 3-13.a.

```
      void
      PhysicalSecurityManager::update(Subject_var, CORBA::Environment&)
      {
        using namespace SecurityAlarm;
        cout << "new alarms to investigate" << endl;
        AlarmList* alist;
        alist = reporterVar->getAlarms (PhysicalViolation,
                AllCauses);

  ②    for(int i = 0; i < alist->length(); i++)
        {
          cout << (*alist)[i].MOClass<< endl;
          cout << (*alist)[i].MOInstance<< endl;
          cout << "Physical Violation"<< endl;// we trust server
          cout << causeStrings[(*alist)[i].cause] << endl;
          cout << (*alist)[i].eventTime<< endl;
          cout << severityStrings[(*alist)[i].severity] << endl;
          cout << (*alist)[i].serviceUser<< endl;
          cout << (*alist)[i].serviceProvider<< endl;
          cout << (*alist)[i].notificationId<< endl;
          cout << (*alist)[i].text<< endl;
          cout << (*alist)[i].data<< endl;
          cout << endl;
        }
        delete alist; // very important, will leak if I don't.
                      // see [CORBA95], pg 16-48 for explanation.
      }
```

LISTING 3-13.b.

Step 3. Write server programs.

The server programs shown in Listing 3-14 and Listing 3-15 are basically the same logic. I wrote them by copying the ones shown in the last section and modifying three things: the header file for the server implementation, the actual instantiation of the implementation object, and the name of the server being provided by the program.

```
// SecurityAlarmReporter_Main.C


#include <iostream.h>
#include <stdlib.h>
#include "Reporter_i.h"

int main()
{
  SecurityAlarm::Reporter_i sar;
  try {
    CORBA::Orbix.impl_is_ready("SecurityAlarmReporterSrv");
  }
  catch (CORBA::SystemException &sysEx)
  {
    cerr << "Unexpected system exception" << endl;
    cerr << &sysEx;
    exit(1);
  }
  catch(...)
  {
    cout << "Unexpected exception" << endl;
    exit(1);
  }
  return 0;
}
```

LISTING 3-14.

```
// PSManager_Main.C

#include <iostream.h>
#include <stdlib.h>
#include "PhysicalSecurityManager.h"

int main() {

  PhysicalSecurityManager psm;// will automatically instantiate TIE

  try {
    CORBA::Orbix.impl_is_ready("PhysicalSecurityManagerSrv");
  }
  catch (CORBA::SystemException &sysEx)
  {
    cerr << "Unexpected system exception" << endl;
    cerr << &sysEx;
    exit(1);
  }
  catch(...)
  {
    cout << "Unexpected exception" << endl;
    exit(1);
  }
  return 0;
}
```

LISTING 3-15.

Step 4. Write client programs.

The C++ program shown in Listing 3-16 simulates what a real monitoring system might do if it detected that someone was potentially tampering with a cable somewhere in the network being managed by our `SecurityAlarm::Reporter`. It is basically just a little test program that provides the catalyst for starting the scenario depicted in Figure 3-11.

```
// PhysicalMO_Main.C

#include <iostream.h>
#include <stdlib.h>
#include "SecurityAlarm.hh"

using namespace SecurityAlarm;
int main() {
  Reporter_var reporterVar;
  try {
    reporterVar = Reporter::_bind(":SecurityAlarmReporterSrv");
  }
  catch (CORBA::SystemException &sysEx) {
    cerr << "Unexpected system exception" << endl;
    cerr << &sysEx;
    exit(1);
  }
  catch(...) {
    cerr << "Bind to SecurityAlarm::Reporter object failed" << endl;
    exit(1);
  }
  Alarm a;
  a.MOClass = "class1";
  a.MOInstance = "instance1";
  a.type = PhysicalViolation;
  a.cause = CableTamper;
  a.eventTime = "12:00:00";
  a.severity = Critical;
  a.serviceUser = "user1";
  a.serviceProvider = "provider1";
  a.notificationId = "id1";
  // did not initialize correlatedIds
  a.text = "this is text for the cable tampering incident";
  a.data = "this is data for the cable tampering incident";
  try {
    reporterVar->postNewAlarm (a);
  }
  catch (CORBA::SystemException &sysEx) {
    cerr << "Unexpected system exception" << endl;
    cerr << &sysEx;
    exit(1);
  }
  return 0;
}
```

LISTING 3-16.

Step 5.   Register CORBA objects with the ORB.

Step 6.   Run the client programs.

When you run the `PhysicalMO` (i.e., client to the `SecurityAlarm::Reporter`), the scenario depicted in the object interaction diagram shown in Figure 3-11 will unfold, and when the last message in the scenario is received by the `PhysicalSecurityManager` object, it will print a message containing the details of the alarm.

3.8 Common Object Services

CORBA makes it possible to define generic software services that can be provided via an ORB. That is exactly what the OMG has chosen to do as follow-on work to the basic CORBA Specification. Their strategy and the types of services that they intend to define are spelled out in [OSA95]. The OMG defines an "Object Service" by specifying its IDL interface and describing the behavior expected from an implementation of the service.

If the OMG is successful in defining good service specifications, this could ultimately result in the emergence of an industry that produces commodity software components for CORBA. I think this is a very good thing, but my observation is that people are still focusing on components as the ultimate reuse technique. A CORBA component approach to building software has the same limitations as any component-based approach. You still need good frameworks.

Some services, like the Naming Service, which enables objects to locate each other by name, are already defined. Others are more esoteric and still pretty much ill-defined. Very few have been brought to the market in compliant form yet. There are off-the-shelf implementations of the Naming Service and the Event Notification Service [see COSS94], but that's about it.

CHAPTER 4
ODMG-93:
An Object Database Standard

I think many people realized some time ago that the era of object databases was coming. I've seen enough evidence at this point to confidently say that the day has arrived. New multibillion dollar systems are being built on OODBs. Financial institutions have started caching information from huge legacy databases into OODBs. Even those who refuse to give up relational databases are using strange tools to make them look object-oriented.

Even though the era of the OODB is here, it is not possible to put a viable methodology in place that uses the technology without standardization of the programming interface to that technology. Which brings me to ODMG-93 [ODMG93], which is intended to bring just that to the table (no pun intended). It was developed out of the recognition by OODB vendors that this was something they needed to do together if their technology was to take a bite out of, and eventually devour, the relational market.

Of the three components comprising the infrastructure, I was most concerned about ODMG-93 becoming real. CORBA was definitely real, as was STL, as vendors rushed and continue to rush to become compliant on those fronts. But, when it came to ODMG-93 compliance, I noticed an almost lackadaisical attitude on the part of the OODB vendors.

I was attending a class being given by probably the best known of all the vendors, and not once did the instructor even mention ODMG-93. In fact, I approached him during one of the breaks to ask him when his company was going to be compliant. He said something like, "Oh, I think that we were involved in that for public relations. We are supposed to have some level of compliance in an upcoming release, but nobody really cares about it anymore." Excuse me? Did he say nobody cares anymore? I couldn't believe what I was hearing. I certainly cared. A sensible manager would also care, since it may be the only way that he/she will be able to justify migrating to OODB technology: having a second source. I also noticed this attitude, although not quite as blatant, with some of the other vendors that I spoke with.

I remained nervous over this issue until the beginning of 1996, when I saw vendors begin using ODMG-93 as a selling feature. At first there was just one. Now, I am happy to report that other major database players are starting to comply.[1] Thank goodness; because a standard that is adhered to by only one vendor isn't much of a standard, is it? Anyhow, the vendor that emerged first with compliance, and advertised this fact vigorously, was the one I gravitated to when I was looking for a database to build my frameworks with. That vendor was O_2™.

Before reading the rest of this chapter, I'd suggest that you go get your hands on a copy of [ODMG93] and read the chapter on the C++ binding. The C++ binding chapter is really all that we are concerned about, and I found it to be quite readable. In the next section I will very briefly discuss the standard, and then in the last two sections I will illustrate how you use a compliant database.

4.1 High-Level Overview

An object database enables C++ programmers to store the state of objects on disk (i.e., make them persistent). Your C++ class declarations *are* your schema, so the programming language view of the data is consistent with the database view. This offers an advantage over a relational database because it eliminates the "impedance mismatch" between C++ and relational data.[2]

Object databases still retain many of the familiar mechanisms of relational ones. For instance, you will find that an object database still needs to be opened and closed. And when a new persistent object is instantiated, it doesn't just float around in a magical place; it must still be put in a particular named database.

The notion of a transaction is common to both relational and object databases.[3] By designating a section of C++ code as a transaction, you can verify that all state changes

---

1. To keep up with which products are compliant with ODMG-93, you can look at the ODMG Web site (www.odmg.org), which now keeps a list of such products.

2. The "impedance mismatch" between C++ and relational databases refers to the differences between the type system and relationships supported by each. It also refers to the tedious and error-prone programming required to keep C++ code synchronized with relational data that it is working with.

3. A transaction is a sequence of database operations where either all take effect or none take effect. In other words, a transaction makes otherwise separate operations atomic.

made to persistent objects in that section of code can be made before "committing" any of them. Committing an object database transaction means that you have successfully made a sequence of state changes to persistent objects and now want to make them permanent.

You may still need to query for certain objects, based on a selection criteria, just as you would query for certain rows in a relational table. In a relational database, you use the Standard Query Language (SQL). In an object database, you use an Object Query Language (OQL), which carries forward standard SQL syntax where it still applies but augments it with features that bind well with C++.

Although you still have a need for a query language when using an object database, the need is diminished by the fact that relationships between C++ objects are now inherent in your schema (i.e., C++ declarations). For example, consider the following little relational database used by a problem reporting system. Assume it consists of two tables: `trouble_tickets` and `locations`. Now, assuming the database is normalized, to find the name of the location where the `trouble_ticket` with id 123 occurred, you would have to issue an SQL join that looks something like this:

```
select l.name from location l, trouble_tickets t where t.id = 123
and t.loc_id = l.id
```

Now consider how you might deal with this situation in C++, using an object database. Your schema could consist of the following two class declarations:

```
class TroubleTicket {
  public:
    d_Ref<Location> location;
    int id;
};

class Location {
  public:
    const char* name;
};
```

When you are working with a persistent object, you have to refer to it by using the template class d_Ref, which allows you to access the object as though you had a pointer to it. So, assume that d_Ref<TroubleTicket> t is set to refer to a TroubleTicket object with id equal to 123, just retrieved from an object database. We can then find the associated location name by using regular C++ dereferencing syntax: t->location->name. The object database will automatically navigate to the Location object for you, going out to disk to fetch it if necessary (it may already be cached somewhere). You can see from this simple example that the need to manually construct simple joins is greatly diminished because C++ relationship semantics are understood directly by an object database. I guess, in this regard, you could say that an object database is "smarter" than a relational one.

I should also mention that an object database is "smarter" than a relational one in the sense that you can specify relationships directly in your C++ class declarations that instruct the database to maintain referential integrity for you. So, for example, if you specify a one-to-one relationship between two objects that refer to each other, then if one is deleted, the reference to it in the remaining object is automatically reset to a null reference.

For some applications, there may not be any need for queries, only navigation through regular C++ class relationships. But for many, there will still be a need to retrieve objects by query. For example, assume that you are in charge of physical network security at a government installation. Assume also that this installation is using OSI Network Management software. If you are trying to track down the source of a rash of violations that have been occurring in the southwest quadrant between midnight and 3 A.M., you will want to query for the associated alarm objects in the alarm database, and you can do so by embedding OQL in your C++. We will see some embedded queries in examples, a little later in this chapter.

The ODMG-93 C++ binding specifies a variety of component classes. For instance, there are time-related classes specified that you can use in the declarations of persistent objects: d_Interval, d_Date, d_Time, and d_Timestamp. This is good news because it fills a void in STL, which does not have any time-related classes.

Unfortunately, there is a new kind of "impedance mismatch" when you try to use STL, CORBA, and ODMG-93 together. Because of the different lineages of the three standards and the recognition that certain standard components for collections and character strings were needed, each body came up with its own component classes that basically have the same semantics. The ODMG-93 C++ binding specifies a character string class (d_String) and a variety of collection classes (d_Set, d_Bag, d_List, and d_Varray) in which to store persistent objects. ODMG-93 also specifies an iterator class (d_Iterator), but its interface looks very much like an STL iterator, making it possible to process collections of persistent objects with STL algorithms.

Collections can be polymorphic, because the d_Ref class supports the notion of inheritance. For example, suppose the classes Circle and Square are persistent classes and are both derived from the persistent Shape class. If I have a d_Set<d_Ref<Shape> >, then it can contain both Circle and Square objects. Try doing something like that with a relational database!

How do you, as a C++ programmer, actually use an ODMG-93 database? Well, you use standard C++ syntax to first declare persistent classes. Then you run a preprocessor on these declarations, which generates all sorts of magical and mysterious code that's not intended for your viewing. In fact, if you stare at it directly, I suspect that you may turn into a pillar of salt. Next, you write the implementation of your persistent class member functions and the application itself. Then you just compile, link, and run. Oh, you will probably need to start your database server process before running your program. You may also have to do some administrative work, like creating your database.

4.2 The Role of Object Databases in Frameworks

When designing frameworks, we are interested in using ODMG-93 to store objects that consist primarily of data members and accessor functions. We are also interested in storing objects that help us manage collections of persistent data objects. Embedded in the data members of such objects are the collections of persistent objects that they manage.

We generally don't think of persistent objects as being rich in behavior, having a frequently changing state that is mainly transient, and having few instances. Objects that can be accessed via CORBA often fall into this category. But, often you would like some of the state of such objects to be preserved. For example, consider the `Subject_i` class in the OBSERVER pattern that we introduced in the last chapter. A `Subject_i` object keeps a list of those `Observer` objects that are currently attached to it. If the machine that a `Subject_i` object is running on crashes, you'd like the `Subject_i` to come back up with the same list of `Observers`. It is possible to buy ORB product offerings that persistently maintain the state of a CORBA object in a way that is transparent to your code. Orbix is one example of an ORB that offers such features. One of the database vendors that it has partnered with, in fact, is O_2. So, technically, you can design frameworks without consideration of the state of CORBA objects if you choose such a product. But, this is currently a vendor-specific solution, so I am not going to assume CORBA object persistence is a given in this methodology.

4.3 The Impact of Object Databases on Modeling Notation

The only impact object databases have on modeling notation is that a persistent class will be labeled as such, by putting "(persistent)" under the class name in the class box.

4.4 Using an ODMG-Compliant Object Database with C++

We are interested in using an object database for the following:

1. Creating persistent objects
2. Retrieving a persistent object by name
3. Retrieving persistent objects by navigating to them through a "root"[4] object

---

4. A "root" object is one that is persistent and named and has references to other persistent objects as its data members.

4. Retrieving a collection of persistent objects that satisfy a particular criterion

5. Iterating through a collection of persistent objects

6. Modifying persistent objects

7. Deleting persistent objects

I want to demonstrate how to accomplish each of these tasks by showing you complete programs. This will leave no doubt about what portions of the API (i.e., ODMG-93 C++ binding) must be exercised for a given task. I didn't want to try to squeeze all the tasks into one program. It's easy to become confused about which pieces of the API must be used together when many tasks are performed in a single piece of code. In the remainder of this section, all the basic tasks mentioned above will be demonstrated in a primitive, yet complete, application for a mail order catalog operation.

At the core of this application are four persistent classes: `CatalogItem`, `Catalog`, `Order`, and `OrderManager`. The relationships between each of these is depicted in Figure 4-1. A `CatalogItem` is basically a data structure used to describe an item for sale in a `Catalog`. It contains data members for providing a textual description of the item, a unique catalog number, and the price of the item. The `Catalog` class itself has a name, an issue date, and a collection containing references to the items for sale in it. To keep track of catalog orders, I have defined an `Order` class that has data members containing a customer identifier,[5] an order number, and the state of the order. It also contains the catalog numbers of the specific items, and quantities of each, comprising the order. In the interest of simplicity I have completely decoupled `CatalogItem` objects from `Order` objects. I will only associate a collection of item numbers with an `Order`, not even verifying that these item numbers correspond to `CatalogItem` objects. Lastly, I define an `OrderManager` class that encapsulates much of the database-related code required for dealing with `Order` objects. It also provides controlled access to persistent `Order` objects. The notion of having a persistent data class and an associated data manager class is an important design technique for developing applications that use an ODMG-93-compliant database. So, pay particular attention to the design of the `OrderManager`.

---

5. I don't include any other information about customers in this application.

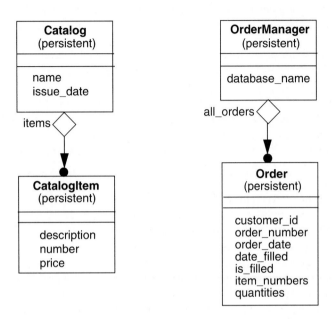

FIGURE 4-1.

I'll build this application in two steps. First, I'll talk about `CatalogItem` and `Catalog` and show you programs for creating and deleting persistent `CatalogItems` (task 1 and 7 mentioned above). This will be followed by a program that prints all `CatalogItems` in a particular `Catalog`. This will illustrate tasks 2, 3, and 5. I will then introduce the declarations and implementations of the `Order` and `OrderManager` classes, which are more thoughtfully designed than `CatalogItem` and `Catalog`, as I'll explain. And lastly, I will show you a program for

- Creating an `Order`
- Filling an `Order`
- Printing all `Orders` that have not been filled and are older than a user-specified number of days

These programs will illustrate some important design techniques, as well as tasks 1 through 6, a few at a time.

`Catalog.h` contains the declarations of `CatalogItem` and `Catalog`, along with their `inline` functions, and is shown in Listing 4-1. This file will be processed by a tool, provided with your database, to make `CatalogItem` and `Catalog` persistent. It will do this by generating code, as I mentioned before. The tool may, in fact, modify `Catalog.h` directly, making the class declarations of `CatalogItem` and `Catalog` derived from another class containing persistence mechanisms. The implementations that you provide for the member functions of these classes are unaffected by generated code.

```
// Catalog.h

class Catalog;
const char* _items = "items";
const char* _catalog = "catalog";

class CatalogItem {
  public:
    CatalogItem(const char* description, const char* number,
               float price);
    const char* get_description() const;
    const char* get_number() const;
    float get_price() const;

  protected:
    const char* description;
    const char* number;// uniquely identifies item.
    float price;
    d_Rel_Ref<Catalog,_items> catalog;
};

inline const char*
CatalogItem::get_description() const { return description;}

inline const char*
CatalogItem::get_number() const { return number; }

inline float CatalogItem::get_price() const { return price; }
```

LISTING 4-1.a.

```
    class Catalog {
      public:
        Catalog(const char* name, d_Date issueDate);
        void add_item(d_Ref<CatalogItem>);
        const char* get_name() const;
        d_Date get_issue_date() const;
        const d_Set<d_Ref<CatalogItem> >& get_items() const;

      protected:
        const char* name;
        d_Date issue_date;
 ❷      d_Rel_Set<d_Ref<CatalogItem>,_catalog> items;
    };

 ❸  inline void Catalog::add_item(d_Ref<CatalogItem> i)
    {items.insert_element(i);}

    inline const char* Catalog::get_name() const { return name; }

    inline d_Date Catalog::get_issue_date() const { return issue_date; }

    inline const d_Set<d_Ref<CatalogItem> >&
    Catalog::get_items() const { return items; }
```

LISTING 4-1.b.

CatalogItem is a typical data class. Many of its functions are small and can actually be
inline. They are mostly accessors or state-setting functions. The only thing that is really
noteworthy in the declaration of CatalogItem is the catalog data member ❶ . This
member serves one purpose: to specify that the database should enforce referential
integrity with the items data member in the Catalog class. When a CatalogItem
object is deleted from the database, any reference to that object in a Catalog object's
items member will be made null. The suite of ODMG-93 template classes with names
that start with "d_Rel_" exists for specifying such relationships.

The Catalog class isn't very exciting either. Every Catalog object will contain a set of
references to CatalogItem objects ❷ . Notice that I used the d_Rel_Set class for the
items data member. It has the exact same interface as the d_Set class, which is what I
would have used if I didn't care about referential integrity. The add_item() function is
used to actually add a CatalogItem to a Catalog ❸ . Inserting elements into a
d_Rel_Set requires a slightly different syntax than inserting into an STL set
(i.e., set::insert() versus d_Rel_Set::insert_element()).

The only non-`inline` functions associated with `CatalogItem` and `Catalog` are their constructors. They are shown in Listing 4-2.[6]

```
// Catalog.C

#include "Catalog.h"
#include <iostream.h>

CatalogItem::CatalogItem(const char* d, const char* n, float p) :
description(d), number(n), price(p),
{
}

Catalog::Catalog(const char* n, d_Date d) : name(n), issue_date(d)
{
}
```

LISTING 4-2.

After you run the preprocessor on `Catalog.h` and compile the generated code, along with `Catalog.C`, you are ready to write programs that can use the object database to store persistent `CatalogItem` and `Catalog` objects. The first program that I wrote adds a `CatalogItem` to a `Catalog` and is shown in Listing 4-3.

The program starts by prompting the user for all the information needed to construct a new `CatalogItem` **1** . The catalog database is then opened **2** . It is assumed to be created already through an administration interface. ODMG-93 does not specify a way to create a database with C++. Then, a transaction is started **3** , which will encapsulate the actual instantiation of the `CatalogItem` object and subsequent addition to the `Catalog` object.

Immediately after starting the transaction, I try to retrieve a reference to the `Catalog` object of interest **4** . If it doesn't exist yet, I create a persistent instance **5** . As you can see, the way to create a persistent version of an object is to use an overloaded version of the `new` operator that accepts a pointer to a `d_Database` object as an argument. I could have created a transient instance by using the version of `new` that does not take any arguments.[7] After creating a persistent `Catalog` object, I name it **6** . It is very important to remember to name it. If I don't, next time a program is started that needs to fetch that `Catalog` object, it won't be able to find it! Persistent objects that are directly fetched from the database (i.e., "root" objects), are retrieved by name.

---

6. For O_2, I was actually required to also initialize the items and catalog data members with the this pointer.

7. That is, other than the hidden size argument.

```
// add_item.C
#include <iostream.h>
#include <stdlib.h>
#include "Catalog.h"
// database-specific includes
const int bufSize = 256;
int
main(int argc, char* argv[])
{
    // database-specific initialization
    char catalogName[bufSize];
    cout << "Catalog Name:" << ends;
    cin.getline(catalogName,bufSize);
    cout << "Item Description: " << ends;
    char itemDescription[bufSize];
    cin.getline(itemDescription,bufSize);

    cout << "Item Number: " << ends;
    char itemNumber[bufSize];
    cin >> itemNumber;
    cout << "Item Price: " << ends;
    float itemPrice;
    cin >> itemPrice;
    d_Database database;
    database.open("catalogBase");
    d_Ref<Catalog> catalog;
    d_Transaction addIt;
    addIt.begin();
    if((catalog = database.lookup_object(catalogName)) == NULL)
    {
        catalog =
         new(&database) Catalog(catalogName, d_Date::current());
        database.set_object_name((d_Ref_Any&)catalog,catalogName);
    }
    d_Ref<CatalogItem> item =
    new(&database) CatalogItem(itemDescription,itemNumber,itemPrice);
    database.set_object_name((d_Ref_Any&)item,itemNumber);

    catalog->add_item(item);
    catalog->mark_modified();  // do I need this, write explanation.
    addIt.commit();
    database.close();
    // database-specific cleanup
}
```

LISTING 4-3.

Next, the CatalogItem is instantiated ⑦ and named ⑧ . It is then added to the Catalog ⑨ . After this, the Catalog object is marked as modified ⑩ so that when the transaction is committed, it is guaranteed that the changes made to it are written to disk. If you've been paying close attention, you may be asking where the mark_modified() function came from. It certainly doesn't appear in the declaration of Catalog shown in Listing 4-1. The answer goes back to what I told you earlier about the code generator provided with the database. The code generator actually gives Catalog a base class that provides this function. I should also note that it may not be necessary to make this call, but, for portability, do it to be safe. The last part of the program commits the transaction ⑪ and closes the database ⑫ .

The program in Listing 4-4 illustrates how you can delete a persistent object, a CatalogItem object, specifically. It's pretty straightforward. First, the user is asked for the item number corresponding to the name of the object to be deleted ① . Remember, in the previous program we explicitly named CatalogItem objects with the same string as their number data member. The database is then opened ② and a transaction is started ③ . Next, a reference to that object is retrieved ④ and the object is then deleted ⑤ . Last, the transaction is committed ⑥ and the database is closed ⑦ .

The call to delete_object() ⑤ removes the CatalogItem object from memory and the database. Notice that the dot operator is used, because delete_object() is a member of d_Ref, not the CatalogItem object being referenced. Also recall that, because of the relationships established between Catalog and CatalogItem classes, when the CatalogItem object is removed from the database, any references to it in Catalog objects will automatically be set to null, leaving no dangling references.

```
     // delete_item.C
     #include <iostream.h>
     #include <stdlib.h>
     #include "Catalog.H"
     // database-specific includes
     const int bufSize = 256;

     int
     main(int argc, char* argv[])
     {
         // database-specific initialization

         char itemNumber[bufSize];
(1)      cout << "ItemNumber:" << ends;
         cin >> itemNumber;

(2)      d_Database database;
         database.open("catalogBase");

         d_Ref<CatalogItem> item;
(3)      d_Transaction deleteIt;
         deleteIt.begin();

(4)      if((item = database.lookup_object(itemNumber)) == NULL)
         {
           cerr << "No such Item" << endl;
         }
         else
         {
(5)        item.delete_object();
         }
(6)      deleteIt.commit();
(7)      database.close();
         // database-specific cleanup
     }
```

LISTING 4-4.

The program shown in Listing 4-5 prints all CatalogItems in a Catalog. It illustrates how to retrieve persistent objects by navigating from their "root" object. A Catalog object can be retrieved by name and contains a collection (i.e., Catalog::items) of references to CatalogItems. A Catalog object is, therefore, considered the "root" of all CatalogItems that it has a reference to. The additional spin put on this example is that an iterator class (d_Iterator) specified in ODMG-93 helps us retrieve the objects referenced in Catalog::items.

The program starts by retrieving the Catalog name from the user **1** . Then a transaction is started **2** . Even though we are only going to be reading the database, the ODMG-93 standard specifies that any interaction to the database must be done from within a transaction. Once the transaction is started, we look up the reference to the Catalog **3** , print the title **4** , and then print each of its items **5** . The retrieval of each item reference illustrates the coding idiom for using the d_Iterator class.

You will notice two things about how we dealt with Catalog and CatalogItem objects in the programs just presented. First, every time we wrote a new program, we had quite a bit of database housekeeping to do. Second, because we named each CatalogItem object, any program could retrieve one from the database and read, modify, or delete it. There was no control over access to these objects. That may be okay for very simple applications, but large, complex applications certainly can't be designed this way.

```
   // print_catalog.C
   #include <iostream.h>
   #include <stdlib.h>
   #include "Catalog.h"
   // database-specific includes
   const int bufSize = 256;

   int
   main(int argc, char* argv[])
   {
       // database-specific initialization
       database.open("catalogBase");

       char catalogName[bufSize];
①     cout << "Catalog Name:" << ends;
       cin.getline(catalogName,bufSize);
       d_Ref<Catalog> catalog;
       d_Transaction prnt;
②     prnt.begin();
③     if((catalog = database.lookup_object(catalogName)) == NULL)
       {
         cout << "No Such Catalog" << endl;
       }
       else
       {
④         cout << catalog->get_name() << "\t\t"
             << catalog->get_issue_date() << endl;
           cout <<
           "_____"
           << endl;
         const d_Set<d_Ref<CatalogItem> >& items = catalog->get_items();
         d_Iterator<d_Ref<CatalogItem> > iter = items.create_iterator();
           d_Ref<CatalogItem> i;
           while(iter.next(i))
           {
⑤             cout << i->get_description() << "\t" <<
               i->get_number() << "\t" <<
               i->get_price() << endl; //":::" << cn << endl;
           }
       }
       prnt.commit();
       database.close();
       // database-specific cleanup
   }
```

LISTING 4-5.

As we now turn our attention to the ordering features of this little application, we will focus on removing much of the database housekeeping from the sight of the application programmers by means of the `Order` class. We will also try to provide a little more control over how these persistent objects are accessed.

The `Order` and `OrderManager` class declarations are shown in Listing 4-6. The only aspect of `Order` that might be in need of some explanation is the association between `item_numbers` and `quantities` ❶. Each `item_number` is a string that is expected to correspond to the name of a `CatalogItem` object (although I don't actually verify this). The order may include one or more of a particular item, so we need to associate a quantity with an item. The quantity of an item in `item_numbers` is assumed to be the element in `quantities` with the same index. This just saves us from having to introduce another data structure.

`OrderManager` is a persistent class that provides a home for all `Order` objects (i.e., the extent of `Order`) in a particular database. The design of `OrderManager` employs a technique that requires access to all "official" persistent `Order` objects be through an `OrderManager` object. There is no way to programmatically prevent a stand-alone program from creating and naming a persistent `Order` object that no other program is aware of. `Order` objects that are put in the database via an `OrderManager`, on the other hand, cannot be accessed in any other way. They have no names and therefore can only be navigated to by the implementation of `OrderManager`, which has access to the `all_orders` collection that contains references to them.

An `OrderManager` object is instantiated as a transient object from within a user application (i.e., as an automatic variable or by using the regular `new` operator), using the public constructor ❷. The protected constructor ❸ is used by the `OrderManager` itself to pull in the `Order` objects from the database. Notice that I have not specified `d_Rel_Set` for `all_orders` ❹. It really isn't necessary since persistent `Order` objects are closely managed through this one class.

```
// Order.h

class Order {
  public:
    Order(const char* customer_id, const char* order_number);
    void add_item(const char* item_number, unsigned quantity);
    void order_filled();
    int is_order_filled() const;
    unsigned days_since_placed() const;
    d_String get_order_number() const;
  protected:
    d_String customer_id;
    d_String order_number;
    d_Date order_date;
    d_Date date_filled;
    int is_filled;
    d_List<d_String> item_numbers;
    d_List<int> quantities;
};
inline void Order::add_item(const char* i, unsigned q)
{
    item_numbers.insert_element_last(i);
    quantities.insert_element_last(q);
}

inline void Order::order_filled()
{date_filled=d_Date::current(); is_filled++;}

inline int  Order::is_order_filled() const { return is_filled; }

inline d_String Order::get_order_number() const
{ return order_number; }

class OrderManager {
  public:
    OrderManager(const char* database_name);
    void place_order(const Order&);
    void order_filled(const char* order_number);
    void print_unfilled_orders(int days_old) const;
  protected:
    OrderManager();
    d_Set<d_Ref<Order> > all_orders;
    const char* database_name;
};
```

LISTING 4-6.

Listing 4-7 contains the implementation of Order and OrderManager. The Order::days_since_placed function ❶ introduces another ODMG-93 class: d_Interval, which enables you to determine intervals of time by treating d_Date objects as arithmetic values that can be added and subtracted. The public constructor of OrderManager ❷ , which is assumed to be used for transient instances, will create the one and only persistent OrderManager object if it does not exist. This persistent instance is the "shadow" of all transient instances. Your program can have multiple transient OrderManager objects, and you can deal with any one of them. They all work with the one and only persistent "shadow" object, which has the same name as the class itself (i.e., "OrderManager"). The protected OrderManager constructor ❸ is used by the OrderManager itself to create the persistent shadow.

And now, turning our attention to the member functions of OrderManager (Listing 4-7.b and 4-7.c): you will notice that each one encapsulates the logic for:

- Opening and closing the database

- Starting and committing a transaction

This logic helps with our goal of removing housekeeping responsibilities from the application programmer.

OrderManager::place_order() ❹ accepts a reference to a transient Order object as an argument. It then constructs a persistent version of that object and inserts it into the all_orders element of the shadow. Notice I never touch the all_orders that is local—it is just a dummy copy.

OrderManager::order_filled() ❺ illustrates the use of OQL. Every ODMG-93 collection class[8] has a select_element member function that accepts a string containing an OQL query. The function returns a reference to the persistent object satisfying the query. In this case, the object returned is a reference to the Order to be designated as filled. As I am putting together the query, notice that I use the phrase "this.get_order_number" ❻ . This is the OQL syntax for invoking Order::get_order_number() on each Order object in the shadow's all_orders as it is being checked to see if it satisfies the query criteria. Yes, you can embed function calls in OQL queries, as long as those functions don't take arguments.

The last member function, OrderManager::print_unfilled_orders() ❼ , will print orders that have not been filled and are at least as old as the input argument specifies. Again we use OQL, but this time we will be getting back more than one object as a result of the query. All ODMG-93 collection classes have a member function called query to process an OQL query expecting a multiple object result ❾ . I define a set of references to objects ❽ for the query results to be placed in. When the query function

---

8. I didn't mention it before, but all collection classes are derived from d_Collection.

returns, I then iterate through the results (now in `unfilled`) to print the unfilled order numbers.

```
// Order.C
#include <stdlib.h>
#include <stdio.h>
#include <strstrea.h>
#include <iostream.h>
#include "Order.h"
const int bufSize = 256;

Order::Order(const char* c, const char* o) : customer_id(c),
order_number(o), is_filled(0)
{
}

unsigned
Order::days_since_placed() const
{
    d_Date today;
    d_Interval i = today - order_date;
    return i.day();
}

OrderManager::OrderManager(const char* db) : database_name(db)
{
    d_Database database;
    database.open(database_name);
    d_Transaction t;
    t.begin();
    d_Ref<OrderManager> om;
    if((om = database.lookup_object("OrderManager")) == NULL)
    {
      om = new(&database) OrderManager;
      database.set_object_name((d_Ref_Any&)om,"OrderManager");
      om->mark_modified();
    }
    t.commit();
    database.close();
}

OrderManager::OrderManager()
{
}
```

LISTING 4-7.a.

```
    void
4   OrderManager::place_order(const Order& o)
    {
        d_Database database;
        database.open(database_name);
        d_Transaction t;
        t.begin();
        d_Ref<OrderManager> shadow;
        if((shadow = database.lookup_object("OrderManager")) == NULL)
        {
            cerr << "Error: could not lookup OrderManager" << endl;
        }
        d_Ref<Order> order = new(&database) Order(o);
        shadow->all_orders.insert_element(order);
        shadow->mark_modified();
        t.commit();
        database.close();
    }


    void
5   OrderManager::order_filled(const char* order_number)
    {
        d_Database database;
        database.open(database_name);
        d_Transaction t;
        t.begin();
        d_Ref<OrderManager> shadow =
            database.lookup_object("OrderManager");
        d_Ref<Order> order;
6       d_String query = "this.get_order_number = \"";
        query += order_number;
        query += "\"";
        if((order = shadow->all_orders.select_element(query)) != NULL)
        {
            order->order_filled();
            order->mark_modified();
        }
        t.commit();
        database.close();
    }
```

LISTING 4-7.b.

```
    void
(7) OrderManager::print_unfilled_orders(int days_old) const
    {
        d_Database database;
        database.open(database_name);
        d_Transaction t;
        t.begin();
        d_Ref<OrderManager> shadow =
            database.lookup_object("OrderManager");
        char query[bufSize];
        ostrstream strm(query,bufSize);
        strm << "this.is_order_filled = 0 and this.days_since_placed >= "
            << days_old << ends;
(8)     d_Set<d_Ref<Order> > unfilled;
(9)     shadow->all_orders.query(unfilled,query);
        d_Iterator<d_Ref<Order> > iter = unfilled.create_iterator();
        d_Ref<Order> order;
        while(iter.next(order))
        {
            cout << order->get_order_number() << endl;
        }
        t.commit();
        database.close();
    }
```

LISTING 4-7.c.

A program for placing an order is shown in Listing 4-8. The most significant point to make about this program is that a transient `Order` object is built up through interaction with the user before the transaction that creates a persistent `Order` is initiated. This prevents the situation where a portion of the database is locked up while a customer is deciding how many turtlenecks to order and what colors they should be.[9] Notice also that we've been fairly successful at purging database housekeeping code from this program.

```cpp
// place_order.C
#include <iostream.h>
#include <stdlib.h>
#include "Order.h"
#include "Catalog.h"
// database-specific includes
const int bufSize = 256;
int
main(int argc, char* argv[])
{
    // database-specific initialization
    char customerName[bufSize];
    cout << "Customer Name:" << ends;
    cin.getline(customerName,bufSize);
    char orderNumber[bufSize];
    cout << "Order Number:" << ends;
    cin.getline(orderNumber,bufSize);
    Order* order = new Order(customerName, orderNumber);
    while(1)
    {
        cout << "Item Number and quantity" << ends;
        unsigned quantity;
        char item_number[bufSize];
        cin >> item_number >> quantity;
        order->add_item(item_number,quantity);
        cout << "Another Item? (y or n)" << ends;
        char answer;
        cin >> answer;
        if(answer != 'y')
        {
            break;
        }
    }

    OrderManager* manager = new OrderManager("catalogBase");
    manager->place_order(*order);
    t.commit();
    // database-specific cleanup
}
```

LISTING 4-8.

---

9. The degree of harm that this would cause depends, in part, on your database architecture. Different databases have different locking granularity.

Programs for filling an order and printing unfilled orders are shown in Listing 4-9 and Listing 4-10, respectively. They are quite trivial, as you can see. Again, this is because we pulled much of the housekeeping into the implementation of the persistent classes themselves.

```cpp
#include <iostream.h>
#include <stdlib.h>
#include "Order.h"
#include "Catalog.h"
// database-specific includes
const int bufSize = 256;
int
main(int argc, char* argv[])
{
    // database-specific initialization
    char orderNumber[bufSize];
    cout << "Order Number:" << ends;
    cin >> orderNumber;

    OrderManager* manager = new OrderManager("catalogBase");
    manager->order_filled(orderNumber);
    // database-specific cleanup
}
```

LISTING 4-9.

```cpp
#include <iostream.h>
#include <stdlib.h>
#include "Order.h"
#include "Catalog.h"
// database-specific includes
const int bufSize = 256;
int
main(int argc, char* argv[])
{
    // database-specific initialization
    cout << "How many days old?" << ends;
    int days_old;
    cin >> days_old;

    OrderManager* manager = new OrderManager("catalogBase");
    manager->print_unfilled_orders(days_old);
    // database-specific cleanup
}
```

LISTING 4-10.

To sum up the discussion about the `Order` and `OrderManager` classes, we have virtually purged the need for the user of the `Order` class to know how to deal with the subtleties of using ODMG-93. We have also tightened up access to persistent `Order` objects. The only way to make an order "official" is by entering it into the database through the use of the `OrderManager` class. Once you've made it persistent through an `OrderManager` object, the only way to get back at it again is through an `OrderManager` object. There is less likelihood that buggy code will inadvertently modify `Order` objects in a way that is not logical. With this design, you can now do things like add your own logging, or build security features into the `OrderManager` so that only certain applications/users can perform certain operations on `Orders`.

Summarizing the entire example: this is just an embryonic version of what a real catalog operation would require, but it actually has a lot of generic behavior woven into it. If we were to invest in scaling this up into a full-blown mail order software system, it would be nice to separate out generic behavior into frameworks, so it could be reused in other applications. In this methodology, the first step in doing this is referred to as "domain analysis", and is the subject of Chapter 5. As you will see, we will analyze the "mail order" domain in much greater detail in Chapter 5 to demonstrate the procedures of domain analysis.

4.5 Example Application Using CORBA and ODMG-93: Security Alarm Reporting

The Security Alarm Reporting example that I presented in the last chapter was intended to demonstrate the use of CORBA. Clearly, the design of that example cannot be used in a real application because alarm information is lost when the `SecurityAlarm::Reporter` process is terminated.[10] Our infrastructure mechanism for addressing this is, of course, ODMG-93. In this section, we discuss how to modify that example to make alarm data persistent, and we also modify the design such that CORBA is used for strictly lightweight communication between distributed objects.

The new and improved CORBA/ODMG-93 design is shown in Figure 4-2. You may want to compare this to the original design shown in Figure 3-10 on page 72. In the spirit of minimizing the volume of information communicated via the ORB, I stripped back the original design so that the basic OBSERVER pattern is the only part of the design that communicates via the ORB. The application is now working more directly with an OODB, using the data manager technique that I introduced in the last section. This allows us to retain the event notification mechanism, which provides loose coupling between objects reporting alarms and those that process them, yet does not require the extra

---

10. The list of all Observers expecting alarm notification is also lost, but I'm not going to address this problem.

marshalling and unmarshalling of alarm data across the ORB. This does require that the code posting a new alarm now do so in two steps instead of one:

1. Write the alarm to the OODB.

2. Notify the appropriate `Subject` that is responsible for "spreading the word" about the new alarm to interested `Observers`.

Security Alarm Reporting: Class Structure with CORBA and ODMG-93

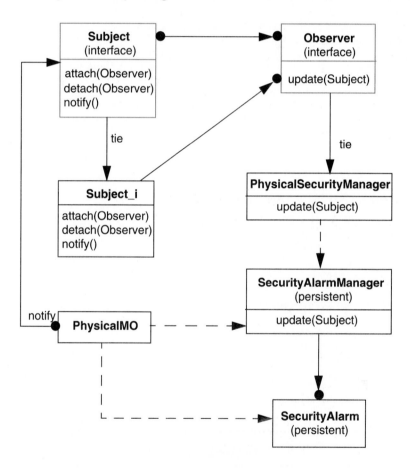

FIGURE 4-2.

If you recall, alarm information was originally defined in IDL (see Listing 3-9). Now it is a persistent class called SecurityAlarm (see Listing 4-11.a). A persistent SecurityAlarmManager class is declared in Listing 4-11.b. Notice the parallels between the interface of SecurityAlarmManager and OrderManager (Listing 4-6).

```
// SecurityAlarm.h

struct SecurityAlarm {
    enum Type{IntegrityViolation,OperationalViolation,
        PhysicalViolation, SecurityService,
        TimeDomainViolation, AllViolationTypes};

    enum Cause{DuplicateInfo, InfoMissing, InfoModDetected,
        InfoOutOfSequence, UnexpectedInfo, DenialOfService,
        OutOfService, ProceduralError, OtherOperational,
        OtherPhysical, OtherSecurity, CableTamper,
        IntrusionDetection, AuthenticationFailure,
        BreachOfConfidentiality, UnauthorizedAccessAttempt,
        DelayInformation, KeyExpired, OutOfHoursActivity,AllCauses};

    enum Severity {Critical, Major, Minor, Warning, Cleared,
        Indeterminate};

    typedef d_String NotificationId;

    SecurityAlarm();
    SecurityAlarm(d_Ref<SecurityAlarm>);
    d_String MOClass;
    d_String MOInstance;
    Type type;
    Cause cause;
    d_Timestamp eventTime;
    Severity severity;
    d_String serviceUser;
    d_String serviceProvider;
    NotificationId notificationId;
    d_List<NotificationId> correlatedIds;
    d_String text;
    d_String data;
};
```

LISTING 4-11.a.

```
class SecurityAlarmManager {
  public:
    SecurityAlarmManager(const char* database_name);
    void add(const SecurityAlarm&);
    void get_alarms(d_List<d_Ref<SecurityAlarm> >& result,
        SecurityAlarm::Type, SecurityAlarm::Cause);

  protected:
    SecurityAlarmManager();

    d_Set<d_Ref<SecurityAlarm> > all_security_alarms;
    const char* database_name;
};
```

LISTING 4-11.b.

Listing 4-12 contains the implementations of SecurityAlarm and
SecurityAlarmManager. Notice that the constructors of
SecurityAlarmManager ❶ ❷ are implemented with the same coding idioms used
for the constructors of the Order class (Listing 4-7.a.).

SecurityAlarmManager::add() ❸ takes a reference to a transient
SecurityAlarm object as an argument and makes it persistent by inserting it into the
all_security_alarms element of the shadow SecurityAlarmManager object.
The SecurityAlarmManager::get_alarms() ❹ function retrieves a list of all
SecurityAlarm objects having a particular Type and Cause. Notice that the objects
inserted into result are instantiated by using the built-in new ❺ operator, so the objects
retrieved are actually transient copies of the ones in the database. I do this instead of
returning references to the actual persistent SecurityAlarm objects to prevent the
programmer from changing their state.

```
// SecurityAlarm.C
#include <stdlib.h>
#include <stdio.h>
#include <strstrea.h>
#include <iostream.h>
// database-specific includes
#include "SecurityAlarm.h"
const int bufSize = 256;

SecurityAlarm::SecurityAlarm(){}

SecurityAlarm::SecurityAlarm(d_Ref<SecurityAlarm> other)
{
    MOClass = other->MOClass;
    MOInstance = other->MOInstance;
    type = other->type;
    cause = other->cause;
    eventTime = other->eventTime;
    severity = other->severity;
    serviceUser = other->serviceUser;
    serviceProvider = other->serviceProvider;
    notificationId = other->notificationId;
    correlatedIds = other->correlatedIds;
    text = other->text;
    data = other->data;
}
```

①
```
SecurityAlarmManager::SecurityAlarmManager(const char* db) :
database_name(db)
{
    d_Database database;
    database.create(database_name,"SecurityAlarm");
    database.open(database_name);
    d_Transaction t;
    t.begin();
    d_Ref<SecurityAlarmManager> sam;
    if((sam = database.lookup_object("SecurityAlarmManager"))==NULL)
    {
      sam = new(&database) SecurityAlarmManager;
      database.set_object_name((d_Ref_Any&)sam,
             "SecurityAlarmManager");
      sam->mark_modified();
    }
    t.commit();
    database.close();
}
```

②
```
SecurityAlarmManager::SecurityAlarmManager(){}
```

LISTING 4-12.a.

```
    void
 3  SecurityAlarmManager::add(const SecurityAlarm& a)
    {
        d_Database database;
        database.open(database_name);
        d_Transaction t;
        t.begin();
        d_Ref<SecurityAlarmManager> shadow;
        if((shadow=database.lookup_object("SecurityAlarmManager"))==NULL)
        {
            cerr << "Error: could not lookup Manager" << endl;
        }
        d_Ref<SecurityAlarm> alrm = new(&database) SecurityAlarm(a);
        shadow->all_security_alarms.insert_element(alrm);
        shadow->mark_modified();
        t.commit();
        database.close();
    }

    void
 4  SecurityAlarmManager::get_alarms(
        d_List<d_Ref<SecurityAlarm> >&result,
        SecurityAlarm::Type type, SecurityAlarm::Cause cause)
    {
        d_Database database;
        database.open(database_name);
        d_Transaction t;
        t.begin();
        d_Ref<SecurityAlarmManager> shadow =
            database.lookup_object("SecurityAlarmManager");
        d_Iterator<d_Ref<SecurityAlarm> > iter =
            shadow->all_security_alarms.create_iterator();
        d_Ref<SecurityAlarm> a;
        while(iter.next(a))
        {
            if((a->type == type  ||
                type == SecurityAlarm::AllViolationTypes) &&
               (a->cause == cause || cause == SecurityAlarm::AllCauses))
            {
 5              result.insert_element(new SecurityAlarm(a));
            }
        }
    }
```

LISTING 4-12.b.

Let's discuss how the design of `PhysicalSecurityManager` (see Listing 3-12 and
Listing 3-13) must change. In `PhysicalSecurityManager.h`, all we need to do is
include `SecurityAlarm.h` and `Subject.hh` instead of
`SecurityAlarmReporter.h` (see Listing 4-13). I should point out that the use of
STL `map` is retained, so this example actually shows CORBA, ODMG-93, and STL used
together. Next, we need to modify the `update()` member function of the
`PhysicalSecurityManager`, as shown in Listing 4-14. And finally, the main
program where the `PhysicalSecurityManager` object is instantiated must be
changed to bind with a `Subject` instead of a `SecurityAlarmReporter` (not
shown).

```
// PhysicalSecurityManager.h

#include "SecurityAlarm.h"
#include "Subject.hh"
#include "Observer.hh"
#include <map.h>

class PhysicalSecurityManager {
  public:
    PhysicalSecurityManager();
    virtual void update(Subject_var, CORBA::Environment &);

  protected:
    Subject_var reporterVar;
    map<SecurityAlarm::Cause,const char*,
        less<SecurityAlarm::Cause> > causeStrings;
    map<SecurityAlarm::Severity,const char*,
        less<SecurityAlarm::Severity> > severityStrings;
};
DEF_TIE_Observer(PhysicalSecurityManager)
```

LISTING 4-13.

```
void
PhysicalSecurityManager::update(Subject_var, CORBA_Environment &)
{
    // database-specific initialization

    d_Database db;
    db.open("alarmBase");
    d_Transaction t;
    t.begin();

    d_List<d_Ref<SecurityAlarm> > alist;
    SecurityAlarmManager* manager =
        new SecurityAlarmManager("alarmBase");
    manager->get_alarms (alist,SecurityAlarm::PhysicalViolation,
        SecurityAlarm::AllCauses);
    d_Iterator<d_Ref<SecurityAlarm> > iter= alist.create_iterator();
    d_Ref<SecurityAlarm> a;
    while(iter.next(a))
    {
        cout << a->MOClass<< endl;
        cout << a->MOInstance<< endl;
        cout << "Physical Violation"<< endl;// we trust server
        cout << causeStrings[a->cause] << endl;
        cout << a->eventTime<< endl;
        cout << severityStrings[a->severity] << endl;
        cout << a->serviceUser<< endl;
        cout << a->serviceProvider<< endl;
        cout << a->notificationId<< endl;
        cout << a->text<< endl;
        cout << a->data<< endl;
    }
    delete manager;
    t.commit();
    // database-specific cleanup
}
```

LISTING 4-14.

Listing 4-15 shows the `PhysicalMO` program. First, the `SecurityAlarm` object is created ① and added to the database ② . After that, the alarm is reported to the `Subject` charged with notifying interested observers ③ .

```
      #include <iostream.h>
      #include <stdlib.h>
      // database-specific header files
      #include <CORBA.h>
      #include "SecurityAlarm.h"
      #include "Subject.hh"
      const int bufSize = 256;
      int
      main(int argc, char* argv[])
      {
          // database-specific initialization
          d_Database db;
          db.open("alarmBase");
          d_Transaction t;
          t.begin();
①        SecurityAlarm a;
          a.MOClass = "class1";
          a.MOInstance = "instance1";
          a.type = SecurityAlarm::PhysicalViolation;
          a.cause = SecurityAlarm::CableTamper;
          a.eventTime = d_Timestamp::current();
          a.severity = SecurityAlarm::Critical;
          a.serviceUser = "user1";
          a.serviceProvider = "provider1";
          a.notificationId = "id1";
          // did not initialize correlatedIds
          a.text = "this is text for the cable tampering incident";
          a.data = "this is data for the cable tampering incident";
          SecurityAlarmManager* manager =
              new SecurityAlarmManager("alarmBase");
②        manager->add(a);
          t.commit();
          // database-specific cleanup.
          Subject_var reporterVar;
          try {
              reporterVar = Subject::_bind(":SubjectSrv");
          }
            catch(...) {
          cerr << "Bind to SubjectSrv object failed" << endl;
          cerr << "Unexpected exception " << endl;
          exit(1);
          }
③      reporterVar->notify();
        return 0;
      }
```

LISTING 4-15.

An alarm is reported and processed as shown in Figure 4-3.

Object Interaction in Security Alarm Reporting with CORBA and ODMG-93

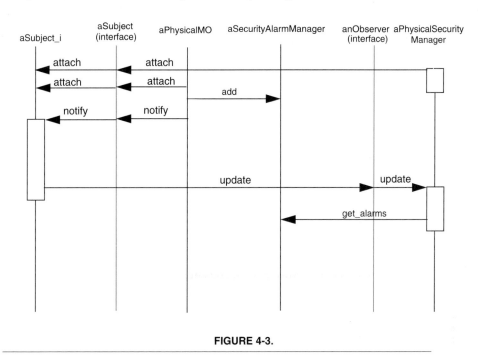

FIGURE 4-3.

So there you have it: CORBA, ODMG-93, and a little STL used together. I'm sure you still see some inadequacies with this design. Performance is still a question. One possible performance enhancer is to make it so that an `Observer` can attach to a `Subject` with a filter. Instead of being notified for every new alarm, an observer could be notified for certain types of alarms. Otherwise, you may have a bunch of observers hitting the database at the same time, querying about new alarms.

You may also be uncomfortable with the fact that anyone can post a new alarm without being authenticated. Designing software to be truly secure is a very complicated task and could dramatically influence your design. And, if you incorporate it into your design, you are delving into something that is very personal to the end user. It is quite possible that the end user will not like your security strategy and either bypass it, or worse, not use your software at all. I think it prudent to employ "separation of concerns" in this case, handling security at a higher level of design than I have shown in this example.

PART 2
Methodology

CHAPTER 5
Domain Analysis

In Chapter 1, we went through a hypothetical example of how to use a framework-based approach to develop an application for "Honest Joe's Autos." We started by determining Joe's requirements. Then, before starting to develop any software, we generalized Joe's problem. This generalization activity is called *domain analysis.*

Domain analysis is, in my view, the most important phase of development. Without it, there can be no frameworks. This became very apparent to me when I started teaching a 10-day OO workshop, which had been taught for a couple of years before I got involved.

Prior to teaching it myself, I decided to attend the workshop as an observer. During the last half of the workshop, the students were given requirements for a simple video game. They were asked to develop the game in C++, using the techniques taught in the lecture material. The project was not complicated, but the students seemed to struggle with it.

I noticed that the workshop did not address domain analysis, so I added the topic to the lecture material. I also required students to perform a simple analysis of the "video games" domain prior to the design phase of their project. The differences between the game designs with and without domain analysis were dramatic. Without it, all C++ classes comprising the game were very specific to the requirements. Adding new features required changing the interfaces and implementations of many of the existing classes. When domain analysis was performed, however, a small framework naturally emerged. With this framework, new features could easily be added to the game by deriving new C++ classes, instead of hacking up existing ones. At first I wondered if this was just a fluke, so I went back and studied the designs from all the workshops taught previously. I found that the only design that separated out behavior that was general to all video games was the one from the workshop where I made the students do a domain analysis first. I taught the workshop four times, and the results were consistent: a framework always emerged as a result of performing a domain analysis. If domain analysis has such a positive effect on this "toy" project, imagine its importance to an industrial-strength project.

Significant efforts have been made to address how domain analysis should be conducted. I looked at a number of the domain analysis process documents that are publicly available (e.g., [PRIETO91], [JODA93]). Although they were developed with the noblest of intentions, I am not going to incorporate any of them here for two reasons. First, you would be bored to death, and I would risk having you throw my book on the shelf (or worse) and not getting to the really fun chapters. Second, although such processes may be suitable for building large frameworks in a very formal development setting, they are too laborious for building small frameworks in a business environment, which is where the vast majority of frameworks will emerge.

In the remainder of this chapter, I present a domain analysis procedure that is lightweight enough for development staffs to digest and accept. It is also formal enough to foster the building of a large repository of small frameworks. Before getting into the actual steps, there is some very important background information that I need to convey, to help you understand how the procedures came about.

Very often, when a specific problem domain is analyzed, behavior is identified that applies to other domains as well. For example, in Chapter 1 we discussed how insurance claim processing, fixed-income derivatives trading, a cable television operation, mail order processing, and mortgage processing are all concerned with workflow. If such generic aspects, or *facets*, of a domain are factored out of a domain description and described in their own right, then there is the potential for two-tiered reuse. The partitioning of a problem domain from generic facets of that domain is a very important goal that I strive to achieve with the procedures in this chapter. If this is accomplished, the descriptions of generic facets can often be used to build horizontal frameworks, and the domain descriptions can be used to build vertical frameworks that rely on them. The bottom line is that we will be able to build more reusable software.

5.1 Steps in Domain Analysis

Some of the steps that I am about to describe may sound very mechanical and rigid. In actuality, no step can be defined with surgical precision. They are intended to be guidelines that will lead you toward the goal of producing concise and complete framework requirements specifications. In the end, however, your good sense and intuition are the most important determinants of success.

After describing the steps, I will demonstrate with an example. I suggest that you read through this section quickly the first time. Then, as you read through the example, reread the details of each step as it is demonstrated in the example. This will help you internalize the procedure by relating it to something concrete.

Domain analysis consists of the following steps:

1. Categorize the problem.
2. Research similar problems.
3. Prepare a domain description.
4. Analyze generic facets of the domain.
5. Repeatedly review and refine the analysis.

I will describe each step in subsequent subsections. Before I do, however, I must stress that you need at least one customer with a specific problem before you can start domain analysis. A customer's requirements document is the initial input to domain analysis.

As you begin a domain analysis, I'd suggest that you forget you are a software developer. Never approach a problem assuming a particular development paradigm. One of the biggest mistakes a developer can make is to march into a project determined to do an object-oriented design before understanding the problem. If you are biased by a particular paradigm, you may miss the true nature of the problem. Instead, you will be trying to fit the problem into the paradigm. It just doesn't work well that way. Immerse yourself in the problem as if you were a potential user of the application.

There's one other thing I must mention. I assume that a software repository exists or that you intend to start one. The notions of domain analysis and repository are indivisible. Domain analysis is where the requirements specifications for frameworks in the repository come from, and the repository must be searched as part of the domain analysis process. Domain analysis *might* produce one or more framework requirements specifications. I say *might*, because if a repository already contains all of the specifications needed to solve a particular problem, there is no need to write any or develop any frameworks.

5.1.1 Categorize the Problem (Step 1)

There are two reasons why it's important to categorize the customer's problem. First, you can't expect to build a repository containing frameworks unless you can categorize them by the type of problem they address. Second, when you determine that a problem is in an existing repository category, you can reuse the framework in that category.

In this book, we categorize problems by *industry* and the *problem domain* with respect to that industry.[1] The United States government has already gone to the trouble of identifying

---

1. The software industry must come to agree on the categories before a framework industry can emerge.

industries. The Office of Budget Management has a complete list of Standard Industry Codes (SICs) that can be used if you plan to build a large repository.[2]

When we speak of a problem domain, we are referring to a type of problem that is unique to firms doing business in a specific industry. For example, "power plant management" is a problem domain in the "utilities" industry (SIC 4939) ; "financial risk management" is a problem domain in the "financial" industry (SIC 6211).

This can get a little confusing. For example, large utilities companies may manage their own pension funds and, of course, would be concerned with risk management of those funds. Does this mean that risk management is also a problem domain in the utilities industry? No, because it is not unique to that industry. It just so happens that one aspect of the utilities operation looks like it is operating in the financial industry.

Assuming that you have discovered a new problem domain, assign it a number that is unique in the industry that it applies to and register it with the repository. For example, suppose that your repository currently has frameworks addressing two problem domains in the financial industry: bond trading and credit risk analysis. You have been asked to attack a problem involving options trading. Since this is the third problem domain that has been addressed in this industry, you would assign it the number 3. If the industry code is 6211, the full category number for the problem domain is then 6211.3. Once you are done with this, you're ready to move on to step 2.

5.1.2 Research Similar Problems (Step 2)

There are several ways to research problems that are similar to your current one. First, try to use your current customer as a problem domain expert if that person has significant experience with similar problems. Second, if you have several years of experience as a software developer, chances are good that your current problem resembles one or more of the problems that you were involved in solving on previous projects. Dust off your old specifications, design documents, and source listings and study them for similarities. Take notes; nothing formal. Think about things you'd do differently if you were told you had to do all those projects over again.

Not everyone has a dull career—doing the same kind of project over and over again. If you are one of those people, make your colleagues feel important by asking them if they ever had to solve a problem like the one you are working on. If so, use them as your domain experts.

---

2. The complete Standard Industry Classification (SIC) Manual was originally written in 1987. It is currently available on the Internet at http://www.osha.gov/oshstats/sicser.html. I should also mention that the Economic Classification Policy Committee is working on a new system called the North American Industry Classification System (NAICS) that may ultimately replace SICs.

Take the time to sit down with the people who have been involved in your business since before you were even writing software. Try knowledge engineering techniques that have been applied to building expert systems for years. When you do this, think in general terms. For example, if a domain expert in avionics is explaining something to you about an F-14, you have to instinctively be translating the vision of an F-14 into a generic aircraft. If he is discussing the F-14's limitations when flying in certain surroundings, you have to ask the question, "Is that just for the F-14, or does this problem exist for all classes of aircraft?"

Use the Internet and your local library, if necessary. The World Wide Web is probably your best source for conducting research into just about any type of problem. Study the home pages of other firms in your industry, checking for common terminology and concepts. Post questions to newsgroups, asking for old-timers who understand the subtle details of your problem. Ask them to explain those aspects of the problem that are general to all problems that they have seen like it.

After you have conducted your research, check the repository to see if there is a framework that you can use before executing the next step unnecessarily.

5.1.3 Prepare a Domain Description (Step 3)

At this point, you should have a lot of notes; some probably scribbled on the back of envelopes. It's time to go off on your own for a while, to formalize the notes into a domain description.

In this step, a problem domain is described in a semistructured fashion. In the process of doing this, you will potentially identify facets of the domain that are common to other domains. These will be factored out of the problem domain description, and descriptions will be started for them as well. So, there are potentially multiple facet analyses spawned as a result of preparing the domain description, each of which will be conducted to completion in step 4. Now let's begin to discuss how to prepare the domain description.

First, you should prepare a glossary containing definitions of domain-specific entities. Always define potentially ambiguous terms, so that there is no misunderstanding of their meaning when a design is evolved from the analysis. Domain-specific terminology is often interpreted differently by people involved in a given domain. This glossary should be used like a contract between the developer and the users.

Second, you should create a numbered list of characteristics that describe the problem domain. This list will be refined through a seven-pass process. It was arbitrarily broken into seven passes with the intention that you will checkpoint your progress after each pass. This way, if you completely screw up a pass, you won't have to start all over again. Start each new pass with the results of the previous one. The seven-pass procedure is as follows.

PASS 1:   Create list of characteristics describing problem domain.

Create a numbered list of characteristics describing the problem domain. Each characteristic should be between one and four complete sentences. Brevity is necessary to force you to zero in on the essence of the characteristic. There should be no more than 50 characteristics. If you are having problems doing this, then you are either being too specific or the problem domain is just too large to approach with this technique. If you feel that the reason is the latter, shrink the boundaries of the problem domain and try again.

The following are additional guidelines that you should follow as you are writing each characteristic:

- Each characteristic should be described in general terms, but not to the point where it sounds unnatural. For example, instead of saying "John must fill out form 5217-A-0821 and give it to Lauren for approval when he wants to purchase PCs for a new project," say something like "Managers are required to seek approval from their managers for purchases in excess of a certain dollar amount. A business justification must accompany the request."

- Do not repeat information in more than one characteristic.

- Do not use any unnecessary words. For example, instead of saying "A piece of equipment usually has a fixed physical location, but under certain circumstances may be mobile, if it was on a truck, for example." Say: "Equipment usually has a fixed location." [STYLE79] is an excellent reference for tips on brevity.

- Choose one word to describe a concept, and use it consistently. Purge all synonyms of this word. Synonyms are a Domain Analyst's worst enemy.

Save a copy of the results of this pass under source code control. You will be doing this for each pass. This provides a history of the domain analysis process that is invaluable for refining that process through later study.

PASS 2:   Reword characteristics to be more like requirements.

In this pass, you are going to make the domain description more like requirements of systems used in this domain. This also brings more consistency to the various characteristics. First, regroup characteristics such that the ones most related to each other appear together. Generally, those that share domain-specific terms are related, and the characteristics that share the most domain-specific terms are most related.

Next, change the wording of each characteristic to use future tense, satisfying the following guidelines:

- Use "shall" instead of "must" or "will." For example, "Such systems shall authenticate users."

- Use "could" instead of "might," "may," or "can."

- You can use the word "usually," never the word "sometimes." "Sometimes" implies that this is more likely a problem-specific characteristic.

- Use the phrase "such systems" in conjunction with "shall" and "usually," where appropriate (e.g., "Such systems shall do such and such" or "Such systems usually do such and such").

- Use the term "mechanism" instead of "feature," "function," or some other term used to describe something that such systems do. For example, "Such systems shall use a timer mechanism." "Mechanism" is a generic term that is not tainted by overuse.

As you read through each characteristic, if you can't comfortably use one of these rules where applicable, then maybe you should rethink whether this is a general characteristic of the domain. When you have followed all the guidelines, save a copy of the results of this pass under source code control.

PASS 3: *Separate domain-specific characteristics from generic ones.*

In this pass, you are going to separate the characteristics into two lists: those that are specific to the problem domain and those that are not.

Start a second list. Go through each characteristic on the original list and ask yourself the following question: "Are there any words or concepts in this characteristic that are specific to the domain being analyzed?" If the answer is no, move the characteristic to the new list. If you are not sure, leave it on the original list. Renumber the characteristics so that each list starts from 1 and runs sequentially.

As you go through this exercise, refine the wording of characteristics that you are not content with. Save a copy of the results of this pass under source code control.

PASS 4: *Graphically partition domain-specific characteristics from generic ones.*

Start with a blank piece of paper and draw a line down the middle. On the left side, draw a circle for each characteristic on the original list. Put the number of the characteristic in the center of the circle. On the right side, draw a circle for each characteristic on the new list, with the number of the characteristic in the center of the circle. When you are done with this pass, you'll have a diagram that looks something like the one shown in Figure 5-1.

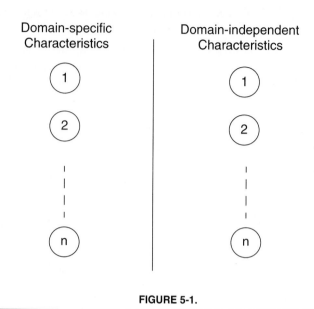

FIGURE 5-1.

PASS 5:   Create new generic characteristics.

For each characteristic on the original list, try to create one or more new ones by
rewording the characteristic such that it does not contain any domain-specific terms or
concepts. In other words, try to create domain-independent versions of domain-specific
characteristics. The glossaries of facet descriptions already in the repository should be
explored first when you are attempting to find the right domain-independent terminology.

Put new generic characteristics on the domain-independent list, and add corresponding
circles on the right side of the diagram. Draw an arrow from the circle representing the
original domain-specific characteristic to the generalized ones born of it.

Make sure that you partition independent generic concepts into different characteristics.
For example, consider the following domain-specific characteristic: "A single allocation
of switch bandwidth shall not exceed a prespecified percentage of the remaining free
bandwidth. The choice of the next switch allocated to, is based on a load balancing
algorithm." Although this characteristic is obviously a telecom-related example, it is easy
to extract two general statements of behavior from it: 1) "The usage capacity that could be
allocated from a particular resource is constrained by rules that consider how much of that
resource's capacity is currently available" and 2) "The choice of resource to be assigned is
based on a load balancing algorithm."

PASS 6:   *Identify facets by graphically clustering the generic characteristics.*

The following defines the rules for partitioning generic characteristics into clusters. The rules that appear earlier in the list take precedence over those appearing later.

1. Characteristics that are self-contained concepts should not appear in any cluster.
2. Mutually dependent characteristics should appear in the same cluster.
3. Characteristics with a common theme should appear in the same cluster.

Encircle groups of characteristics (actually the circles representing those characteristics) on the right side of the diagram, using the rules above. Each independent generic characteristic and cluster of generic characteristics is a facet of the problem domain.

Be very careful; if a generic characteristic stands on its own, do not encircle it, even if it defines terms or concepts that other generic characteristics depend upon. This mistake will, potentially, lead to the creation of a large cluster of characteristics with more than one theme, where independent characteristics inadvertently bind unrelated ones.

You should perform some informal reachability analysis on all clusters by seeing if you are able to logically relate every characteristic in a cluster to every other characteristic in the same cluster via transitivity. For example, should the following three characteristics be in the same cluster?

1. A timer mechanism shall be employed to check for time-out conditions and record the duration of certain activities.
2. All error conditions shall be cleared within a prespecified time period.
3. User response time is recorded.

No, because the first characteristic describes an independent timer component. But, suppose you didn't realize this and put them in the same cluster because you saw a common "timer" theme. If you tried to apply transitivity to relate the characteristics to each other, you'd find that it can't be done. Both characteristic 2 and 3 relate to 1, but not to each other. So, this can't be a cluster.

PASS 7:   *Create separate lists of characteristics for each cluster and show existing assets from the repository.*

Now you should create a separate list for each cluster. Also, remove the individual circles from inside a cluster; any arrows to them should now just terminate on the cluster boundary.

Any facet recognized as having an implementation in the repository should be shaded and labeled with the facet name. All new facets should be given a name that is appropriate for its theme.

You should now have a *proposal* for the domain description. I say proposal, because you really can't claim that it is complete until it has been affirmed by your domain experts. So, you should get them to review the output of PASS 7. They may be a bit baffled by the fact that you are being so general. That's okay. But, something is wrong if any of them tell you that the characteristics are incorrect.

Inevitably, the first time around, you will miss the mark somewhere. When you do, you need to correct it. Depending on how far you missed the mark, you may have to repeat this entire step, starting with a rework of the glossary. The description is deemed complete when none of your domain experts can claim that any characteristic is incorrect.

5.1.4 Analyze Generic Facets of the Domain (Step 4)

In step 3, we identified the generic facets of the domain. Hopefully, there will be assets in the repository that address some of these. Those that are newly discovered, however, must be thoroughly analyzed in this step, because the descriptions of facets that come out of a domain description are probably inadequate and usually have some bias toward the domain in which they were identified.

Facet analysis is basically a scaled-down version of domain analysis. Don't be fooled into thinking that the task is easier, however. In some sense, facet analysis is actually much harder because the concepts may be more abstract, and now you need to consider the needs of multiple domains. Facet analysis consists of the following steps:

1. Name the facet.
2. Research the facet from the perspective of different domains.
3. Prepare a facet description.
4. Repeatedly review and refine the analysis.

You can see that this is very similar to domain analysis itself. The first distinction is in the research phase, which requires more work in facet analysis because you have to research multiple domains to accumulate evidence that the facet spans domains. If you can't accumulate evidence, terminate the facet analysis and subsume the facet back into the problem domain in which it was originally discovered.

After researching the facet, prepare a facet description. First, prepare a glossary containing definitions of facet-specific entities. Second, create a numbered list of characteristics that describe the facet, using the guidelines given in PASS 1 and PASS 2 of step 3. There should be no more than 25 characteristics, and they should be between one and four sentences each. The third and last thing you need to do is go to the repository and determine which, if any, assets in the repository this facet depends on. Those assets identified should be listed.

I don't formally specify discovery procedures at the facet level as I do at the domain level. This is not to say that you won't identify new potentially independent abstractions at the facet analysis level, but initially they will be specified in the facet description. A separate extraction procedure should be specified for periodically going through the repository and pulling out such abstractions when a critical mass of reuse potential is identified.

5.1.5 Repeatedly Review and Refine the Analysis (Step 5)

These procedures alone are not mechanical enough to get you to a domain or facet description that spells out every last detail. They are not supposed to. They are supposed to get you to the point where you have enough information to intelligently start designing a framework and other reusable software that it uses: rough boundaries of domains and facets. As you start designing, you can expect to go back and refine the domain analysis over and over again as you find that the boundaries you established were not quite right. Yes, you will be modifying requirements as you are building the actual framework that supports those requirements. This is not an indictment of the analysis; rather, it is a natural discovery process. So, please, don't "baseline" your domain analysis until the framework developed as a result is actually out and running in several applications.

On a final note, terminology is particularly fragile and volatile in the first few iterations of a domain analysis. It is very common to find yourself adjusting terminology in the glossary as you learn more details in each iteration. It is very easy to inadvertently drag terminology that is too specific into the description of a facet or a domain.

5.2 An Example Domain Analysis for "Mail Order"

Assume that I've been asked to automate the ACME Tool Company's mail order division. Let's go through an abbreviated version[3] of what the domain analysis of this problem might look like, using the procedure discussed in the previous section.

Step 1. Categorize the problem.

The problem is in the Retail Sales Industry (SIC 5961). The problem domain is "mail order." I am just starting a new repository and I have to assign the mail order domain in the Retail Sales Industry a unique number. How about 1? I am now done with step 1.

Step 2. Research similar problems.

I looked through the dozens of mail order catalogs that I get and checked for similarities. For example, at home I've got flower and seed catalogs, golf club component catalogs,

---

3. I am going to ignore some aspects of the operation, like payroll and taxes.

many clothing catalogs, tool catalogs, specialty item catalogs, computer supply catalogs, business supply catalogs, etc. I reviewed the catalog item descriptions, ordering procedures, and terms of sale for accepted practices. I called up a few of these companies and asked the sales people if they could take a few minutes to explain how their operation works. Most know pretty much how things work, especially in smaller operations, and are happy to talk about it to break the monotony of taking orders. I also just found an article in the business section of today's paper that talked about how mail order businesses are making themselves more competitive and what difficulties they are encountering with rising postal costs. This provided helpful insight into what frameworks will be required to do in future mail order operations.

Step 3.   Prepare a domain description.

Glossary:

back-ordered item – an item that is not in stock currently, but for which an order has been placed to replenish inventory. Customer orders are being accepted for that order and will be shipped when the item becomes available, free of additional shipping charge.

catalog – a collection of items. The catalog will exist in both electronic and hardcopy form.

customer – anyone with an address who has placed, or is currently placing, an order.

inventory – items on hand that have not been shipped to customers.

item – something to be sold. An item has a description, price, number, and sometimes a picture associated with it.

order – a request to purchase one or more items.

sales clerk – someone who takes orders by mail.

sales person – someone who takes orders from customers.

shipping clerk – someone who packages and ships items to customers, based on an order.

PASS 1:   Create list of characteristics describing problem domain.

Characteristics:

1. Customers can order items from the catalog by phone, the Internet, or mail. When placing an order, the customer needs to provide the catalog number and quantity for each item requested. If not already on file, the customer must also provide an address.
2. When items are ordered by phone, a sales person takes the order. The customer will be given a total, order number, and the status of back-ordered items. The customer must pay by credit card.

3. Phone orders are distributed to sales people as they become available. If customers are not being serviced within a certain time limit, management should be notified.

4. When items are ordered by mail, a sales clerk processes the order. A credit card number or check must accompany the order. If something is out of stock, the customer is sent notification of when it will be available.

5. When items are ordered by Internet, software processes the order. The customer is shown the order total, order number, and the status of items that are back-ordered. A credit card number must be provided.

6. When orders are placed, this implies a pending reduction in inventory.

7. When orders are packaged and shipped, this reduces inventory. Accounts receivable is also notified and funds are collected unless deferred payment arrangements have been made.

8. Orders are distributed to shipping clerks. If shipping clerks are not filling orders in a timely fashion, management should be notified.

9. Inventory levels should be sufficient to fill incoming orders.

10. When orders are placed to restock inventory, accounts payable is notified.

11. When a shipment of inventory items is received, accounts payable is notified and funds will be dispersed.

12. The managers determine the workflow of the business and may change it periodically.

13. There is an accounting department.

14. There is a shipping/receiving department.

PASS 2: Reword characteristics to be more like requirements.

Characteristics:

1. Customers shall order items from the catalog by phone, the Internet, or mail. When placing an order, the customer shall provide the catalog number and quantity for each item requested. If not already on file, the customer shall provide an address.

2. When items are ordered by phone, a sales person shall take the order. The customer shall be given a total, order number, and the status of back-ordered items. The customer shall pay by credit card.

3. Phone orders shall be distributed to sales people as they become available. If customers are not being serviced within a certain time limit, management shall be notified.

4. When items are ordered by mail, a sales clerk shall process the order. A credit card number or check shall accompany the order. If something is out of stock, the customer shall be sent notification of when it will be available.

5. When items are ordered by Internet, software shall process the order. The customer shall be shown the order total, order number, and the status of items that are back-ordered. A credit card number shall be provided.

6. When orders are placed, this implies a pending reduction in inventory.

7. When orders are packaged and shipped, inventory shall be reduced. Accounts receivable shall be notified and funds shall be collected unless deferred payment arrangements have been made.

8. Orders shall be distributed to shipping clerks. If shipping clerks are not filling orders in a timely fashion, management shall be notified.

9. Inventory levels shall be sufficient to fill incoming orders.

10. When orders are placed to restock inventory, accounts payable shall be notified.

11. When a shipment of inventory items is received, accounts payable shall be notified and funds shall be dispersed.

12. The managers shall determine the workflow of the business and could change it periodically.

13. There shall be an accounting department.

14. There shall be a shipping/receiving department.

PASS 3:   *Separate domain-specific characteristics from generic ones.*

Domain-specific characteristics:

1. Customers shall order items from the catalog by phone, the Internet, or mail. When placing an order, the customer shall provide the catalog number and quantity for each item requested. If not already on file, the customer shall provide an address.

2. When items are ordered by phone, a sales person shall take the order. The customer shall be given a total, order number, and the status of back-ordered items. The customer shall pay by credit card.

3. Phone orders shall be distributed to sales people as they become available. If customers are not being serviced within a certain time limit, management shall be notified.

4. When items are ordered by mail, a sales clerk shall process the order. A credit card number or check shall accompany the order. If something is out of stock, the customer shall be sent notification of when it will be available.

5. When items are ordered by Internet, software shall process the order. The customer shall be shown the order total, order number, and the status of items that are back-ordered. A credit card number shall be provided.

6. When orders are placed, this implies a pending reduction in inventory.

7. When orders are packaged and shipped, inventory shall be reduced. Accounts receivable shall be notified and funds shall be collected unless deferred payment arrangements have been made.

8. Orders shall be distributed to shipping clerks. If shipping clerks are not filling orders in a timely fashion, management shall be notified.

9. Inventory levels shall be sufficient to fill incoming orders.

PASS 3   Continued.

Domain-independent characteristics:

1. When orders are placed to restock inventory, accounts payable shall be notified.
2. When a shipment of inventory items is received, accounts payable shall be notified and funds shall be dispersed.
3. The managers shall determine the workflow of the business and could change it periodically.
4. There shall be an accounting department.
5. There shall be a shipping/receiving department.

Commentary: At this point, I'm a little uncomfortable moving any characteristic that refers to an "order" over to the domain-independent list, since "order" implies a sale that is indicative of mail order, as opposed to an operation where a sale is made face to face, and goods are usually taken at that time by the customer. I am confident that the list above contains only domain-independent characteristics.

PASS 4:   Graphically partition domain-specific characteristics from generic ones.

Domain-specific
Characteristics

Domain-independent
Characteristics

① ①

② ②

③ ③

④ ④

⑤ ⑤

⑥

⑦

⑧

⑨

PASS 5:   Create new generic characteristics.

Domain-independent characteristics:

1. When orders are placed to restock inventory, accounts payable shall be notified.
2. When a shipment of inventory items is received, accounts payable shall be notified and funds shall be dispersed.
3. The managers shall determine the workflow of the business and could change it periodically.
4. There shall be an accounting department.
5. There shall be a shipping/receiving department.
6. Work shall be distributed to workers as they become available. If the work is not completed within a certain time limit, management shall be notified. **(new)**
7. It shall be possible to reserve items in inventory. **(new)**
8. When a customer sale reduces inventory, accounts receivable shall be notified and funds shall be collected unless deferred payment arrangements have been made. **(new)**
9. Inventory levels shall be monitored based on historical rates of depletion. **(new)**

Commentary: As I went through the original domain-specific list of characteristics, I saw five that could be interpreted in a more generic light. Two of them (3 and 8) were really just discussing how workers were allocated new work, regardless of what it was they were actually doing. Domain-specific characteristic 6 was really just saying that inventory items could be reserved, and it is irrelevant that this is done through mail order. Domain-specific characteristic 7 is really just saying that a customer is required to pay for something when he/she takes possession of it. Domain-specific characteristic 9, which states that "Inventory levels shall be sufficient to fill incoming orders," implies that you must know how often specific items are removed from inventory. This is a very general task that involves studying depletion rates and has nothing to do directly with mail order.

PASS 5   *Continued.*

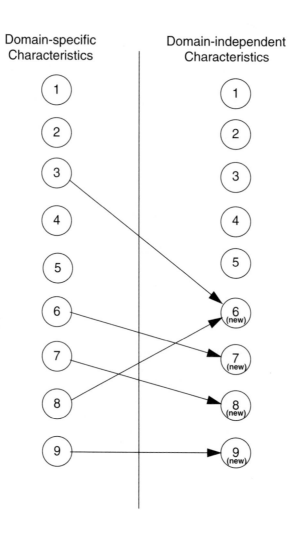

PASS 6:   *Identify facets by graphically clustering the generic characteristics.*

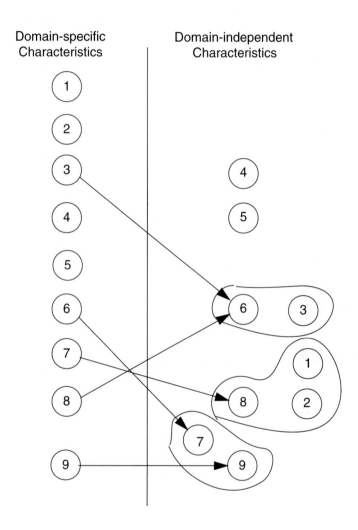

Commentary: Characteristic 3 and 6 were grouped because they both pertain to a workflow theme. Characteristics 1, 2, and 8 all involve relationships between inventory and accounting. Characteristics 7 and 9 were grouped because they both pertain to inventory alone.

*PASS 7:   Create separate lists of characteristics for each cluster and show existing
assets from the repository.*

Facets:

- **Accounting**

- **Shipping/Receiving**

- **Workflow**

1. The managers shall determine the workflow of the business and could change it
   periodically.
2. Work shall be distributed to workers as they become available. If the work is not
   completed within a certain time limit, management shall be notified.

- **Inventory/Accounting Relationships**

1. When a shipment of inventory items is received, accounts payable shall be notified and
   funds shall be dispersed.
2. When orders are placed to restock inventory, accounts payable shall be notified.
3. When a customer sale reduces inventory, accounts receivable shall be notified and
   funds shall be collected unless deferred payment arrangements have been made.

- **Inventory**

1. It shall be possible to reserve items in inventory.
2. Inventory levels shall be monitored, based on historical rates of depletion.

PASS 7   Continued.

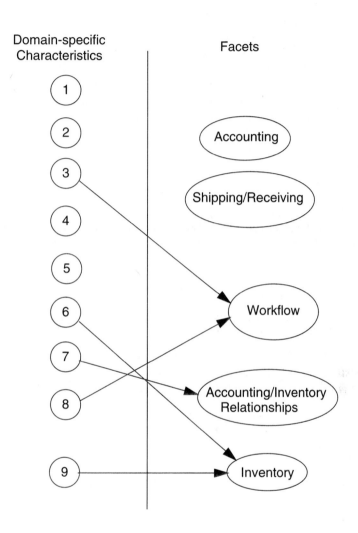

Step 4. Analyze generic facets of the domain.

I'm not going to analyze any of the facets here; the workflow facet will be analyzed in great detail in Chapter 10, where we actually implement a horizontal framework for workflow. Each of the facets, except for one of them, looks as though it is self-sufficient and probably a good basis for a horizontal framework.

The Inventory/Accounting Relationships facet is the one exception. It does satisfy the definition of a facet; it has a common theme and none of the wording is specific to the mail order domain. But, as worded, it is obviously dependent on the Inventory facet and the Accounting facet. It may end up being folded back into the domain description, or maybe we have identified a useful abstraction that can be molded into a general-purpose convention, component, or framework for "snapping" two facets together. The word "notified" appears in every one of its characteristics. Perhaps this is telling us that this is actually something more general, like a "notification" facet, and that I didn't quite word the characteristics in a generic enough way. This rambling paragraph is intended to convey the "stream of consciousness" nature of this step.

Step 5. Repeatedly review and refine the analysis.

The list of characteristics that we ended up with is probably too vague to start designing a framework for mail order. But it's a good starting point. You will surely have to review and refine the characteristics.

CHAPTER 6
Framework Design Standard

The aspects of a framework design that are influenced by this standard are:

- The class structure of the framework

- The overall responsibilities of certain classes in the framework

- The behavior expected from certain member functions of classes in the framework

- The syntax of C++ declarations of classes in the framework

When designing a framework, you will be faced with many situations requiring selection from design alternatives. This standard specifies the alternatives that should be used for many such situations. The benefit of having such a standard is threefold. First, if followed, it raises the likelihood that a high-quality framework will be produced, because it is based on tested design alternatives. Second, developers will be able to produce a framework much faster, because design knowledge is being reused. Third, all the frameworks developed according to the standard will have designs that are more consistent with each other, which is essential for building a framework repository.

Some design alternatives are dictated in a way that is very abstract, and applicability is often subjective. These types of alternatives will be specified in *design patterns*. Other design alternatives are dictated in very concrete fashion, and there is little question as to whether or not an alternative applies to a given situation. These types of alternatives will be specified in *design rules*.

6.1 Introduction to Design Patterns

Design patterns are not unique to software. In fact, they are used in many human endeavors. Consider the design of a typical, modern house. Have you ever seen a toilet in the kitchen? Although some may have a life style that finds this arrangement to be convenient, your average individual would not. When houses are designed, toilets are put in bathrooms. This is a simple design pattern. There are also patterns that are important to the structural integrity of the house, like: "joists and rafters are secured to a sill with 2 toenailed 10d nails" and "a two-story house can be safely studded with 8-foot 2x4s spaced 16 inches on-center." There are other patterns that accommodate the life style of the inhabitants. For example, "bedrooms are generally clustered in one part of the house" and "a dining room is usually adjacent to the kitchen."

There are four key points to note about these house-related patterns. First, they can exist together for one specific house and, in fact, some may depend on others. For example, it would be rather difficult to realize any of the patterns relating to life style without those that guarantee structural integrity. The second key point is that the patterns are general enough to accommodate vast variety. This is evident in the enormous number of house styles. The third point is that a vocabulary exists that makes it possible to express a lot of precise information with few words. For example, architects and builders everywhere know exactly what you are talking about when you use phrases like "toenailed 10d nails" and "16 inches on-center."

The fourth and final point pertains to the origin of the patterns. When looking at the collection of design patterns working in concert to create acceptable living conditions, we may be inclined to think they were logically and scientifically produced by a very clever group of engineers that sat down one day and figured out how a house should be built. In actuality, the patterns now employed are the result of many years of trial and error, passed down through apprenticeship. Their evolution was, and is, influenced by culture and advancements in technology. Although there are reasons why the patterns are the way they are, there are many other ways that they could have evolved. For example, in another universe or distant land, perhaps front doors are hinged on the right or don't have hinges at all.

The first three points that we noted about house-related patterns are also applicable to software design patterns:

1. They can exist together, and some may depend on others.

2. They are general enough to accommodate vast variety.

3. A vocabulary exists that makes it possible express a lot of information with few words.

The fourth point about the origin of software design patterns differs from the house-related ones in a very significant way. Software design patterns have a very short history. Yes, there has been some trial and error, but over the course of a few years as opposed to hundreds of years. Also, until very recently, very few design patterns having anything to do with software have been passed down to apprentice software developers, let alone those patterns that lend themselves well to the design of frameworks. Every developer that I know starts his or her career equipped with the same bare-bones knowledge of how to design software, with little or no benefit of the hard-won "wisdom" that experienced designers have accumulated over their careers. So, they too have to start their learning process from first principles, making their apprenticeship a long and sometimes tumultuous experience. It's analogous to a junior architect having to design a few houses that come crashing to the ground before he finally gets it right. That just doesn't happen— unlike software, which always crashes a few times before it actually works right.

To be fair to the software profession, this could not really be helped. Every time wisdom was acquired, rapidly changing technology usually rendered it obsolete. But, I think that infrastructure standards are bringing us into a period of more stability in technology, and it's time to start disseminating design "wisdom," albeit wisdom that has been accumulated over a very short period of time.

Design patterns are an integral part of the methodology presented in this book. Now that we have established, through analogy, what they are, let's discuss why they are so important to the methodology.

First and foremost, documenting design patterns starts developers inexperienced in designing frameworks higher on the learning curve. Pattern descriptions guide the developer down a path that has a higher likelihood of success, because the patterns represent tested concepts.

Second, if a methodology sanctions only the use of specific design patterns (i.e., makes them part of the standard), there will be more consistency between the designs of the frameworks developed using that methodology. Without consistency, it is not practical to attempt to build large repositories of frameworks. Why? Because the users of a repository have neither the time nor the patience to learn how to use every framework from scratch. When they think they found one that addresses a problem domain that they are not familiar with, they should not have to struggle with both learning about the domain and the idiosyncracies of a maverick framework designer. If you know the methodology, you will already know something about the semantics and syntax of all the frameworks and, consequently, how to start using any one of them.

There is a third, and final, reason why patterns are important to the methodology: they will shape a framework design to be able to take advantage of the object infrastructure introduced in Part 1. The patterns sanctioned by the methodology partition designs such that they will be able to "plug" the framework into the infrastructure.

The notion of design patterns and frameworks are very similar. In some instances, a pattern description contains class interfaces and C++ implementations of those interfaces, such that you actually have the makings of a small horizontal framework before you. A pattern may dictate the exact syntax of interfaces of classes involved in the pattern, as well as the behavior that must be supported by the class implementations. However, the pattern *never* dictates the specific code implementing the member functions of classes in the pattern. This is where the fuzzy line that separates patterns from frameworks is drawn, because a framework always includes some member function implementations that can't be overridden or are expected to be used. If you did have a framework where all the classes comprising the framework were abstract and all the member functions of all the classes were virtual, it would also be a pattern because no piece of the implementation is dictated down to the line of code. But, I've never seen a framework like that.

6.2 Catalog of Design Patterns

The patterns sanctioned by this methodology are documented in the catalog presented at the end of this section. The catalog is fairly small and should be viewed more as a foundation upon which your organization can build a larger catalog that is tuned to your problem domain. In essence, you need to build and maintain a pattern catalog along with the framework repository. When you add a pattern to the catalog, you should document it in the same style and with the same level of rigor as the ones presented here. You must also educate developers through patterns seminars, and every developer should have electronic access to the catalog. As time goes by, a particular pattern may become so prevalent and precisely understood that you want to build a small horizontal framework that implements that pattern.

The patterns in this catalog are geared toward framework development using C++, CORBA, and an ODMG-93 database. The patterns are definitely domain independent, but not technology independent. This defies the typical definition of design patterns, which usually states that patterns are technology independent, but we are trying to mold a methodology that increases productivity through the use of a standards-based infrastructure.

I tried to leverage off the pattern work presented in [PATTERNS95], which is the landmark work on the subject of OO design patterns. You may want to get your hands on a copy of this book, because I do refer to patterns in it. Some patterns in [PATTERNS95] are inherent in our assumed infrastructure and do not really need much consideration anymore. The ITERATOR pattern is a good example. Both STL and ODMG-93 incorporate iteration into their APIs. As you will see later, I use iteration heavily in the Workflow Framework developed in Chapter 10. There is really no need for us to think about iteration abstractly anymore, because this pattern has been incorporated into the concrete standards implementation comprising our infrastructure. There are other low-level patterns that were more applicable before we had such a rich infrastructure—an infrastructure that now either incorporates them or relieves us of the need to use them.

I rewrote the descriptions of two very important patterns that can also be found in the [PATTERNS95] catalog: INTERPRETER and OBSERVER. I rewrote the INTERPRETER description largely because I didn't think that the motivational discussion was compelling enough. The OBSERVER description was rewritten to reflect the fact that we will be implementing the pattern with CORBA.

I don't want you to get the impression that I just recycled patterns from [PATTERNS95]. In fact, most of the ones in this catalog originated from framework-related work that I have done over the past few years. I have been fortunate enough to work in both the telecom and financial industries. Many of the patterns in this catalog were discovered by studying common aspects of applications that I have been associated with in these completely different industries.

I don't try to categorize patterns. This is in contrast to [PATTERNS95], which tries to categorize patterns into three categories: creational, structural, and behavioral. I think that many patterns are actually hybrids of these categories, and any attempt to pick one category would be far too subjective to really mean anything. Besides, I don't subscribe to the view that grouping them really buys you anything. What you really need is a guide to proper selection: a *Pattern Roadmap*. So, I opt to put the patterns in the catalog in alphabetical order. In Chapter 8, I will present the pattern roadmap and how to use it in the course of your development.

I use the pattern documentation template shown on page 151. It is quite similar to the one known as the "Gang of Four Template" taken from [PATTERNS95]. The template that I use has one additional section: "Optional Details." Some patterns have a very basic underlying model and a number of optional details that may, or may not, be relevant in a given situation. Instead of introducing a different pattern for each permutation of details, I introduce the "Optional Details" section, which usually contains a flowchart. The potential user of the pattern can follow the flowchart and incrementally tailor the pattern to his or her needs by adding the details that are relevant to his/her situation. The OBSERVER pattern is a good example to go through to see how this works.

The "Related Patterns" section assumes a central role in the template. It forms the basis of the patterns roadmap that will be presented in Chapter 8. The roadmap is constructed on the premise that the use of one pattern often "sets the stage" for using another pattern. So, if you can find the first major pattern or two, the roadmap will help you identify others that are also likely to be applicable.

There is one very important convention that you must know as you read the pattern descriptions. It must be very clear to you which syntax is dictated in the declarations of the classes participating in a pattern, and which is just used to illustrate an example usage of the pattern. Any syntax that is dictated always appears in the class diagram that is presented in the Structure section of the pattern description. Any syntax in the class diagram that is in italics is *not* dictated. All other syntax must be used when the pattern is employed.

Before presenting the catalog, you should be familiar with two terms that I use quite frequently in the pattern descriptions: *fine-grained object* and *coarse-grained object*. Their definitions are as follows:

> A ***fine-grained object*** is primarily a data structure with little, if any, behavior.

> A ***coarse-grained object*** has significant member function implementations.

Pattern Documentation Template

PATTERN # - Pattern Name
The pattern's name becomes part of your generic vocabulary.

Intent
A short statement that conveys what the design pattern is supposed to accomplish.

Also Known As
Other names for the pattern, if any. Give references.

Motivation
Scenarios illustrating a design problem and how the pattern helps solve it.

Applicability
The situations in which the design pattern must be applied.

Structure
Class Diagram, and perhaps an Object Diagram, showing static relationships between classes participating in the pattern. See Appendix B for notation to use. There may also be a table that shows other patterns used in this one and what roles are played by classes in this pattern.

Participants
The classes and other software entities participating in the design pattern, along with their responsibilities.

Collaborations
How the participants collaborate to carry out their responsibilities. An Object Interaction Diagram is generally put in this section (see Appendix B for notation to use).

Optional Details
This section may include a flowchart that shows how the pattern can be tailored.

Consequences
List design trade-offs and side effects of using this pattern, pieces of the infrastructure, components, and environmental factors required for implementing the pattern.

Implementation
Techniques to consider when implementing the pattern.

Sample Code and Usage
More discussion on how the pattern can be usefully applied, accompanied by C++ code fragments that illustrate how you might implement the pattern.

Known Uses
Examples of the pattern found in real applications.

Related Patterns
List 1) Patterns that are "Stage Setters" for this pattern 2) Patterns that this pattern "Sets Stage For."

CATALOG OF DESIGN PATTERNS

PATTERN 1 - BLACKBOARD

Intent

To reduce the amount of information that needs to be studied and processed simultaneously, by partitioning heterogeneous data objects into groups and studying the properties of each group as a whole.

Motivation

This is one of the patterns that I have seen applied in both telecom and finance applications. In both cases, a huge stream of incoming data needed to be analyzed quickly.

I worked on a telecom project for a couple years, and, in retrospect, the entire purpose of the system that we were delivering revolved around this pattern. The task was to develop an expert system to help technicians keep a colossal network operational. The switches that were at the heart of this network were, at that time, twenty-something years old. As you can imagine, many versions of software and hardware had crept into the network over that time. There were also many adjunct systems surrounding these switches that were added over time, contributing to the complexity of what was already an enormously complex system. The manuals describing the error messages that could be generated by the switches occupied a 4-foot bookshelf. There was a small army of technicians sitting in a control center monitoring ASCII consoles, which were always scrolling with error messages from the 100+ switches comprising the network. Needless to say, sometimes critical error messages were missed. This had to be corrected. The only way to correct it was to take the many error messages, of varying types and origins and reduce them into a few messages, telling the technicians what actually needed to be fixed. The way we did this was to group related messages based on heuristic rules and tell the technician only what a group of messages implied.

When I worked on Wall Street, I saw the same type of problem, only with completely different data and a completely different set of system goals. Data feeds pumped in a plethora of raw time-series data, including stock prices, bond prices, options prices, commodity prices, economic statistics, interest rates, news events, etc. The goal was to take in as much of this data as possible and reduce it into a set of predictions about the future value of financial instruments—predictions that would result in the highest reward for a given risk. As with the telecom example, data was grouped based on domain-specific rules. For instance, all closing prices for IBM for the past two years might be stored in one collection. You might also want to associate IBM-related news items with this same collection in order to explain and filter out anomalies in the prices. The statistics for the time-series price data, such as high and low prices and volatility, would then be used as the basis for investment decisions.

The following can be observed for both of these types of applications:

- Data of potentially varying types is aggregated according to rules.
- A higher-level view of this aggregation is presented, based on analysis of the aggregated data.
- The raw data is historical. So, once it is instantiated, it does not change state.
- Data is quite often shared across aggregated views (e.g., many traders watching IBM, each with his own buy/sell algorithm; or many technicians studying the same switch alarms, each looking for a different type of problem).
- The results of the analysis of raw data should be shared, perhaps factoring into even higher-level analysis.

This pattern can be used to solve problems that have these characteristics. The pattern is, in large part, a suite of other patterns: OBSERVER, one of the variations of SINGLETON and CORBA-FRIENDLY. There is a synergy between these patterns that helps us solve problems of the nature that I've discussed.

Applicability
This pattern should be used whenever analyzing a large body of heterogeneous time-series data, from a variety of perspectives.

Structure

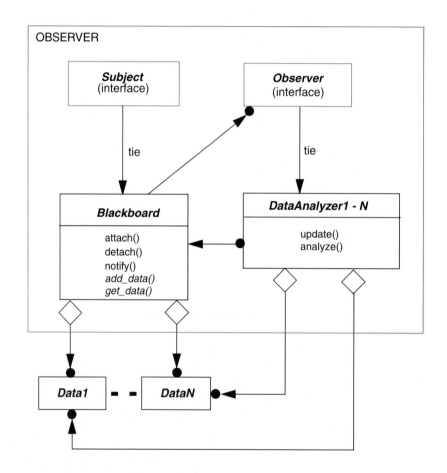

Pattern Used	Role	Role Played By
OBSERVER	*Subject*	*Subject*
OBSERVER	*Subject_i*	*Blackboard*
OBSERVER	*Observer*	*Observer*
OBSERVER	*Observer_i*	*DataAnalyzer1–N*
CORBA-FRIENDLY CLASS	*Server_i*	*Blackboard*
CORBA-FRIENDLY CLASS	*Server_i*	*DataAnalyzer1–N*

Participants

- *DataAnalyzer1–N*
  - Each of these classes provides an implementation of an *Observer* that analyzes data objects as they are added to the *Blackboard*.
  - The implementation of the update function will determine if a new piece of data is relevant to the *DataAnalyzer* object and, if so, will keep a reference to it or a copy of it.
  - The analyze function will iterate through a group of data objects, performing a domain-specific algorithm that produces a higher-level view of a group of data objects.
  - When the view of a group of data objects under scrutiny by a *DataAnalyzer* object changes, it may be necessary to notify other objects of this change. If so, the results of the analyze function can be placed directly on the *Blackboard*. Interested *Observer*s would then be notified by the *Blackboard* object.
  - There will be, potentially, many *DataAnalyzer* objects, each with different implementations, in an application using this pattern.

- *Blackboard*
  - Manages all shared data (i.e., instances of *Data* objects).
  - Is often a transient SINGLETON, as described in [PATTERNS95], or a PERSISTENT DATA MANAGER, which is actually a special type of PERSISTENT SINGLETON.
  - When a new *Data* object is added, the *Blackboard* object will notify any *DataAnalyzer* object that has attached and specified an interest in data of that type. The OBSERVER pattern is employed to provide notification, so this class provides the implementation of the *Subject* interface. Some of its member functions, therefore, must be tied to this interface. Other member functions can be called directly by the *DataAnalyzer*. As you can see, this must be a CORBA-FRIENDLY class.

- *Data1–N*
  - There are one or more domain-specific data types associated with this pattern. All data objects are fine-grained, playing a passive role in the pattern. *Data1* can be the same as *DataN* if it is logical to partition objects of the same type into different collections. Remember the example of how you might want to keep closed Orders in one collection and open Orders in a different collection?
  - *Data* objects can contain the results of analysis performed by *DataAnalyzer* objects.

- *Subject*
  - IDL interface, as described in OBSERVER pattern.

- *Observer*
  - IDL interface, as described in OBSERVER pattern.

Consequences

  – There is a design issue that you will need to resolve when you implement a *DataAnalyzer* class: Do you want the *DataAnalyzer* objects to store one specific group of objects or any group of objects that satisfy a given set of rules? For example, suppose you are building a network management application that notifies users of power failures. It has one simple rule for determining this: "When three or more shutdown alarms are received from the same location, a power failure is assumed and should be reported for that location." Is each location monitored by a separate *DataAnalyzer* object, or are all shutdown alarms handled by the same *DataAnalyzer* object?

  – Assumes that an ORB is available.

Implementation

  – Depending on how you implement the *Blackboard,* data may be referenced by the *DataAnalyzer* using either C++ pointers, ODMG-93 object references (i.e., `d_Ref`), or a string identifier.

Sample Code and Usage

This pattern is used in the Risk Monitoring Framework presented in Chapter 11, but since this is such hard pattern to conceptualize, I will present the simple "Power Failure Analysis" example described in the Consequences section, using STL and transient data. It is assumed that all power failures will be detected and handled by one `PowerFailureAnalyzer` object. I'm not going to show the entire implementation, just the class declarations, the implementation of `PowerFailureAnalyzer`, and a typical scenario using an Object Interaction Diagram.

Although I show only one type of analysis, you should be able to see how easy it would be to extend the application to diagnose many different types of fault conditions, using data in the *Blackboard*. For example, I could add another class that analyzes parity errors in data being transferred through switches.

The mapping of roles is as follows:

Role	Role Played By
Blackboard	AlarmManager
Blackboard::add_data()	AlarmManager::add()
Blackboard::get_data()	AlarmManager::get()
DataAnalyzer1	PowerFailureAnalyzer
Data1	Alarm

```cpp
struct Alarm {
    string id;
    string type;
    map<string,string,less<string> > attributes;
};

class AlarmManager {
  public:
    static AlarmManager* instance();
    void add(Alarm*);
    void attach(Observer_var);
    void detach(Observer_var);
    void notify();
    Alarm* get(const char* alarm_id);
  protected:
    AlarmManager();
    vector<Alarm*> all_alarms;
  private:
    static AlarmManager* _instance;
    list<Observer_var> attached_observers;
};

class PowerFailureAnalyzer {
  public:
    PowerFailureAnalyzer();
    void update(const char* new_alarm_id);
  protected:
    virtual void analyze(vector<Alarm*>&);

        // key is location name, value is list of alarms
        // received from that location.
    map<string,vector<Alarm*>,less<string> > open_alarms;
    map<string,int, less<string> > power_failures;
};

void
PowerFailureAnalyzer::update(const char* new_alarm_id)
{
    AlarmManager* alarm_manager = AlarmManager::instance();
    Alarm* a = alarm_manager->get(new_alarm_id);
    if(a->type == "shutdown")
    {
        vector<Alarm*>& alarm_group
            = open_alarms[a->attributes["location"]];
        alarm_group.push_back(a);
        analyze(alarm_group);
    }
}
```

```cpp
void
PowerFailureAnalyzer::analyze(vector<Alarm*>& alarm_group)
{
    if(alarm_group.size() >= 3)
    {
        string location =
            alarm_group[0]->attributes["location"];
        cout << "Possible Power Failure at "
            << location << endl;
        power_failures[location]++;
        alarm_group.erase();

        // you may want to notify other Observers here, or
        // put the fact that there has been another power
        // failure on the Blackboard
    }
}
```

The following shows a Power failure scenario, where three "shutdown" alarms are received from the same location.

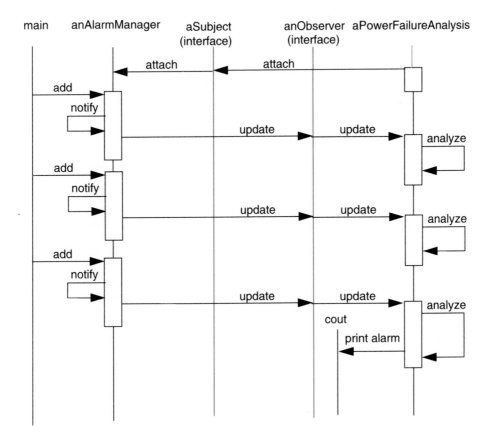

Known Uses
Switching System Fault Diagnosis, Portfolio Management, and Risk Measurement.

Related Patterns

Sets Stage For: THRESHOLDING

PATTERN 2 - CORBA-FRIENDLY CLASS

Intent

To design classes of coarse-grained objects such that critical functionality is "tieable" to a CORBA interface.

Motivation

If you design a class without recognizing that it may need to be accessed via an ORB, this can really come back to bite you later if it does need to be accessed. You will either have to wrap the class or redesign your interface, which can have a nasty ripple effect.

Maybe you can't efficiently provide an interface that completely maps to the CORBA C++ binding without significant sacrifices. If that is the case, the primary mode of usage must be to instantiate the class in the same process space as the client objects. However, you should still design with the goal that you will accommodate remote usage with a subset of functionality. This way, the heavy-duty users of a class get the benefit of a class interface that was not watered down so that it could be used via an ORB, when it may be perfectly acceptable for them to directly link it into their C++ program. But there may be lightweight users of the class that only need to use a few functions, perhaps for querying, and may want to share the same object over an ORB. Maybe they are Java clients. So, you want the class, or at least some portion of its interface, to be made accessible by remote objects by using the tie approach.

Applicability

Use this pattern whenever it is anticipated that a class may need to be accessed via an ORB.

Structure

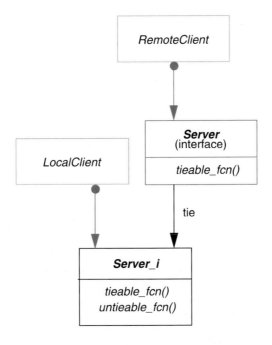

Participants

- *Server*
    - Interface that makes a subset of *Server_i* member functions available via an ORB.
- *Server_i*
    - Instances of this class are coarse-grained objects.
    - Has some functions that can be accessed via an ORB and some that cannot.
    - No part of the implementation of this class should be CORBA dependent, so that it can be linked into a stand-alone program.

Consequences

- Unfortunately, you will probably have to tweak your ORB's tie macro in order to implement a class that doesn't depend on CORBA. For Orbix, I had to manually remove the ENV argument that is automatically assumed to be passed to the object being tied to.

- You can't overload function names in IDL, so if your class uses overloading, you will have to distinguish the names in the IDL. For example, instead of `Foo(const char*)` and `Foo(long)`, you will need something like `Foo1(in string s)` and `Foo2(in long l)`.

- Assumes that an ORB is available.

Implementation

- The functions that can be tied to an ORB must have arguments with types that can be promoted to/from the C++ types mapped to IDL. Please see Table 3-1 on page 51 for the mapping of IDL types to C++ types.

- To be CORBA friendly, no tieable functions can return `const char*` and must allocate a returned string on the heap.

Sample Code and Usage

Please refer to the design of the `Workflow_Manager` class in section 10.2.

Related Patterns

Stage Setters: OBSERVER

PATTERN 3 - DETAIL FILTERING

Intent
To be able to view multiple subsets of a large collection of hierarchical data.

Also Known As
Drilling down.

Motivation
Very often, complex systems need to be built such that hierarchical data can be viewed with details filtered out, either because the system is just too complex to comprehend all aspects of it at once or you are only concerned with certain aspects of the system at a particular point in time.

Remember the old encyclopedias you had on your bookshelf as a kid? If you looked up "Human Body," chances are that you would have found a stack of transparencies. When all were stacked together, you saw all the guts inside a person. How does this mess actually work? you might have asked. So, you started to flip through the transparencies. If you looked at just one transparency, you might just see the circulatory system or bones. When you looked at a couple together, you could focus on the relationships between certain systems in the body. Perhaps you just wanted to see how the circulatory system carried blood to vital organs. This is one simple example of how some clever encyclopedia authors made it easier to understand complex hierarchical data by allowing details to be selectively filtered out.

Detail filtering is not always a matter of visually separating pieces of a system. It may also involve filtering other types of data. For example, a bank has many individual depositors, but the bank auditor doesn't study them all at once. He or she may be looking at one account at a time or be looking at a summary of all deposits.

This pattern provides the basis for what is often referred to as *drilling down* into a hierarchy. This is most often done by a person looking at a GUI, as would be the case for a Risk Manager of a large brokerage house who is navigating through screens to zero in on the trading group assuming the most risk, and not necessarily producing the highest rate of return. Or, what about the guy troubleshooting a network, traversing through graphical depictions of a network topology to where a problem is manifesting itself, and then drilling down into a detailed view of those pieces of equipment and links that are most likely the culprits?

There is one very important thing to take note of with the examples that I have given. In each case, the viewer of the system was viewing a subset of the all information associated with the system. Aggregation is the primary OO mechanism at work. This is different from what I call *data rendering*, where the data being viewed is an approximation of reality, not just a subset of it. Like DETAIL FILTERING, data rendering helps the viewer more easily grasp what's going on in a complex system. Unlike DETAIL FILTERING, data rendering is done when the system is simply too complex to store and process all associated data in a timely fashion, and it is creatively transformed into a simpler approximation.

Applicability
Use the structure specified in this pattern whenever you are designing a system where users are required to analyze a large amount of hierarchical data.

Structure

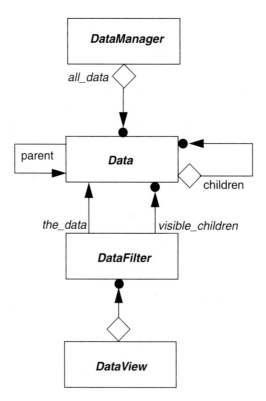

Participants

- **DataManager**
  - Either a SINGLETON [PATTERNS95] or a PERSISTENT DATA MANAGER, whose state includes a collection of *Data* objects that are related hierarchically.

- **Data**
  - Base class for fine-grained objects that are inherently hierarchical.
  - Contains a collection of references to its children, which are assumed to be objects also derived from *Data*.
  - Contains a reference to its parent.

- **DataFilter**
  - A class that contains a reference to a *Data* object, and a collection of references to some or all of that object's children (i.e., its visible children).
  - The visible children of a *Data* object are those that are relevant in a particular *DataView*.
  - This class is responsible for verifying that visible children are legitimate references to children of *the_data* object being filtered.

- **DataView**
  - A class containing a collection of *DataFilters*. A *Data*View captures a subset of all *Data* objects comprising a given data hierarchy.
  - Either *DataView,* or a class derived from it, will have member functions for displaying and/or navigating through the view.
  - If no *DataFilter* is associated with a *Data* object for a given *DataView*, it is assumed that the *Data* object is fully visible if traversed through that *DataView*.

Consequences

  - Requires either an ORB or STL, depending on whether the data is persistent or transient.

Implementation

  - There are two variations of implementations that you will see when you use this pattern. One implementation will employ STL for transient hierarchical data. The other will employ the ODMG-93 API for persistent hierarchies.
  - The *Data* class will probably have at least one attribute that derives its value from its children. We see this in the Risk Monitoring Framework presented in Chapter 11, which employs Detail Filtering.

Sample Code and Usage

The STL version of this pattern might look something like this:

```
struct Data {
    string      id;
    Data*       parent;
    set<Data*,less<Data*> >  children;
};

class DataFilter {
  public:
    friend DataView;
    class InvalidChild {};   // exception class

    DataFilter(Data* the_data);
    void add_visible_child(Data*);

  protected:
    Data*       the_data;
    set<Data*, less<Data*> >  visible_children;
};

class DataView {
  public:
    DataView(const string& view_name);
    void add(DataFilter*);
    void display() = 0;

  protected:
    string          view_name;
    set<DataFilter*,less<DataFilter*> >  filters;
};

class DataManager {
  public:
    static DataManager* instance();
    void add(Data*);
  protected:
    DataManager();
    set<Data*, less<Data*> > all_data;
  private:
    static DataManager* _instance;
};


DataFilter::DataFilter(Data* d) : the_data(d) {}
```

```
void
DataFilter::add_visible_child(Data* child)
{
    // find() is an STL algorithm
    if(find(the_data->children.begin(),
            the_data->children.end(),child))
    {
        visible_children.insert(child);
    }
    else
    {
        throw InvalidChild();
    }
}


DataView::DataView(const string& n) : view_name(n) {}

DataView::add(DataFilter* f)
{
    filters.insert(f);
}

// DataManager implementation not shown
```

The ODMG-93 version of *Data* might look something like this:

```
struct Data {
    d_String id;
    d_Rel_Ref<d_Ref<Thing>,children> parent;
    d_Rel_Set<d_Ref<Thing>,parent> children;
};
```

Using d_Rel_Ref and d_Rel_Set instead of just d_Ref and d_Set keeps the responsibility of referential integrity with the database itself. Please note the implications of the above implementation. We would not be able to protect data with the PERSISTENT DATA MANAGER pattern because there is a trail of d_Refs that makes it very difficult to protect that *Data* and still make it available to application code without a complete transformation. If we really require data protection, the following, less efficient, implementation could be used. In this case, navigating the hierarchy can be done in a *DataManager* class, using OQL instead of simply dereferencing:

```
struct Data {
    d_String id;
    d_String parent;   // id of parent
    d_Set<d_String> children;   // keeps ids of children
};
```

Known Uses

Chapter 11 gives an example of the STL style implementation being used in a Risk Monitoring Framework. In Chapter 11, we have `Portfolio`, `PortfolioFilter`, `PorfolioView`, and `PortfolioManager`, instead of *Data*, *DataFilter*, *DataView*, and *DataManager*, respectively.

This pattern can be used in Portfolio and Risk Analysis, Hardware Fault Diagnosis, Managing Physical Topology of a telecom network, or any type of application that requires modeling complex hierarchical, physical structures (e.g., computer equipment, urban areas, organisms).

Related Patterns

Shares some similarities with the FLYWEIGHT pattern [PATTERNS95]. They both help you deal with a collection of objects that will be used in multiple contexts.

Sets Stage For: COMPOSITE [PATTERNS95]

Sets Stage For: PERSISTENT DATA MANAGER

Sets Stage For: SINGLETON [PATTERNS95]

Stage Setters: COMPOSITE [PATTERNS95]

PATTERN 4 - GENERIC ALGORITHM

Intent
To create a template function that can execute an algorithm on any class that satisfies a set of preconditions.

Motivation
It is desirable to generalize an algorithm like *sort*, putting it in its own separate function, instead of having to provide it as a member function of each class of objects that needs to be sorted. There would be less duplicated code and smaller class interfaces.

Algorithms are made generic through the use of templates. You want to avoid making an algorithm less general by having that logic assume the existence of a particular class; requiring anyone who would like to use that logic to introduce new classes into their object model or, worse yet, force them to use multiple inheritance.

Consider a graph library that provides traversal algorithms, one of which enables you to retrieve an upstream path in a tree structure. An example is shown below.

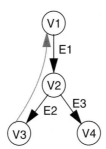

upstream path from V3 to V1 is: {V3,E2,V2,E1,V1}

An algorithm like this is very useful in the telecom domain for tracking down the source of a problem in a network. For example, if a customer calls up complaining of a problem, you'd like to know all the physical devices comprising the path to that customer, in order to isolate the cause. The following is bad design for such a general algorithm:

```
void upstream_path(const Vertex*,set<Vertex*>&,set<Edge*>&);
```

When this function is called, the `sets` passed by reference will be populated with pointers to all the `Vertex` and `Edge` objects comprising an upstream path from the `Vertex` pointed to by the first argument. The problem with this function is that you've required the caller to introduce the `Vertex` and `Edge` classes into their design.

It is better to develop a generic algorithm with a signature like this:

```
template<class VERTEX_PTR, class EDGE_PTR>
void upstream_path(const VERTEX_PTR,
                   set<VERTEX_PTR>&, set<EDGE_PTR>&);
```

Now the user does not necessarily have to change the structure of his or her object model. The only thing the user must ensure is that the classes in the model that have the qualities of vertexes and edges (directed, in this case) satisfy preconditions of the algorithm.

For example, assume the generic version of upstream_path() has the following implementation:

```
template<class VERTEX_PTR, class EDGE_PTR>
void upstream_path(const VERTEX_PTR child_vertex,
set<VERTEX_PTR>& vertexes, set<EDGE_PTR>& edges)
{
    VERTEX_PTR v = child_vertex;
    EDGE_PTR e;
    while(e = v->get_parent())
    {
        edges.insert(e);
        v = e->get_source();
        vertexes.insert(v);
    }
}
```

As you can see, there are preconditions for using this algorithm. The preconditions are placed on the class that plays the role of a vertex (i.e., the vertexlike class) and the one that plays the role of an edge (i.e., the edgelike class). A vertexlike class must have a get_parent() member function that returns a pointer to an edgelike object that links it to its parent vertexlike object. An edgelike class must have a member function called get_source() that returns a pointer to the vertex from which this directed edge originates.

A designer of a cable network application can now develop a domain-specific model to utilize this algorithm:

```
class CoaxCableDevice {
  public:
    d_Ref<CoaxCableRun> get_parent() const;
};
class CoaxCableRun {
  public:
    d_Ref<CoaxCableDevice> get_source() const;
};
main()
{
    // database initialization code goes here
    set<d_Ref<CoaxCableDevice> > devices;
    set<d_Ref<CoaxCableRun> > cable_runs;
    d_Ref<CoaxCableDevice> child_device =
        database.lookup(argv[1]);
    upstream_path(child_device,devices,cable_runs);
}
```

Notice how the persistent nature of the vertexlike objects (i.e., `CoaxCableDevice`) and edgelike objects (i.e., `CoaxCableRun`) is transparent to the algorithm.

Applicability
Use this pattern if a function can be made into a template that can process multiple types of objects, not related to each other through inheritance. Look for independent functions (i.e., those that do not depend on any state that existed before the call) that take objects as arguments and those objects are accessed in a simple way.

Participants
- *Algorithm*
  - A C++ template function that processes objects of the template argument type(s).
  - Depending on the nature of the algorithm, it can also process built-in types.
- *Class1–N*
  - There should be many different types of classes to which the algorithm can be applied; otherwise, the algorithm may not be general after all.
  - Every target class must satisfy preconditions, which are a set of member function signatures that are required by the algorithm. Quite often, these are overloaded arithmetic operators (e.g., operator++).

Consequences

- Employing this pattern has the wonderful side benefit of gradually causing classes designed for completely different applications to have similar interfaces, as application programmers try to take advantage of the generic algorithms modifying their classes to satisfy the preconditions.

Implementation

- Because you are working with C++ templates whenever you use this pattern, you have the same potential for illogical use that you do for STL algorithms. You may want to copy and change the STL_Lint program in Appendix A for new algorithms that you introduce into your software repository.

Sample Code and Usage

Just look at any STL algorithm or the standard deviation algorithm that was developed in section 2.5.

Known Uses

This pattern is an integral part of the design of STL.

Related Patterns

Stage Setters: PROTOCOL (actually, a prerequisite)

PATTERN 5 - INTERPRETER

Intent

To make it easy to modify an object's behavior at runtime, with minimal impact on the rest of the application, by defining a language to specify the object's behavior.

Motivation

Suppose you are charged with developing a bottle-washing control system. You have to design it so that you can vary the washing process without having to recompile. For example, you may want to vary things like the amount of soap used, the rinsing duration, the number of scrub cycles.

The specification of the washing process can't be changed unless the machine is cleared of bottles and is shut down. At this point, you realize that you should follow the SPECIFICATION-ENGINE pattern when you design this system. But where does the specification originate? It might be entered into an ASCII file, or it might be entered via a GUI. What form do you want the *Specification* object to take when the *Engine* receives it? How about using a language? Then, the *Specification* object can simply be a string, which the *Engine* will translate and use as the basis for executing a specific bottle-washing procedure. You can keep this string in a flat file or get it from a GUI. If you want to get fancy, you can front-end the language with a bunch of dialog boxes, buttons, scrolling lists, and other cool stuff. But, you now have the option to use a simple, text-entry widget.

Speaking more generally about why you would want to use a language to specify an *Engine* object's behavior, consider the following. If the specification is stored in an ASCII file, there may be no impact on code surrounding the *Engine* when the language changes. If you define one language with another, then the *Engine* itself may not have to change. An example of how and when you might want to do this is discussed in the Sample Code and Usage section.

The INTERPRETER pattern occurs when an *Engine* takes an ASCII string for its *Specification*. This pattern is described at great length in [PATTERNS95]. I chose to write my own description because I think it is an extremely powerful pattern for framework development, and I felt that a more compelling motivational argument was in order than was presented in [PATTERNS95].

Applicability

Use this pattern whenever you must design a coarse-grained object that:

—   Has many variations in behavior that may have to change at runtime.

—   Will have its behavior specified in a portable, readable fashion.

—   Needs its behavior specified or modified in a nontrivial way via an ORB.

—   Needs its behavior specified or modified via a public interface of an abstract class in a framework. THRESHOLDING is a good example of this.

Structure

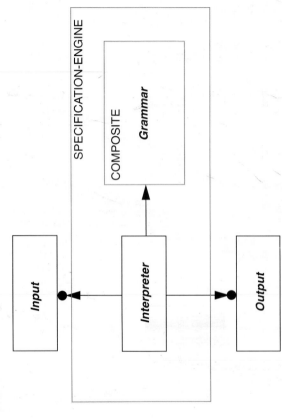

Pattern Used	Role	Role Played By
SPECIFICATION-ENGINE	*Specification*	*Grammar*
SPECIFICATION-ENGINE	*Engine*	*Interpreter*

Participants

- **Input**
  - Contains the string(s) of characters to be parsed according to the *Grammar*. This is usually an STL `string`, a `const char*`, or some kind of input stream (e.g., `ifstream`, `cin`).
- **Grammar**
  - Together, this group of objects comprise the rules that the *Interpreter* uses for parsing input (i.e., the *Specification* for the *Engine*). The objects form a structure that matches that of the COMPOSITE pattern [PATTERNS95].

- ● **Interpreter**
  - – A coarse-grained object that reads *Input* and parses it to produce *Output*. The *Grammar* specifies how this translation should occur. The *Output* may be domain specific; however, NAME-VALUE PAIRS can also be used in the *Output* class to generalize the *Interpreter*. In other words, name-value pairs can be passed from *Input* to *Output*, with no type translation being performed by the *Interpreter*.
  - – *Interpreter* can use *Output* to control its own behavior or simply pass it on to some other object, acting as nothing more than a translator.
- ● **Output**
  - – A class of fine-grained objects that are a logically equivalent representation of the information captured by the *Input* character string(s). There may actually be more than one such class required to completely represent the *Input*.

Consequences

- – Interpretation is slower than working with native objects.
- – To implement the INTERPRETER pattern, you really need a good, regular expression class. The problem here is how to buy a good one and not violate Rule 12, which states that your design should not be tightly coupled to a particular vendor. Ideally, you would like to put one good regular expression class in your repository and not have to drag a huge library along with it. You also want to make sure that you purchase the source for that class—not to change it, but to have it as an insurance policy against vendor dependence.

Sample Code and Usage

Many of today's applications are dedicated to converting data from one form to another, and this is usually a hardcoded translation that must be written and supported by a programmer. As time goes by, this problem is only going to get worse as more and more applications are written in isolation. At some point in their life cycle, most such applications must either provide information to, or get information from, another system that was also written in isolation. On Wall Street and in telecom, where there is a tremendous amount of data that needs to be shared among systems, the situation is at a crisis level.

Quite often, ASCII is used as an intermediate form for translation of data from one format into another. You may be concerned with retrieving input data from a legacy database, a news wire, a configuration file, etc., and translating it into C++ objects, without having to hardcode all of this translation. The problem just occurs too often to build and maintain customized hardcoded translation programs. By my observation, translating ASCII data from one form to another consumes more human resources than any other software development activity.

This is particularly significant to framework development, because frameworks must acquire state from somewhere, and that somewhere is often another system. A technique that can dramatically simplify ASCII data loading is to use two instances of the INTERPRETER pattern to decouple the input data format from the code that processes the data.

The *Output* of the first *Interpreter* is the *Grammar* of the second, which specifies how to parse incoming ASCII data (see figure below).

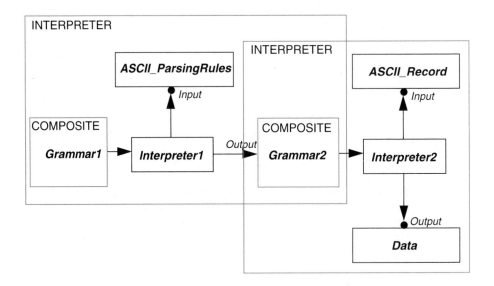

The rules for parsing the ASCII records containing the actual data to be loaded, then, is defined by the *Input* to *Interpreter1*, which is just ASCII as well. Think about that. The rules for parsing the data can be sent with the data itself. The real beauty of this is that the input data format can vary, and the implementation of the *Interpreter2* class does not have to change to be able to parse it. Further, if the data attributes haven't changed, only the format that they are received in, then the *Output* of *Interpreter2* is unchanged, and the code using the *Output* remains unaffected.

This is a great way to build reusable software. For example, suppose you wanted to build and sell a financial data analysis package. Such a package will only be marketable on a large scale if you can design it to work with large amounts of data, received from potentially many sources. Using this technique, a user can simply modify an ASCII file that specifies how to translate data into the format expected by the analysis software.

Let's take a look at a simple example. Assume that you want to build an
interpreter that will enable you to read statistics about a financial instrument (e.g.,
a stock, bond, commodity). Your first grammar will allow you to define the rules for
parsing an input string that contains statistics about one instrument. It might look
like the following (specified in BNF):

```
instrument ::=        record instrument_type { header delimiter attribute* };
attribute ::=         { attribute_name " regex " }
header ::=            " regex "
delimiter::=          " regex "
attribute_name::=  [A-Za-z_]+
instrument_type::= [A-Za-z_]+
```

where regex is UNIX egrep regular expression syntax. The interpreter assumes
that an instrument will be specified in one record (i.e., a line in an ASCII file) and
that the instrument type corresponding to a record can be determined by checking
for a match on a header. The interpreter will also assume that the attributes in a
record are positional if a delimiter is non-null. Finally, the value of an attribute is
assumed to be the first subexpression in the regular expression associated with
that attribute (i.e., that contained in the first matching pair of parentheses () in the
regular expression).

There will be a COMPOSITE object structure reflecting this BNF playing the
Grammar1 role. The *Input* to *Interpreter1* could be a string that looks like this:

```
record Stock
{
        "Stock:"  ""
        { symbol   "Symbol=([A-Za-z0-9_]+)" }
        { high     "High=([0-9]* [ 0-9/]*)" }
        { low      "Low=([0-9]* [ 0-9/]*)" }
        { close    "Close=([0-9]* [ 0-9/]*)" }
};
```

This just defines how to parse a Stock record from one source. You may define
how to parse other instruments as well or, perhaps, another format for a Stock
sent from another source. For example, a Stock might also be parsed in a
positional fashion like this from another source:

```
record Stock
{
        "NYSE"  ":"
        { symbol   "([A-Za-z0-9_]+)" }
        { high     "([0-9]* [ 0-9/]*)" }
        { low      "([0-9]* [ 0-9/]*)" }
        { close    "([0-9]* [ 0-9/]*)" }
};
```

The *Interpreter1* will turn these record format strings into a COMPOSITE that becomes *Grammar2*. So, from one source IBM data might come in like this:

```
Stock: Symbol=IBM High=80 Low=78 1/2 Close=79
```

which would match the first format. In another, it might come in like this:

```
NYSE:IBM:80:78 1/2:79
```

which would match the second. In either case, The *Output* of the *Interpreter2* could be a collection of objects with the following structure:

```
struct Stock
{
    string symbol;
    float  high;
    float  low;
    float  close;
};
```

Known Uses

This pattern can be seen in many systems. One example is the X Toolkit, in which the visual appearance of a particular screen can be customized through resource files. CASE tools often work the same way.

The INTERPRETER pattern is assumed in the implementation of classes that support some of the services defined in [COSS94]. For example, in the Life Cycle Service [COSS94], a `GenericFactory` interface assumes that constraints for creating new objects will be passed to the factory implementations by use of a constraint language. So, constraints like "<= 10 objects per workstation" can be passed to the factory implementations, which will then be responsible for interpreting them.

This pattern has a place in large financial institutions, where legacy back-office databases must communicate with newer front-office client/server applications. It can also be applied in network management where many legacy Manager-Agent interfaces are still based on ftp.

This pattern is also used to develop compilers.

Related Patterns

Sets Stage For: FACTORY METHOD [PATTERNS95]

PATTERN 6 - NAME-VALUE PAIRS

Intent
To customize a fine-grained object at runtime.

Motivation
Consider the following design problem. You have to design a framework that deals with telecom network topology. One of the most basic properties that must be associated with all physical entities comprising a topology is their location. A location could be a street address, a zone, a gps coordinate of a device on a ship, or a polar coordinate of a satellite. It could be something else that varies with culture. For example, Saudi Arabia has no notion of street address; they use the closest landmark. So, what am I, as a framework designer, going to do—have a different class for each of these? No, I don't think so.

From the perspective of the framework, it is important that an association can be made between a physical entity and a location, but location attributes are irrelevant to the framework. Assume that it has been determined that a persistent collection `Location` objects should be maintained by this framework. Name-value pairs provide a design option:

```
struct Location {
    d_String id;
    d_String type;
    d_Rel_Ref<Location,children> parent;
    d_Rel_Set<Location,parent> children;
    d_List<d_String> attribute_names;
    d_List<d_String> attribute_values;
    };
```

This class is designed to include the absolute minimum information that I know will be associated with every location, leaving all the details to the framework user. A user could turn this into a U.S. postal address by simply setting name-value pairs for state, street, building number, and zip code. Or, the hierarchical nature of a U.S. postal address can be accounted for in this structure (e.g., states have counties, counties have towns, towns have streets, streets have buildings) by creating a separate location for each county, town, street, and building, applying a combination of name-value pairs and parent-child relationships. Notice that this would also set the stage for DETAIL FILTERING. For example, you could set up a `LocationView` that referenced all addresses in Point Pleasant, New Jersey, and another one that referenced all counties in New York and New Jersey.

It may well be that the application is translating different "Location" data structures from different applications into this one generic Location data structure. This would be an example of what I call *data multiplexing*.

Applicability

Use this pattern when it has been determined that a framework is responsible for maintaining a collection of fine-grained objects that

- Have many variations in structure, not all of which are known in advance of the framework design.

- Inheritance is overkill.

- The framework is not concerned with the variations and is not required to verify the validity of the variations.

Consequences

- When you employ this pattern to a class provided with a framework, you are giving application code more flexibility and simplifying class structure. You are also giving application programmers more responsibility, because type checking is no longer done by the compiler and the framework will have no knowledge of the semantics of the name-value pairs (unless you are building a framework with AI capabilities). Validation of the legal values must be performed by the programmer. For example, an attribute called "lastName" should probably be checked to make sure that the first letter is in [A-Z] and the remaining letters are in [a-z]. There is one other inefficiency: values are always kept as strings. If the string value is actually a number, it will occupy more space than a number stored in a numeric type. It will also need to be converted if the number needs to be used in a calculation. The designer of the framework must assess whether or not any of these consequences are too severe after considering how the framework is going to be used. Upon determining that this pattern is just not acceptable, he or she should consider inheritance as an alternative.

Implementation

- The implementation involves embedding an associative array in the fine-grained object. If the data is transient, you can simply use an STL `map<string,string>` or `map<string,float>` to contain the name-value pairs. If the data is persistent, however, there is no associative array collection class, like `map`. ODMG-93 does not define one. I found that the easiest way to do this is with two `d_List`s, one for names and one for values. As long as a name and its associated value are always appended to their respective lists at the same time, they will have the same index. The index can then be used to associate a name with its value. This approach relieves you from having to create another persistent data structure to encapsulate a name with a value.

- Although the name in a name-value pair will always be a character string, the value can be of any primitive type (e.g., float).

Known Usage

Name-value pairs are very useful for passing details through a system in a generic fashion, so they have behavioral benefits in addition to structural ones. For example, the CORBA Life Cycle Service [COSS94] uses name-value pairs for this purpose.

Related Patterns

Sets Stage For: PERSISTENT DATA MANAGER

PATTERN 7 - OBSERVER

Intent

To provide an event notification mechanism, where the notifier (i.e., *Subject*) and the objects notified (i.e., *Observers*) are loosely coupled.

Also Known As

Publish-Subscribe, Event Notification Service [COSS94], Callback Mechanism, Event-Report-Management [STALLINGS93].

Motivation

This pattern grew partially out of the need to support GUI programming. The need to build more efficient systems for trading financial instruments and managing networks in a client/server environment were also major influences on the emergence of this pattern.

Consider what must occur in a Wall Street application, where many stock traders are monitoring their workstations, trying to buy or sell blocks of stock at just the right moment. Their workstations must be instantly notified by a quote server when there is a change in the current price of a stock that is in their portfolios or that they are interested in adding to their portfolios. How could you build this feature into such an application? You can establish a simple protocol between workstation processes and the quote server by using the OBSERVER pattern.

This pattern specifies a protocol with two simple IDL interfaces, one for *Subject* objects and one for *Observer* objects. In this example, the role of the *Subject* is played by the quote server, and the *Observer* roles are played by objects in the trader workstations. The implementation of *Subjects* and *Observers* must know about each other, but only through very simple IDL interfaces. Consequently, the implementations of quote server and workstation objects are minimally coupled and therefore can be maintained and modified independently.

This is just one example of where this pattern is used. I also discussed the need for this pattern at great length in Chapter 3, where we used it to provide event notification in a network management application. An explanation of how this pattern is relevant to GUI applications can be found in the Motivation section of the OBSERVER pattern description in [PATTERNS95].

Applicability

This pattern should be used when one object must provide event notification services to other objects, and the objects to be notified are not known in advance, and may change during the course of system operation.

Structure

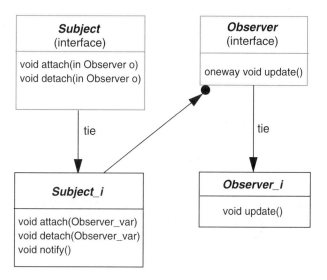

Participants

- **Subject**
  - IDL interface through which *Observer_i* objects attach to a *Subject_i* object.
  - IDL interface through which an *Observer_i* object can detach from a *Subject_i* object, so that it will no longer be sent events.
- **Subject_i**
  - Implements the *Subject* interface.
  - When *Subject_i*::notify() is called, the update() function of each attached *Observer* is called.
  - The *Subject_i* object must maintain a list of references to all attached Observers. For some situations, this list may be transient. For others, however, the list may have to be persistent.
- **Observer**
  - IDL interface through which a *Subject_i* object notifies *Observer_i* objects when an event occurs. Notification occurs when *Observer*::update() is called.

- *Observer_i*
  - Knows how to obtain a reference to a *Subject*, which may or may not be stored as part of its state.[1]
  - Attaches to, and detaches from, *Subject* interfaces.
  - Processes events when its update() function is called.

Collaborations

The following illustrates a scenario for one event, with one *Subject* and one *Observer*. There could just as well be many *Observer*s, in which case, notify() would be followed by a sequence of update() calls. Remember, update() is a oneway call, which means that *Subject_i* doesn't have to wait for one *Observer_i* object to finish its update() call before issuing another. What actually occurs during the activation period of the update is a mystery, from the perspective of this pattern. This scales back the scope of the pattern as described in [PATTERNS95]. You don't necessarily have to go through the same *Subject* interface to determine the details of the event. You can read a database, for example.

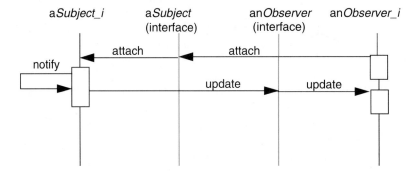

---

1. Because the reference is not necessarily stored in the state of an *Observer_i*, there is no reference relationship drawn on the class diagram.

Optional Details

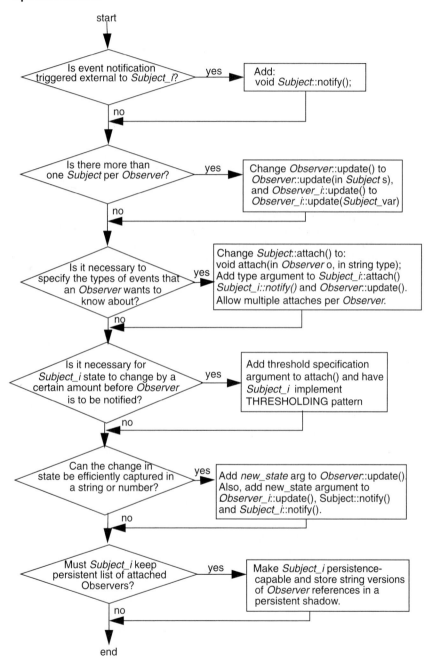

Consequences

- Requires an ORB.

- If *Subject*::notify() is provided, this could be considered a security vulnerability, because there is no way to prevent anyone from calling it. You may have to derive an interface from Subject and provide a more secure protocol for doing this.

- This pattern may appear to be in competition with the CORBA Event Notification Service [COSS94], but that service supports a more complex model, geared toward completely decoupling objects and supporting complex push/pull models. Loose coupling is desirable, but trying to completely decouple objects in the same framework doesn't make much sense, since they are designed to work with each other. Also, complex push/pull semantics are left up to the framework designer and are not included in the pattern.

- This can be used as an event notification mechanism between objects in the same process space, in different processes on the same machine, or on different machines. It is probably not the most efficient approach if you know that the objects will always be in the same process space. But, don't opt for efficiency when you know that you will probably need to distribute objects later.

Implementation

There are two primary ways to implement and use the OBSERVER pattern.

First, you may have a very complex *Subject_i* that contains a rich transient state. In this case, notify() will be called from within the *Subject_i* implementation when its state changes, and there will probably be no access to notify() through the *Subject* interface. When used in this way, *Observer*s will actually be using an interface derived from the *Subject* interface, supplemented with a function, or functions, that enable the *Observer_i* object to retrieve details about state changes in *Subject_i* objects.

In the second type of *Subject_i* implementation, a *Subject_i* object has no state. Instead, it serves only as a an event-notifying delegate of some other object. This type of implementation requires Subject::notify() access. There are several reasons why you may want to do this. First, the object with the interesting state does not have to have the implementation necessary to notify observers. Second, you may want to separate the two so that an application-specific object can do something, like block on an system call, while its *Subject_i* delegate is accepting attach and detach requests. So, you could have a *Subject* IDL (as shown in Listing 3-1), a *Subject_i* class (like the one shown in Listing 3-3), and server program (like the one shown in Listing 3-7) that is compiled once and reused from application to application. The actual object with the state being monitored simply calls *Subject*::notify() when its state changes. *Observer_i* must be designed to know how to retrieve the new state, perhaps from a database, or directly from the object that invoked Subject::notify(). The OBSERVER pattern is employed this way in the Security Alarm Reporting example presented in section 4.5. It is also used this way in the Workflow Framework developed in Chapter 10.

Sample Code and Usage
Please refer to section 3.7.2 to see a complete implementation of a small horizontal framework that implements the OBSERVER pattern and then uses the framework in a small network management application.

Known Uses
GUI Toolkits, Financial Instrument Trading Systems, Network Management Applications, Control Systems.

Related Patterns
Stage Setters: PERSISTENT DATA MANAGER

PATTERN 8 - PERSISTENT DATA MANAGER

Intent
To control access to a collection of independent, fine-grained, persistent objects via a coarse-grained Data Manager object.

Motivation
Consider the example application that we developed in Chapter 4 for managing catalog orders. In that application, we were concerned with one persistent collection containing all `Order` objects. Assume this collection is created, named "All Orders," and is to be your "golden" copy of all orders in the system. Code must then be written to perform basic CRUD[2] operations, as well as other application-specific logic. There are a few design problems you must solve. For instance, how do you prevent ODMG-93 API calls from being peppered throughout your code? Oh, there's another potential problem: once the collection is named, anybody with access to the database can write a program to access the collection by simply invoking `Database::lookup()`. How do you prevent programs from doing harmful things to the data or looking at data that they have no business looking at? The ODMG-93 standard does not address database security, so how do you do this in a portable way? Assume you deal with these problems and build your application. Then, time passes. Many orders go through your system, and you find that the system is getting too slow because the collection of `Orders` is growing too large. You realize that you need to split "All Orders" into "Open Orders" and "Closed Orders" to improve efficiency. Oh no! This really screws up your existing application code. How could you have minimized the impact of this oversight? Uh-oh, your object database vendor is going out of business. No problem, you are using ODMG-93, so you should just be able to plug in another compliant database. What's that? You were using the proprietary database transaction log to generate your reports for management? Wow, now you have to figure out how to generate them for the new database—and make them look just like the old reports. You know how much management hates change. How could you have captured transaction information in a database-independent fashion?

All of these potential problems can be addressed by using this very simple pattern. The PERSISTENT DATA MANAGER pattern makes it easier to 1) encapsulate database semantics, 2) provide a portable security mechanism through object-oriented design, 3) tune the performance of data access through object-oriented design, 4) provide a database-independent transaction log that is tailored to the type of objects kept in the collection, and 5) store information about the collection itself. Let's briefly discuss how the pattern makes it easier to achieve each of these.

---

2. Create, Read, Update, and Delete.

Using an ODMG-93-compliant database when you are developing in C++ is so much easier than using a relational database, but it is still a database. And so, you still have a lot of database semantics to contend with when you are dealing with a persistent collection of objects. Your C++ code still has to open and close the database, begin and commit transactions, look up named objects, etc. Whenever you design a framework that deals with persistent data, you'd like to minimize the framework user's exposure to database semantics. A *DataManager* class can encapsulate a lot of these semantics.

With the advent of ODMG-93, it is now easier to protect data through class design, rather than relying directly on proprietary database administration mechanisms. This pattern describes how to design such that you must access a collection of data by way of the public member functions of a *DataManager* object. If you can do this, you may be able to protect the data with those functions.

The data managed by a *DataManager* object is protected. The way it stores data can, therefore, be changed over time with no impact on the application code that uses it. So, you can separate "All Orders" into two collections: "Opened Orders" and "Closed Orders," affecting only the implementation of the *DataManager*.

A *DataManager* class is designed by using the PERSISTENT SINGLETON pattern, which means that all *DataManager* objects share state. This state can contain information about the collection being managed, including a log of changes to that collection.

Applicability
This pattern should be used whenever a collection of independent fine-grained persistent objects must be maintained. This pattern does not necessarily apply to collections of objects that have embedded d_Refs to other persistent objects unless protection of data is not an issue. The transformation of the data that would be required before it could safely be presented to application code may nullify its benefits.

Structure

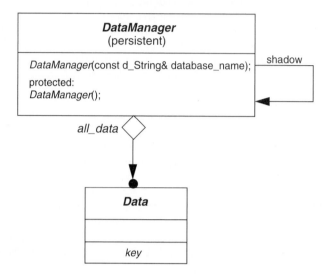

The static class structure is not terribly interesting. The object structure (shown below) is really what is interesting. This diagram indicates that many processes may have a transient instance of a *DataManager* object, but they all work with the state of a persistent shadow, which contains the actual collection of persistent data objects.

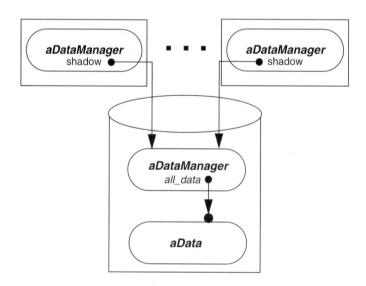

Pattern Used	Role	Role Played By
PERSISTENT SINGLETON	*PersistentSingleton*	*DataManager*

Participants

- ***DataManager***
  - Uses ODMG-93 API as persistence mechanism.
  - Applications work with transient *DataManager* objects.
  - The persistent shadow that a transient *DataManager* object will use is in the database named in an argument passed to its public constructor. If a *DataManager* needs the shadow and finds that it doesn't exist yet, it will instantiate it, using the protected constructor. It will then name the shadow with the same name as the *DataManager* class.
  - All transient *DataManager* objects use the *all_data* collection in the persistent shadow, ignoring their own *all_data* member.
  - *all_data* element is protected and is implemented with an ODMG-93 collection class (e.g., `d_Set`, `d_List`).
  - Persistent data objects put into *all_data* should be instantiated from within a *DataManager* object; otherwise, it is possible that the *Data* objects were named elsewhere and therefore are not protected by the *DataManager*.
  - The attributes and operations of the *Data* objects managed are irrelevant to this pattern.
- ***Data***
  - Will have a *key* attribute that enables a *Data* object to be joined with other objects that represent a different view of the same entity. This is very important for integrating horizontal frameworks, as we'll see in Chapter 8, when we discuss the notion of *object splitting*.

Optional Details

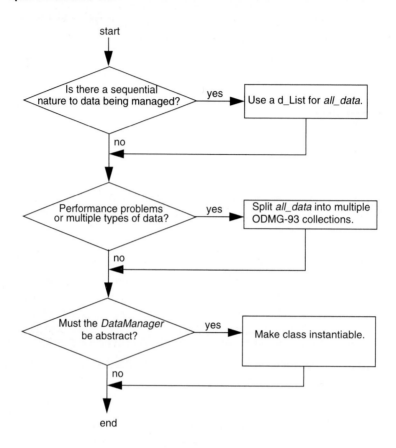

Consequences

– Requires ODMG-93 features.

Implementation

A *DataManager* object must be able to instantiate the *DataManager* class itself in order to create the persistent shadow. However, the transient instances may have to be objects of a class derived from *DataManager*. This is the case for the Workflow Framework presented in Chapter 10. In that framework, the role of *DataManager* is played by the Workflow_Manager class. An application that uses the framework must derive a class from `Workflow_Manager`, to provide implementations for several member functions. In the running application, therefore, you will have transient instances of the class derived from `Workflow_Manager`, and their persistent shadow will be an instance of the *DataManager* base class.

Sample Code and Usage
This pattern is applied three times in this book:

1. In the `OrderManager` class described in section 4.4.
2. In the `SecurityAlarmManager` class described in section 4.5.
3. In the `Workflow_Manager` class described in Chapter 10.

Related Patterns
Sets Stage For: OBSERVER

PATTERN 9 - PERSISTENT SINGLETON

Intent
To have all instances of a class share the same persistent state.

Motivation
Suppose that you have been asked to implement a Finite State Machine that is to be used in a distributed application. The characteristics of a Finite State Machine are such that the SPECIFICATION-ENGINE pattern must be applied. So, there is going to be a class playing the role of *Specification* for a state machine *Engine* class. A specification object will contain all the information about states and transitions that are legal in a given application.

How can you guarantee that all state machine *Engine* objects use the same specification? You don't want to hardcode the specification. You want to have the *Specification* object created once, somewhere, and used by all *Engine* objects, regardless of where they are running. One approach to doing this is to design the *Specification* class such that all instances will use the state of one persistent "shadow" object of the same type.

The same situation may apply to the *Engine* object itself. Suppose you want all instances of the *Engine* to be synchronized. They will also need to work off the state of one persistent *Engine* object (i.e., the *Engine*'s shadow).

Applicability
Use this pattern whenever all of the following conditions are true:

- All instances of a given class must share state.
- The instances are not necessarily in the same process space.
- The state must be persistent.

Structure

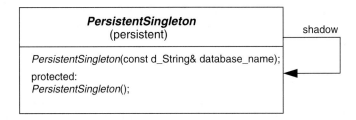

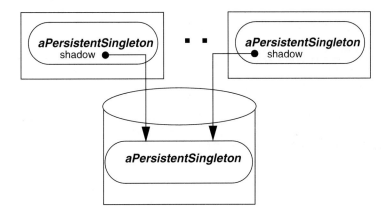

Participants

- ***PersistentSingleton***
    - Uses ODMG-93 API as persistence mechanism.
    - Must have two constructors: one public and one protected. The public one is used to instantiate transient instances of the class, and the protected one is used to instantiate the one and only persistent instance (i.e., the shadow). The shadow is often instantiated in the public constructor.
    - Whenever any public member function is called, the function must be implemented such that it starts a transaction, looks up a reference to the shadow, works with the state of the shadow, and then commits the transaction. This way, any *PersistentSingleton* object instantiated, anywhere, always has the same state.

Consequences

- Efficiency is not necessarily at its highest when interacting with a *PersistentSingleton*. Every public member function call will result in a Database transaction.
- Requires ODMG-93 API.

Implementation

- You may want to encrypt the name of the shadow, so it is less likely that someone will delete it.
- If the state of the *PersistentSingleton* is frozen and efficiency is a problem, you may want to dump its state into a data structure, so you don't have to make any more database accesses.

Sample Code and Usage
See PERSISTENT DATA MANAGER.

Related Patterns
Stage Setters: SPECIFICATION-ENGINE

PATTERN 10 - PROTOCOL

Intent
To give classes with similar behavior a consistent-looking interface, without resorting to the use of inheritance, templates, or other C++ mechanisms.

Motivation
Suppose you have a class in your software repository called `CheckingAccount`, and, to determine the balance of an account, you are required to call a member function called `get_balance()`. Now suppose you have another class called `MutualFund` in your repository, which is not related to the `CheckingAccount` class but obviously shares abstract similarities. To get a mutual fund balance, I would expect to also call a function named `get_balance()`.

It is not possible to build a large repository of software assets if there is not some consistency in the names of member functions that are semantically equivalent. Nobody will ever become proficient in using the software in the repository; they will constantly be required to consult reference manuals. You need to establish guidelines for designing predictable syntax into your frameworks.

Usability and readability are only part of the benefit of using predictable syntax. Consider the `CheckingAccount` class and `MutualFund` class again. What if I wanted to write a function that tallies the balances of both a collection of `CheckingAccounts` and a collection of `MutualFunds`. In fact, I'd like to write one generic algorithm to tally a collection of any kind of account without being required to derive my class from some `Account` base class. Well, I can't unless there is syntax that I can count on when I am accessing any kind of object that represents some sort of account. If there is such a syntax, then I can use a C++ template to implement the algorithm. In the case of accounts, it may be sufficient to assume that there will be a `get_balance()` member function that comes with any accountlike class.

This pattern is the basis of generic programming, which is, as you may recall from Chapter 2, an integral part of the design of STL. As we discussed in Chapter 2, STL has many unrelated collection classes, but they all have a common set of member functions. This common set of functions is called a *protocol*. Because they all have a common protocol and it closely matches the protocol that a programmer uses to work with built-in types, the designers of STL were able to provide dozens of useful, generic algorithms that can be applied to any STL collection or built-in C++ array. There is a significant amount of discussion about this pattern in Chapter 2.

Applicability
If two or more classes have behavioral similarities but are not derived from the same base class, this pattern should be applied.

Structure

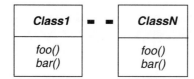

Participants

- *Class1–N*

    - Each of the classes in this group has a common subset of member function signatures. Every class provides implementation that is semantically equivalent to that provided by every other class, for the same function signature. So, if *Class1* has a member function called *foo*, which is part of the common protocol, then *ClassN* will also have a function called *foo* with the same semantics.

Collaborations

All classes with the same protocol will have similar semantics and will likely be used with generic algorithms.

Consequences

    - One of the consequences you may encounter when establishing a protocol common to several classes is that each class may end up having member function names that are a little more general than they would otherwise be.

Implementation

When trying to choose the best syntax for a protocol, start by creating a quiz. Describe the purpose of a member function, and then ask a few programmers what they would expect it to be called. If you have consensus or a majority, by all means use the name.

Known Uses

STL collection class interfaces.

Related Patterns

    Sets Stage For: GENERIC ALGORITHM

PATTERN 11 - SPECIFICATION-ENGINE

Intent
To create a specification for the behavior that a coarse-grained object is to exhibit, prior to instantiating it.

Also Known As
This pattern is similar to MEMENTO [PATTERNS95]. Both a *Specification* and a *Memento* capture the internal state of another object. There is a difference, however. A *Specification* is intended to be initialized outside of the object whose state is to reflect the *Specification*, whereas a *Memento* is initialized only by the object whose state is to be captured.

Motivation
Consider the Finite State Machine class with an interface that looks similar to this[3]:

```
template <class State, class Stimulus> class FiniteStateMachine {
  public:
    class IllegalState{};   // exception
    FiniteStateMachine();
    void  addState(State);
    void  addTransition(State current,Stimulus,State next);
    void  setCurrentState(State);
    void  fire(Stimulus) = 0;
  private:
    State currentState;
    // other implementation details
};
```

The problem with this interface is that you can accidentally start firing through transitions before the state machine is completely initialized, which may result in an exception. There is also no way to prevent a user from changing a specification once one is created, because you don't know when you are finished creating it. The class interface is also harder to understand because it mixes the functions used to set up the state machine with those used to operate it.

There are actually two abstractions lumped into one here:

- the "Specification" of the state machine (i.e., its legal states and transitions)
- the state machine "Engine," which will respond to stimulus differently, depending on its current state.

There are many important "state-machine-like" abstractions. For example, that is exactly what is at the heart of a workflow application. There are states representing the objects performing the tasks, transitions that represent how work

---

3. I've used off-the-shelf implementations of an FSM that were designed more poorly than this one.

flows from task to task under various conditions, and there is an engine that actually transitions the work upon completion of a task. The next task to be performed depends on how the current task was completed (i.e., what "stimulus" was generated by the task).

When you are building up a complex data structure, like a *Specification*, validation of the values being populated in the data structure is best left to a validation function that gets called after the data structure is completely initialized. First of all, this is more efficient than verifying the *Specification* as you are incrementally building up its state. Second, it may be impossible to verify for correctness until the state is finalized. This would be the case when you need to check for connectivity between two nodes on a graph that you are constructing one edge and vertex at a time. You don't know until the graph is completed. Even if you could validate as you go, it is easier on the programmer who is populating the state of the data structure, because now he need not concern himself with the order in which the data structure is populated.

Applicability

Use this pattern whenever you are designing a class with complicated behavior that must be specified, to a large extent, by the user of the class.

Look for the following: employing the services of a coarse-grained object requires making preliminary member function calls in a well-ordered sequence before the object can perform its primary task. This is a good indication that you need to apply the pattern.

Structure

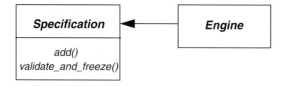

Participants

* *Specification*
  - Defines how an *Engine* object should behave.
  - Will also include the starting state for the *Engine*.
  - Has one or more *add()* functions to incrementally build up the complete specification.
  - Has a *validate_and_freeze()* function that validates the state of the *Specification* and freezes its state. Freezing the state is necessary to avoid the situation where the specification of a running *Engine* object is inadvertently changed, which would result in undefined behavior. If the state does not represent a valid specification, an exception shall be thrown when this function is called.
  - All interaction that occurs from the time a *Specification* is instantiated until the time that its *validate_and_freeze()* function is logically one transaction.

* *Engine*
  - Executes behavior according to a *Specification* object, starting at the state specified in the *Specification* object.

Implementation

  - The code that instantiates and builds up a *Specification* must call *validate_and_freeze()* before the *Engine* object that is going to use it is instantiated.
  - A reference to a *Specification* object can be passed to the *Engine* constructor. A second alternative is to implement the constructor to implicitly know how to find its *Specification*. For example, the *Specification* may be a PERSISTENT SINGLETON.

Sample Code and Usage

Please refer to the Workflow Framework in Chapter 10, where this pattern is employed. The *Specification* role is played by `Workflow_Specification` and the *Engine* role is played by `Workflow_Manager`.

Known Uses

Finite State Machines, Workflow Management, Compilers.

Related Patterns

Sets Stage For: SINGLETON [PATTERNS95]

Sets Stage For: PERSISTENT SINGLETON

Sets Stage For: PERSISTENT DATA MANAGER

PATTERN 12 - THRESHOLDING

Intent

To enable an *Observer* object, whose behavior depends on a numeric value in another object, to be notified when that value has changed by more than an amount specified by the *Observer*.

Motivation

Consider the following situations:

- A doctor wants to know if symptoms persist for more than a certain number of days.
- An inventory manager wants to know when inventory of a particular item falls below a certain level.
- A nuclear power plant operator (except maybe Homer Simpson) wants to know when the water level in the cooling towers falls below a certain height.
- A stock trader wants to know when a particular stock's price has moved by 20 percent, up or down.
- A technician monitoring a telecommunication network wants to know when a particular alarm has been generated three times for the same piece of equipment.
- A financial risk manager wants to know when the value at risk is more than $1,000,000.

In all of these situations, some observer is interested in being updated when a particular numeric value has changed by a specific amount. As you can probably tell by now, this pattern employs a specialization of OBSERVER. The specialization is the addition of the threshold condition. This throws back more responsibility on the *Subject*, which must now selectively update *Observer*s. The *Observer*s will now specify the amount of change that should occur in a numeric value kept in *Subject_i* before they want to be updated.

In a environment where monitored numeric values are kept in different objects that are distributed and change often, this division of responsibility will result in much lower network traffic than you would see if you were employing the basic OBSERVER pattern. For example, suppose you were writing a stock trading system where you had 1) an object that maintained current stock prices and 2) hundreds of other objects, each serving a trader. On a day when a hot IPO called WWW Inc., hits the market, its price will be fluctuating constantly. In the basic OBSERVER pattern, each tick up or down in its price would result in hundreds of updates across the network, followed by hundreds of queries to find out whether it was an up tick or a down tick. Granted, with the THRESHOLDING pattern, you could end up with the same situation if every trader wanted to know about every tick, up or down. You have, however, dramatically improved your ability to prevent huge bursts of network traffic by allowing John to specify that he only wants to know when WWW Inc. has had a price move of 10 percent, up or down, and allowing Sally to specify that she wants to know when the price of WWW Inc., has moved up by 3 points.

Sometimes, you must use a threshold. For example, assume you have an object X that has to perform a real-time calculation whenever a value in object Y changes. If the calculation takes five minutes but the value in Y changes every 30 seconds, you have a bit of a problem, don't you?

THRESHOLDING actually uses a combination of the OBSERVER pattern, the SPECIFICATION-ENGINE pattern, and the INTERPRETER pattern. The OBSERVER pattern is extended by:

- Adding two arguments to *Subject::*attach() and *Subject_i::*attach() to allow an *Observer* to specify threshold conditions that should be satisfied before it is notified (i.e., its update function is called). The specific value to which the threshold applies must be identified by the first argument.The second argument is a string that specifies that actual threshold.

- Adding two arguments to *Observer::*update() and *Observer_i::*update(): one argument to identify the numeric value that changed and another to pass its new value.

- Adding an argument to *Subject::*detach() and *Subject_i::*detach() to specify which value the *Observer* is no longer interested in.

Applicability

Use this pattern whenever there are many objects that must be notified of changes in the numeric state of another object and it is necessary to vary the granularity of the change that causes notification events.

Structure

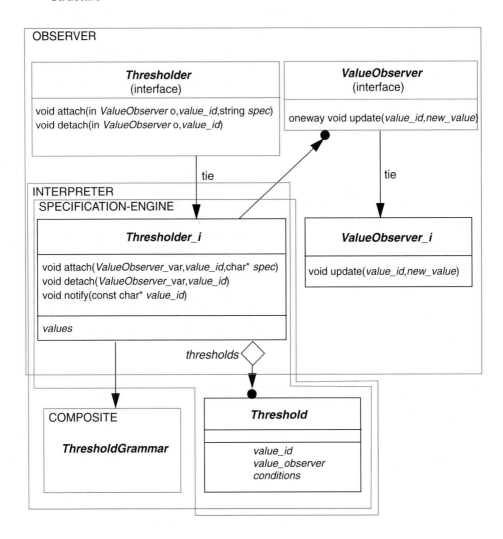

Pattern Used	Role	Role Played By
OBSERVER	*Subject*	*Thresholder*
OBSERVER	*Observer*	*ValueObserver*
OBSERVER	*Subject_i*	*Thresholder_i*
OBSERVER	*Observer_i*	*ValueObserver_i*
INTERPRETER	*Input*	*char* spec*

Pattern Used	Role	Role Played By
INTERPRETER	*Output*	*Threshold*
INTERPRETER	*Interpreter*	*Thresholder_i*
INTERPRETER	*Grammar*	*ThresholdGrammar*
SPECIFICATION-ENGINE	*Specification*	*Threshold*
SPECIFICATION-ENGINE	*Engine*	*Thresholder_i*

Participants

- **Thresholder**
  - IDL interface used to register an interest in being notified of changes in numeric values maintained by *Thresholder_i*.

- **Thresholder_i**
  - Creates *Threshold* objects by parsing the *spec* argument passed to attach().
  - Maintains one or more non-const numeric values as part of its state.
  - Notify() is called after a value in the *values* collection changes, perhaps due to a recalculation or a new record received from a data feed. When notify() is called, threshold conditions specified in the *Threshold* objects, are checked. Each threshold met will result in an update of the *ValueObserver* indicated in the *Threshold* object corresponding to the met threshold.

- **ThresholdGrammar**
  - Grammar containing the parsing rules for the *spec* argument passed to attach() function of the *Thresholder_i* class.

- **Threshold**
  - Fine-grained object that identifies an element in *Thresholder_i::values* that is being monitored by a *ValueObserver*, who the *ValueObserver* is, and the threshold conditions that must be met before the *ValueObserver* is notified.

- **ValueObserver**
  - IDL interface that *Thresholder_i* uses to notify a *ValueObserver* of changes in numeric *values* contained in its state.

- **ValueObserver_i**
  - Special type of *Observer* that knows the grammar for specifying threshold conditions to a *Thresholder_i* object. It must also know the semantics of the *values* maintained in the *Thresholder_i*.
  - Can accept a notification of a change in a *Thresholder_i* value via its update function. What it does with the new value is outside the scope of the pattern.

Optional Details

- Previous *values* can be maintained for purposes of checking threshold conditions that depend on a relative change in value. For example, a threshold condition may have been specified as "the temperature increases by 10% from its current value."
- One variation that you may want to incorporate into your implementation of this pattern is an authentication ID that legitimizes the update. This may be important because anyone with a reference to a *ValueObserver* would otherwise be able to make an undetected bogus update. The design trade-off here is between coupling and security at the framework design level.

Consequences

- Because INTERPRETER is used to specify threshold conditions, IDL remains very simple and immune to changes in the implementations of *Thresholder_i* and *ValueObserver_i*.

Implementation

- We use the pull model in basic OBSERVER and the push model in THRESHOLDING. In the update we push an id of a numeric value and the actual new value itself. This doesn't really compromise the design by too much coupling, because this is still a very generic protocol.

Sample Code and Usage

The Risk Monitoring Framework presented in Chapter 11 illustrates the use of this pattern. I also want to show you a simple general-purpose grammar that can be used for specifying threshold conditions. If this grammar is suitable for your situation, you can write a little parser for it, plop it into your *Thresholder_i* class, and call it in its attach function. The grammar (in BNF) is as follows:

```
Trigger ::=  Expr [or Expr]
Expr ::=     increased | decreased To | By
To ::=       to Number
By ::=       by Number[%] [from original]
Value ::=    Number[%]
Number ::= [0-9]*[\.[0-9]*]
```

With this grammar, you can specify conditions like the following:

"increased by 10% or decreased by 20%"

"increased to 100"

"increased by .25 or increased by 5%"

"decreased by 1 from original"

Related Patterns
Similar to "aspects" ([PATTERNS95] bottom of page 298), only far more powerful because of the arithmetic semantics associated.

Stage Setters: OBSERVER

6.3 Design Rules

Rules are generally simpler and more definite than patterns. Both patterns and rules are based on experience. The rationale behind a rule, however, is more easily understood because it is based on logic rather than heuristics and existence proof, as is usually the case with patterns. Some rules are just conventions to improve code readability and establish more consistency in interfaces.

Some design rules are really just a documentation of sensible ways that the C++ language should be used. Many originated in various textbooks and articles but now exist as popular styles and idioms among seasoned C++ developers, with the origins of the rules now faded into the distant past. I personally use all of them, but I forget which I picked up through my own trial and error and which I first read about somewhere and found to be useful. Since these rules are a part of the methodology standard, I view their contribution to be critical to the quality of designs that employ them. As with patterns, your organization should add to the Rules Catalog. I will present rules in the format of the following template. Rules are simply enumerated.

Rule Documentation Template

Rule Number

Intent
A short statement conveying what the rule accomplishes.

Applicability
The situations in which the design rule must be applied.

Designer Responsibilities
The actions that must be taken by the designer when faced with the situation described in the Applicability section.

Rationale
The rationale, if not obvious from Intent.

Example

CATALOG OF DESIGN RULES

RULE 1

Intent
To minimize the likelihood that you will have to modify a base class later.

Applicability
Use whenever designing a base class.

Designer Responsibilities
Design base classes to be "inheritance friendly," by making data members and functions `protected` instead of `private`, unless you have a good reason to do otherwise. Make all `protected` member functions virtual. Make the destructor virtual.

RULE 2

Intent
To establish a consistent error handling strategy.

Applicability
Use whenever an error condition is encountered.

Designer Responsibilities
Never return error conditions from function calls. Use exceptions for all error reporting. Exception classes should be nested in the declarations of the class that they are thrown in. Please note that there is a subtle difference between failure and "not found." This rule only applies to failures.

Rationale
By now, many of you have probably already adopted this. It sure beats the old days where everybody checked return codes, and you spent a significant amount of time deciding whether you wanted 1 or 0 to mean success and whether you wanted -1, -2, or -3 to represent an error condition.

RULE 3

Intent
To establish read-only access to persistent data.

Applicability
Use when neither PERSISTENT SINGLETON nor PERSISTENT DATA MANAGER suffices.

Designer Responsibilities
Name each persistent object, allowing anyone to get a reference to that object by name. However, such objects should only have public member functions that are `const`. So, unless the accessor is a `friend`, there is read-only access.

RULE 4

Intent
To eliminate catastrophic bugs due to dereferencing bad character-string pointers.

Applicability
If possible, use when designing any function call signature that requires character strings.

Designer Responsibilities
Make arguments to functions `string` or `d_String` instead of `const char*`, to avoid core dumps due to dereferencing null. This rule applies unless you want to pass a character string as an optional argument, in which case you can use a `const char*` set to null to indicate that the argument is not passed.

RULE 5

Intent
To make classes easier to use when character strings are passed as arguments.

Applicability
Use in all classes that have member functions with character string arguments.

Designer Responsibilities
Use `const char*` instead of `char*` whenever possible.

Rationale

Every once in a while, I will find a class that I need to use, but it accepts `char*` when it is only reading the string. Therefore, I can't pass `string::c_str()` as an argument. Instead, I have to first dump the string into a buffer just to pass it to the function!

RULE 6

Intent

To establish a convention for returning something from a function that has been allocated on the heap.

Applicability

Use whenever a function call allocates something on the heap and then returns it to the caller.

Designer Responsibilities

Use the following contract between caller and callee: if non-const pointer is a return value, the caller is responsible for deleting the space pointed to when finished using the return value.

Rationale

This will cut down on memory leaks and, when it becomes a commonplace idiom, will make it easier for programmers to learn how to use new classes.

RULE 7

Intent

To improve efficiency when returning values and help establish consistency in class interfaces.

Applicability

Apply whenever a member function or nontransitive operator returns a value.

Designer Responsibilities

When returning one small value to a caller, return it by value, using the `return` statement (e.g., `int foo() { return 1; }`). To return one large value, fill in a non-const reference to an object passed in by the caller (e.g., `void foo(BigType& result)`). This saves a copy.

RULE 8

Intent
To maintain predictability and consistency in operator semantics.

Applicability
Apply whenever a binary operator is overloaded.

Designer Responsibilities
For transitive operators, always make the value returned by the `return` statement a reference to the object performing the operation (i.e., `return *this;`).

RULE 9

Intent
To establish a convention for passing arguments by reference.

Applicability
Apply whenever an argument of a non-built-in type is passed to a function.

Designer Responsibilities
If a function argument is not of a built-in type, it should be passed by reference. When passing information into a function by reference, the reference must be constant. This prevents the function being called from inadvertently modifying the argument.

Rationale
A non-const reference is assumed to be used to return information to the caller, as explained in Rule 7. This rule used in conjunction with Rule 7 establishes a readability standard, whereby the user can tell exclusively by looking at a function signature which information is going into a function and which is going out.

RULE 10

Intent
To keep the public portion of a class interface as simple as possible.

Applicability
Applies to all classes.

Designer Responsibilities
Never add a member function whose purpose can be satisfied with a combination of other member functions and trivial logic. Further, you should create the minimum number of member functions possible that can provide the required behavior. Doing otherwise creates clutter. If programmers really need to combine member functions, let them write an `inline` to do it.

Rationale
Programmers are turned off by classes that are too complicated, which happens as more functions are added. Remember, there is a tension between the desire to make something have more widespread appeal and the desire to keep it simple. You want to take a minimalist approach, even if in some cases the user may have to massage an input argument or two before invoking your member function. I've seen many valuable classes become almost unapproachable because they have had so many public member functions added to them, many of which are redundant.

Example

```
class Stock {
  public:
    float price();
    float pe_ratio();
    float earnings(); // get rid of this, can be calculated.
                      // Chose to get rid of this instead
                      // of pe_ratio() because pe_ratio is
                      // a more valuable piece of data.
};

class Person {
  public:
    date birthday();
    float age();         // get rid of this, any date class
                         // worth its salt will be able to
                      // convert a date into an age for you.
                         // Worst case, you have to divide by
                         // 365.
};
```

RULE 11

Intent
To prevent name clashes and simplify names.

Applicability
If your tools support `namespace`, define one for your framework.

Designer Responsibilities
Assign a `namespace` to every framework. The name should indicate the domain or facet that the framework addresses.

Rationale
I remember in the olden days when we used to go to great lengths to avoid name clashes by prefixing type names with what appeared to be, and often was, an arbitrary string of characters: like Xm for Motif®. Failing to do this would result in clashes that required all kinds of annoying tricks to get around, especially when the clashes occurred between two libraries that you had not developed.

RULE 12

Intent
To keep a framework portable and vendor independent.

Applicability
This rule applies to all frameworks.

Designer Responsibilities
Don't build frameworks that have any dependency on a specific GUI API! A GUI API should only be accessed from within application code.

Rationale
There are a number of reasons for this. First, you may already be familiar with the notion of Model-View-Controller (MVC), which is an instance of the OBSERVER pattern. MVC suggests that a business model, the screens that drive the model, and the physical device drivers that control the view should be designed independently of each other. A framework captures a business model. To remain true to MVC, therefore, the framework should have nothing to do with the GUI.

The practical statement of the value of using this rule can be summed up as follows. Textbook models exist for things like insurance claim processing, payroll, inventory control, etc. But you can bet that every firm and establishment that has software to help them drive these models will have a different preference for what the user interface should look like and how navigation should occur. Translation: models do not vary from application to application, but human factors do. So don't build human factors-related aspects into a framework or you will severely limit the potential users.

There is another very practical reason. There are an overwhelming number of options for constructing user interfaces these days. For example, you could use one of the many Rapid Application Development (RAD) tools that are now on the market, which allow you to rapidly construct very simple applications that have these magnificent GUIs. You could also choose from the dozens of C++ GUI toolkits that have a widget library and a layout tool. Maybe you want to use HTML as your front end, or how about Tcl/TK? This is one area of application building that is in desperate need of standards and where none currently exist.[4] To pick one for use in a framework would be "frameicide". You will have cheapened the generalness of the framework by making it not only sensitive to human factors, but vendor specific as well (except in the case of HTML).

RULE 13

Intent
To keep a framework portable and vendor independent.

Applicability
This rule applies to all frameworks.

Designer Responsibilities
Don't design a framework that relies on nonstandard components or tools, unless you have the source code for it.The exception would be simple components like a regular expression or date class that you could replace without a great deal of difficulty, as long as there was a straightforward transformation for porting code to a new component. It may be no big deal to pump your source code through a conversion script, but don't go buying into a vendor-solution that ties your success to theirs.

Rationale
I've seen this kill projects again and again. Sometimes vendors go out of business; other times your project direction is inconsistent with the direction of the vendor's product line.

---

4.   Although, if I were a betting man, I would bet that when one does emerge, it will be HTML/Java related.

<u>**RULE 14**</u>

Intent
To keep a framework scalable.

Applicability
This rule applies to all frameworks.

Designer Responsibilities
Use the ORB sparingly, preferably for control information being passed between coarse-grained objects or passing small amounts of simple data (e.g., a sequence of floats). If possible, a fine-grained object (e.g., a data structure) should not be made into a CORBA object.

Rationale
CORBA is a wonderful mechanism for object distribution, but there are complexities associated with object distribution that require the incursion of overhead. That's why you want to be careful about how many objects you make accessible via an ORB. One source of overhead is object references. These references take up space that can become very significant if you are trying to have millions of CORBA objects talk to each other. The space required for references affects your process size and the amount of information being sent over the ORB. Too many references also places significant demands on object-lookup services, like the Naming Service. This methodology recommends accessing fine-grained objects via a Persistent Data Manager class that links directly into your program (see PERSISTENT DATA MANAGER pattern).

CHAPTER 7
Framework Design Metrics

A *metric* is "a standard of measurement" [DICTIONARY85]. A *software metric* is a standard measurement of some aspect of a piece of software. The value associated with the measurement implies something about the quality of that software. Metric values can either be measured directly or calculated based on measured and/or estimated values.

Software metrics can be very valuable tools for both managers and developers. Managers can use them to help assess the quality of software that their people are producing, without having to personally get involved in design and code reviews. Developers can use them to methodically improve the software that they produce.

I have not personally seen many managers or developers even try to use metrics. This is unfortunate, because I believe that in certain instances, a good metrics process could mean the difference between order and chaos. Part of the problem is that collecting metrics has not, traditionally, been an automated part of software manufacturing.

Compiler vendors, in general, have completely shunned the incorporation of features that enable the collection of metrics. I don't know why: most are fairly easy to extract from code. The so-called CASE tool vendors have done the same thing, which is even more difficult to understand. As far as I'm concerned, Computer-Aided Software Engineering means using a tool that will tell me how to improve my design. The only way that a tool can do this is to extract metrics from the design parameters that I enter into it.

In the remaining sections of this chapter, I introduce metrics that enable you to measure the quality of frameworks, consistently and objectively. This chapter introduces you to metrics that are consistent with the methodology and establishes the benefits of applying them.

The metrics I discuss in this chapter can be used to identify potential weaknesses in the design of a framework. All the metrics can, and should, be applied throughout the life cycle of a framework. At some point in the life cycle, they can all be calculated objectively by extracting statistics directly from C++ code. Some can be calculated early in the life cycle, and others, not until the framework has been in use for some time. All, however, should be estimated early on and held as quantifiable design goals. As I go through each metric, I will explain when it should be used.

I assume that developers are designing in good faith by following the patterns and rules put forth in the design standard (Chapter 6) and not attempting to "beat the system" by taking advantage of weaknesses in metrics. These metrics will have no validity if the design standard is not followed.

The larger and more formal the development effort, the more beneficial it could be to establish metrics guidelines. The guidelines could establish thresholds of metrics values that are considered acceptable. These thresholds could be used as criteria for determining if a framework is suitable for incorporation into a repository.

7.1 Inheritance Depth Metric

I was sitting in on an OO RAD[1] tool demo recently, and the vendor was bragging about how much faster their product was than their competitor's, especially when it comes to using inheritance. He said, in fact, "We encourage deep inheritance hierarchies, six or more levels deep because that's when we truly shine." Wow, that's impressive! Now all they need to do is find people that are capable of understanding such hierarchies.

Here's another inheritance story that illustrates the danger of overusing inheritance. I have a friend who has been developing and maintaining software for 20 years now. He's what I characterize as a "master software mechanic." I've seen him decipher some pretty disgusting code and make it dance. Not too long ago he called me and didn't sound his usual jovial self. There was a definite nervous tone to his voice. He said, "Greg, I'm really terrified. For the first time in my career, I've been given an assignment I don't know if I can do." He went on to explain how a 50,000-line C++ library had been dumped on him to maintain, and the stakes were very high. I said, "So what? You've done that before." Then he began to tell me how classes were derived from classes, which were derived from other

---

1. RAD stands for Rapid Application Development. RAD tools are often used to build prototypes quickly.

classes, etc. He said matters were made worse because multiple inheritance was used everywhere. He finally summed up the situation when he said, "I just can't visualize the whole picture, and I can't trace through any scenarios." The designer obviously went overboard trying to prove himself by deriving as many levels of classes as possible and using multiple inheritance whenever he thought he could.

People can, and do, go overboard with inheritance. The average inheritance depth of a framework is a good metric to study. It has a direct impact on the comprehensibility of a framework design. The more depth, the harder it will be to understand and maintain the framework. You could interpret the average inheritance depth of a framework to be inversely proportional to its quality, when it is greater than some acceptable level. I would recommend that the average be less than two and that under no circumstances should there be instances of inheritance depth greater than three.

7.2 Inheritance Width Metric

Multiple inheritance is one of those touchy subjects that some people get real religious about and, just like inheritance in general, tend to overuse. The story of my friend's problem in the previous section indicated that too much multiple inheritance was part of his problem. It makes a design harder to visualize and introduces the potential for ambiguity in member functions and data.

I never really understood why people getting into OO were so infatuated with multiple inheritance. I went to an interview a couple years back at a very prestigious investment bank. The technical manager came in to interview me and one of the first things he asked me was what my guidelines were for using multiple inheritance. My answer was, and I wasn't trying to be funny or anything, "Avoid it if you can." He looked a bit surprised and went on to tell me about their policy of looking at adjectives or something like that. Being in an interview, I politely sat and listened, but I couldn't help but think how ridiculous what he was telling me sounded. Do people really design their systems based on some arbitrary syntactic relationship with the English language? You can't approach complex problems like that. You actually have to think about the behavior you want to implement.

I personally have very rarely had occasion to use multiple inheritance. But, I understand that under certain circumstances it may be necessary to retrofit a design on top of an older library, and that's why I don't have a rule that forbids its usage.

I think a good metric is to calculate the average number of classes that framework classes are directly derived from. If there is no multiple inheritance, I would expect this number to be less than 1. If this number is greater than or equal to 1, the design should be considered suspect. Also, any class that uses multiple inheritance should be identified and questioned.

This "inheritance width" metric also implies something about how heavily dependent classes in the framework are on a few base classes. If the number is just a little less than 1, there may be too much dependence on a few classes. This was typical in older component libraries, where all the classes were derived from one root class. We would prefer to see a number closer to 0, which would reflect a philosophy of using inheritance sparingly.

7.3 Size Metrics

7.3.1   Overall Framework Size

In general, a framework should be less than 10,000 NCSL.[2] This is primarily my own heuristic. The recommended size is from a few hundred to a few thousand NCSL. This is one of the few metrics that someone can apply right off the bat for judging whether a framework is suspect. If you find that your framework is growing much larger than 10,000 NCSL, this does not definitely mean that you are doing something wrong, but it warrants that you ask yourself the following questions:

- Am I trying to build a framework that is all things to all people?
- Should this framework actually be multiple frameworks?
- Am I making this too problem specific?

If these numbers sound small to you, consider the following:

- Frameworks capture general behavior; not all that much detail. Detail is left as a fill-in-the-blank exercise for the application developer. For example, later we will build a framework for the finance industry that will capture behavior that is general to the task of monitoring financial risk. This is a very difficult domain, and there are many complicated techniques for measuring risk. What you must realize is that the specific technique used varies from firm to firm and should not be hardcoded into a risk monitoring framework. The techniques are subjective and, therefore, by definition, have no place in a framework. Yes, if you aggregate all of the analytics that are being applied to risk measurement, you probably have millions of lines of code. But we are not interesting in building a library of analytics. We are interested in capturing behavior that is commonly applied throughout the industry that uses the results of these analytics. This behavior is far more abstract and not all that large, as we shall see. But this should not be trivialized, because it gives the firms using it the freedom to employ analytics of their choice without rewriting the rest of the firm's software. Remember: separation of concerns!

---

2. NCSL means Non-Commented Source Lines.

- Applications will generally be made up of a bunch of frameworks that are "snapped" together—not one huge one. So, when I say a framework is only 5,000 lines of code, it may depend on five other frameworks that are also 5,000 lines. The user of this small framework is actually leveraging off of 30,000 lines of code.

- Frameworks are not designed well by committee. A framework, like any piece of software that was worked on by more than one person, tends to lose its consistency. A programmer cannot easily conceptualize a class library design if it reaches a certain threshold of complexity. I think that this threshold is about 10,000 NCSL. Hence, if it is desirable to have one lead designer per framework, I believe that it is undesirable to divvy up the work into chunks that are greater than 10,000 lines apiece.

- Frameworks do not contain any GUI-specific code, which is typically a sizeable portion of an application.

- STL, ORBs, and OODBs substantially reduce the coding traditionally required. Evidence of this was presented in Chapters 2 through 4.

7.3.2   Function Size

Not long ago, my supervisor told me that the group he was working in 10 years ago had a strict rule that a function couldn't be longer than 60 lines, so you could see the whole thing on one 8.5×11 printed page. I think that's a great rule, albeit a little dated with respect to the ability of our hardware to present quite a few more lines on an 8.5×11 sheet of paper. The exact number is not as important as the underlying objective: don't make a function any longer than can be seen and conceptualized at one time.

A good metric to measure is the average number of lines in all functions in a framework. Thresholds should be established for minimum and maximum accepted average values. If the average falls below the minimum, your design may be loose, have unnecessary function call overhead, or the need for the framework itself may be brought into question. If the number is too high, you may have gotten carried away with "run on" code that just sprang forth from your stream of consciousness effortlessly but makes no sense to you when you read it a week later.

To account for the inevitable exceptions and to reduce misleading averages, the actual calculation of an average function size for a framework should exclude outlier functions from the calculation. These outliers, however, should definitely be pointed out, by the metrics extraction tool, as functions that should be scrutinized.

7.3.3   Number of Function Arguments

Ideally, you want to design a framework with the smallest possible number of member functions and still maintain an acceptable average for the number of arguments passed to member functions. I think an average of four or less is acceptable, excluding those with default values from the calculation. You can state a rule that says, "Thou shalt never have more than N arguments." But, it is probably also not very good if all the member functions of a given class have N-1 arguments, or none. You need to establish what is an acceptable mean and standard deviation. If this average number of arguments is too high, it could imply that you need to:

- Define more structures
- Put more intelligence into a member function
- Use more member functions with smaller signatures
- Remove some functions from the classes
- Require the application code to do more preprocessing of arguments

This metric has a weakness. You can simply put all arguments into structures, and unless your metrics extraction tool is very smart, this ploy will yield a value of 1 or less, which could be perceived as outstanding. In reality, there may be tons of data being passed between the framework and the application.

7.4 Framework Reusefulness Metric

The metrics we have discussed so far are easy to calculate but are limited in conveying the overall goodness of a framework design. Framework *Reusefulness* is a metric that addresses overall framework design. It will help you:

- Methodically improve the design of a framework
- Determine if one framework should be divided (i.e., if dividing a framework would result in a higher total *Reusefulness* value)
- Determine when an older framework should be redesigned or discarded
- Compare the quality of various framework designs
- Establish a minimum standard of overall framework quality, used to assess whether or not a framework should be included in a repository. If you calculate the Reusefulness of what you know is a good framework design, you can use this value as a baseline.

I'll introduce *Reusefulness* by pointing out that even though horizontal frameworks, by definition, are more general than those specific to a given problem domain, they are not necessarily examples of better framework design. There are actually three factors that determine what makes a good overall framework design:

1. The level of generality
2. The average portion of the framework interface that is used in an application
3. The average value contributed by member functions of classes comprising the framework

Let's discuss each of these factors and show how each can be quantified, which is necessary if they are to be used as variables in the calculation of *Reusefulness*. First, consider the definition of the *generality* of a framework:

> **The *generality* of a framework is the percentage of applications that can use it, in a particular universe of potential applications.**

The universe will be determined by whether:

- Frameworks are developed for in-house use only (i.e., proprietary)
- A particular vertical market is being targeted for frameworks being developed (e.g., the legal profession)
- Frameworks are being developed for a horizontal market

Considering this, the level of *generality* assigned to a vertical framework could be as high as that of a vertical framework, because the relevant universes could be different sizes. The value of *generality* can be between 0.0 and 1.0. For example, a framework that is determined to be useful for 90 percent of the applications in the relevant universe will have a *generality* value of .9.

The value assigned to this factor before a framework is designed is a goal, since it cannot be measured until the framework has been available for a while. Frameworks that are domain specific can have more volatile *generality* values, since their universes are more likely to evolve than those of horizontal frameworks. For example, a software house specializing in the development of software for the telecommunication industry is operating in a universe that is rapidly changing. A framework that can be used in 90 percent of all existing systems may only be useful in 20 percent of systems being used five years from now. On the other hand, the universe of a vendor that develops inventory systems will probably not experience a very dramatic shift in the way inventory systems are built.

The second factor that plays into the quality of a framework design is defined as follows:

> **Framework *utilization* is the average percentage of public member functions called in an application using the framework.**

When the framework is used the first time, we hope it has a utilization close to 100 percent (i.e., *utilization* equals 1.0). If a framework was not designed well for its target usage, as it is used in more applications, you will start to see functions added that will solve one user's problem but have no relevance to anybody else's. Problem-specific functions must not creep into a framework, and this is the only variable that will point out this degradation in design. Extra functions make a framework harder to learn and are distracting. The lower the *utilization* gets, the higher the likelihood that the framework should be broken up or redesigned.

Because this factor is such an important indication of how well a framework is designed, it will weigh heavier in the calculation of a *Reusefulness* metric. As you will see, this factor will be squared in the metric calculation to heavily penalize those who add member functions just because they think that they might be used or to accommodate users with custom functions. Remember, the value is greater than 0.0 and less than or equal to 1.0, so this will exponentially lower the *Reusefulness* value as functions are added that are not widely used.

The last factor that plays a part in determining framework *Reusefulness* is defined as follows:

> **Framework *functionValue* is the average value added by a member function of a class in the framework.**

How exactly is *functionValue* calculated? Well, there are several options. You could simply use the average function-size metric described earlier in this chapter. You may, alternatively, want to average out a complexity measure. Because there are arguments for each, I will not try to dictate which is best here. But, whatever the choice, I will assume that it is normalized to a number between 0.0 and 1.0. I will also assume that outlier member functions that are outside of some multiple of the standard deviation will be discarded from the average. This will reward those who strive to balance the content of member functions and penalize those who try to cram as much as they can into a few functions, which can be a real headache for those maintaining the code.

One of the goals of the *Reusefulness* metric is to provide a uniform way to assess the quality of both framework types: horizontal and vertical. Using this metric, you have grounds for arguing that this horizontal framework is designed better than that vertical one. Or this horizontal framework that can be used in two domains is designed as well as this other one that can be used in ten domains. This is what makes it possible to establish one *Reusefulness* value as a minimum standard of overall framework quality. It should be clear, however, that *Reusefulness* values calculated or estimated in different universes can't be compared.

Now we're ready to present the equation for calculating the *Reusefulness* of a framework:

$$Reusefulness \ = \ generality \times (utilization)^{2} \times functionValue$$

I think it would be helpful, at this point, to illustrate the rationale behind the *Reusefulness* metric by means of a simple development scenario. Consider the case where we are developing two frameworks, FW1 and FW2, for a universe of one application. Why bother building frameworks for just one application? Well, as mentioned early on, a framework does not necessarily have to be reused in multiple applications to be worth the effort it takes to build it, because building an application around a framework makes it easier to add new features to it. But, in this hypothetical case, the reason that frameworks are being built is because it is anticipated that several more projects like the current one are on the horizon, and we don't want to have to start from scratch on each new project.

We know that *generality* equals 1.0 for both frameworks at this point. Presumably *utilization* is also close to 1.0, because of the design rule that states you should not add functions that have no known application that can use them. Last, let's establish a goal of having a *functionValue* of at least .5. If it is less than this, the framework may be designed with too many small member functions.

At this point, we go ahead and build FW1 and FW2, and after a few passes through the metrics tool and some redesigning, we achieve our goal of the minimum *functionValue* of .5. In fact, we find FW1 has *functionValue* = .6 and FW2 has *functionValue* =.9. So, initially the *Reusefulness* of FW1 is .6, and of FW2 is .9, which might indicate that the design of FW1 is not as "tight" as that of FW2.

Next, we build the application with the frameworks and pass the application through the metrics tool. Here we find that, indeed, all of FW1's 20 member functions have been used, and the goal of having *utilization* = 1.0 is maintained. FW2, on the other hand, has used only 25 of its 50 member functions. The designer either misunderstood the requirements or was doing too much daydreaming about how the framework could be used to solve the world's problems. The *Reusefulness* of FW1 is still $1 \times (1 \times 1) \times .6 = .6$, but FW2 now has a measured *Reusefulness* of $1 \times (.5 \times .5) \times .9 = .23$. Warning! Warning! Have the designer of FW2 get rid of enough of those unused member functions to bring this value up to at least that of FW1. The designer convinces the review committee that five of those functions are very likely to be used in future releases of this application, so they are allowed, but the rest are purged. This brings FW2's *Reusefulness* to $1 \times (25/30 * 25/30) \times .9 = .62$. So what FW1 lacks in tightness, FW2 lacks in *utilization*, and the designs are perceived to be of roughly equal quality.

Now, along comes a second project in which only FW2 can be used. FW1's *Reusefulness* in this universe immediately drops to $.5 \times (1 \times 1) \times .6 = .3$ because its *generality* is now .5.

FW2 can be used, but 10 new member functions needed to be added, bringing *functionValue* down a little to .8, and the new project only used 20 of the now 40 total member functions in FW2, so its *Reusefulness* is now $1 \times ((25/40 + 20/40)/2) \times .8 = .45$. You can see that the *Reusefulness* of both dropped with the second project.

This will be typical if you think about it. As any software ages, its usefulness and quality tend to deteriorate, until it gets to the point where a major redesign may be in order. It's just entropy!—the universal law stating that all things tend from a state of order to a state of disorder. What you need to do at some point is revaluate the designs of FW1 and FW2, say, when *Reusefulness* falls below .2. In the meantime, the drop in FW2 was due to *utilization*, so the designer should see if there is anything that can be done to raise it. For FW1, there is nothing that can be done. It is simply a more domain-specific framework. I hope this scenario helps you see how this metric can help you and your managers maintain a minimum standard of framework quality and managing the life cycle of frameworks.

There are certain observations that can be made about the relationship between *generality* and *utilization* in a large universe of potential applications.[3] As you try to make a framework more general, it is increasingly difficult to design it such that everyone using it will require most member functions in most classes. GUI toolkits are classic examples of this. As time goes on, GUI toolkit vendors try to capture a larger market by adding more and more widgets, dialog boxes, etc. Yes, this will satisfy the needs of more and more potential customers, but the typical customer will probably use a smaller subset of the features.

Figure 7-1 represents this tension between *generality* and *utilization* as a linear relationship. At this point there is simply not enough data to establish whether there is any curvature, only an heuristic that the two variables are inversely proportional. The goal of the designer is to maximize the *Reusefulness*, which means striking an optimal balance between these variables. Assuming that *functionValue* is held constant at 1.0 and *generality = 1- utilization*, then *Reusefulness = (1-utilization)* $\times$ *utilization^2*, as shown in Figure 7-2. This figure illustrates that there is a theoretical optimal *Reusefulness* value.

---

3. In a universe of size 1, presumably anything you build will have a *generality* value of 1.0, and *utilization* will be close to 1.0. To design a framework, or any other piece of software for that matter, otherwise, is simply illogical.

Utilization vs. *Generality* in a Large Universe of Potential Applications

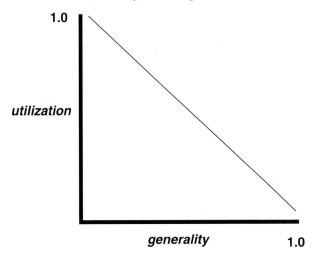

FIGURE 7-1.

Reusefulness vs. *Utilization* in Large Universe of Potential Applications

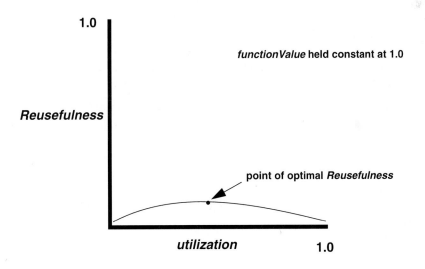

FIGURE 7-2.

In summary, *Reusefulness* is a comprehensive and telling framework design metric. It can be viewed as a measure of the framework's expected usefulness to future applications. This is analogous to a stock analyst's earnings predictions, which are reflected in a stock's price. Like a stock analyst, the metrician may be wrong. And just as the value of a stock price is reevaluated when the actual earnings can be measured, so too will the *Reusefulness* of a framework that has been in use for some time. And also as lower-than-expected earnings cause companies to take action to raise them, so too should designers of frameworks attempt to increase *Reusefulness* when it turns out to be lower than anticipated. And to bring this analogy to a close: just as companies go bankrupt when earnings continually tank and corporate management can't figure out how to change the situation, frameworks will be retired when designers can no longer figure out how to keep *Reusefulness* at an acceptable level.

CHAPTER 8
Framework Development Procedures

Once a domain analysis has been conducted and the need for a new vertical framework has been justified,[1] you should follow the procedure in this chapter to actually build it. The domain analysis has left you with:

- A domain description that can serve as the requirements for a vertical framework
- Descriptions of the generic aspects of the domain (i.e., its facets)

Before starting the development of the vertical framework, you must model each facet and either design a piece of software to implement it or represent the facet in a design pattern. If the facet is captured in software, it will be one of the following:

- Horizontal framework
- Generic algorithm
- Component

If a facet is to be implemented as a horizontal framework, the procedures in the rest of this chapter should be followed. If a generic algorithm needs to be written, use the advice given in the GENERIC ALGORITHM pattern, and follow the lead of STL. If a component needs to be built, you can pretty much still follow the procedures in this chapter. The notion of abstract classes will not be applicable, however.

---

1. In Chapter 9, I provide suggestions for economically justifying the development of a framework.

Before we start to discuss the procedures, it is important to establish what the major activities of development are and the products of each. In the context of our methodology, *framework development* has four activities:

Framework Development Activity	Products of the Activity
Design	Design document and header files (public and protected interfaces only). The design document template is described later.
Implement	Source code for all concrete member functions, updated header files, compiled framework code, manual pages.
Test	Test plan, test programs, and test results.
Document	User Guide and Programmer's Reference Manual.

These activities are sort of chronological, but you usually end up engaging in some of them simultaneously when you get into the throes of development. That's okay. In my experience there is no harm in this, as long as you are only fine-tuning previous activities.

Notice that I don't mention maintenance. That doesn't mean your framework won't need any. It simply means that I consider it a separate activity for which you are going to have to establish your own policies and procedures. Those policies and procedures will vary widely, depending on your staff size, repository size, customer base, etc.

I assume that you have established coding conventions to supplement the standard presented in Chapter 6. Conventions, when followed, give all the source code a consistent look. They are important for maintaining continuity in a project. In the event that somebody leaves and another person in the group must take over the maintenance of his or her code, it should be an easier task if conventions have been followed. There is no need to make up conventions. Books and published papers abound with them. Some are quite thorough. I particularly like one that I pulled off the Internet from Elemtel [ELEMTEL92].

No project that I have ever worked on has fully enforced conventions. It has all been based on trust and gentle nudging. Resources are scarce and people don't have time to make sure that others in the group are following the conventions. One suggestion that I have for correcting this is to select a set of conventions that are simple and either buy or have someone build a little tool to check source code for adherence to the conventions. This tool could be run as part of the build process, so violations are flagged right along with compiler warnings.

The following sections discuss what you should be doing in each of the development activities. I don't present much in the way of examples. Part 3 of the book demonstrates the development procedures with real frameworks.

8.1 Designing a Framework

There are quite a few steps involved in the design activity. The order in which I present the steps roughly matches the order in which you should perform them. As with the entire development process, however, you may be engaging in multiple steps simultaneously. There is also going to be a good deal of iteration. You should complete all steps during the first iteration. In subsequent iterations, however, you may perform only some of the steps.

Step 1.   Identify applicable design patterns.

In Chapter 6, I presented a catalog containing 12 patterns that are particularly well suited to framework development. They are summarized in the table below. You can build a lot of frameworks with these patterns, but, as I stated earlier, you should grow this catalog for your domain.

Pattern	Page	Intent
BLACKBOARD	152	To reduce the amount of information that needs to be studied and processed simultaneously, by partitioning heterogeneous data objects into groups and studying the properties of each group as a whole.
CORBA-FRIENDLY CLASS	160	To design classes of coarse-grained objects such that critical functionality is "tieable" to a CORBA interface.
DETAIL FILTERING	163	To be able to view multiple subsets of a large collection of hierarchical data.
GENERIC ALGORITHM	169	To create a template function that can execute an algorithm on any class that satisfies a set of preconditions.
INTERPRETER	173	To make it easy to modify an object's behavior at runtime, with minimal impact on the rest of the application, by defining a language to specify the object's behavior.
NAME-VALUE PAIRS	179	To customize a fine-grained object at runtime.
OBSERVER	182	To provide an event notification mechanism, where the notifier (i.e., *Subject*) and the objects notified (i.e., *Observer*s) are loosely coupled.
PERSISTENT DATA MANAGER	188	To control access to a collection of independent fine-grained persistent objects via a coarse-grained Data Manager object.
PERSISTENT SINGLETON	194	To have all instances of a class share the same persistent state.

Pattern	Page	Intent
PROTOCOL	197	To give classes with similar behavior a consistent looking interface, without resorting to the use of inheritance, templates, or other C++ mechanisms.
SPECIFICATION-ENGINE	199	To create a specification for the behavior that a coarse-grained object is to exhibit, prior to instantiating it.
THRESHOLDING	202	To enable an *Observer* object, whose behavior depends on a numeric value in another object, to be notified when that value has changed by more than an amount specified by the *Observer*.

You should start the design activity by identifying the patterns that are applicable for the framework. To help you do this, I have included the *Patterns Roadmap* on the following few pages. Study the domain/facet description and then go down the first column of the Roadmap, writing down the names of those patterns that definitely apply. When you've gone through all 12 patterns, go back to the rows of each that you know apply and give the patterns mentioned in the third column another look if they are not already deemed to be applicable. Historically, the patterns in the first column "set the stage" for the patterns in the third column. I do reference patterns from [PATTERNS95] in the third column; they are indicated by an asterisk after their names.

The third column in the Roadmap becomes far more valuable as your pattern catalog grows. For instance, if your catalog grows to, say, 500 patterns, it begins to get impractical to search the whole catalog for applicable patterns. Instead, you want the most frequently occurring ones at the top. So, as you descend down the roadmap, you quickly traverse to an applicable set of patterns. The goal of the Roadmap is to optimize the search time and make it less likely that applicable patterns will be missed.

Patterns Roadmap

If this applies:	Then use this pattern:	And check for applicability of:
You must analyze, from a variety of perspectives, a large body of heterogeneous time-series data.	BLACKBOARD	THRESHOLDING
It is anticipated that a class may need to be accessed via an ORB.	CORBA-FRIENDLY CLASS	
You must design a system where users are required to analyze a large amount of hierarchical data.	DETAIL FILTERING	COMPOSITE*, SINGLETON*, PERSISTENT DATA MANAGER
If a function can be made into a template that can process multiple types of objects, not related to each other through inheritance. Look for independent functions that take objects as arguments, and such objects are being accessed in a simple way.	GENERIC ALGORITHM	
You must design a coarse-grained object that satisfies one of the following: • Has many variations in behavior that may have to change at runtime. • You want its behavior specified in a portable, readable fashion. • Needs its behavior specified or modified in a nontrivial way via an ORB. • Needs its behavior specified or modified via a public interface of an abstract class in a framework.	INTERPRETER	FACTORY METHOD*
When it has been determined that a framework is responsible for maintaining a collection of fine-grained objects that: • Have many variations in structure. • Not all the variations are known in advance of the framework design. • Inheritance is overkill. • The framework is not concerned with the variations and is not required to verify the validity of the variations.	NAME-VALUE PAIRS	PERSISTENT DATA MANAGER

If this applies:	Then use this pattern:	And check for applicability of:
One object must provide event notification services to other objects, and the objects to be notified are not known in advance and may change during the course of system operation.	OBSERVER	PERSISTENT SINGLETON, PERSISTENT DATA MANAGER, THRESHOLDING
A collection of independent, fine-grained, persistent objects must be maintained. This pattern does not necessarily apply to collections of objects that have embedded `d_Ref`s to other persistent objects, unless protection of data is not an issue.	PERSISTENT DATA MANAGER	OBSERVER
Use this pattern whenever all of the following conditions are true: • All instances of a given class must share state. • The instances are not necessarily in the same process space. • The state must be persistent. (NOTE: A class that is applying the PERSISTENT DATA MANAGER pattern is also applying this pattern.)	PERSISTENT SINGLETON	
Two or more classes have behavioral similarities but are not derived from the same base class.	PROTOCOL	GENERIC ALGORITHM
You are designing a class with complicated behavior that must be specified, to a large extent, by the user of the class. Look for the following: employing the services of a coarse-grained object requires making preliminary member function calls in a well-ordered sequence before the object can perform its primary task.	SPECIFICATION-ENGINE	SINGLETON*, PERSISTENT SINGLETON, PERSISTENT DATA MANAGER
There are many objects that must be notified of changes in the numeric state of another object, and it is necessary to vary the granularity of the change that causes notification events.	THRESHOLDING	

It is important to realize that when patterns work together, one class often takes on a variety of roles and, consequently, participates in more than one pattern. For example, the PERSISTENT DATA MANAGER pattern and the SPECIFICATION-ENGINE pattern are often used together, where a single class plays the dual role of *DataManager* and *Engine*. This is logical if you think about it. The *DataManager* is coarse-grained and often heavily burdened with algorithms to manage the data. The constraints on the data can be complex and must be determined at the point when the *DataManager* is instantiated. The `Workflow_Manager` class in Chapter 10 is an excellent example of where these two patterns are used together. A framework for managing network topology data could use the same combination of patterns. The constraints on network topology could be prepackaged into a *Specification* and then passed to an *Engine* when it is instantiated. The *Engine* is also the *DataManager* that is responsible for guaranteeing that physical network elements are connected properly before being committed to the database.

Using PERSISTENT DATA MANAGER and OBSERVER together is probably the most important combination of patterns. This combination embodies a very important philosophy about object distribution, which is that object distribution should be achieved through the combined usage of ODMG-93 and CORBA. When you apply these two patterns together, lightweight control information makes its way between distributed objects via an ORB, and large volumes of complex data are distributed, using ODMG-93. Using ODMG-93 gives you direct communication with the database.

If you try to retrieve persistent data indirectly via an ORB, you have two problems:

- "Impedance mismatch"[2]
- Poorer performance

The impedance mismatch is introduced because you now have to map structures generated by an IDL compiler to the actual persistent C++ classes. The performance hit is taken because now, instead of going directly to the database, you must:

1. Retrieve data objects from the database into a CORBA server.
2. Copy the persistent data objects into the structures generated by the IDL compiler.
3. Send the data over the ORB to the client that wants it.

This philosophy of how to use the CORBA/ODMG portion of the infrastructure is shared by the ODMG itself. They formally present their stance on just this issue in Appendix B of [ODMG-93]. This stance is, of course, biased because all the members of the ODMG are trying to sell databases. But, it is also shared by some of the best-known technical proponents of CORBA. I was just at a CORBA seminar; Steve Vinoski and Doug Schmidt, whose names are becoming synonymous with CORBA in technical circles, both

---

2. "Impedance mismatch" means that the type system of the database does not match the type system that the application is using.

gave talks. Both echoed the view that CORBA is very good for communicating control information to help you manage your data, but you shouldn't necessarily try to pump the data itself over an ORB.

DETAIL FILTERING and NAME-VALUE PAIRS make an interesting combination. Take the following example:

```
struct Data {
    Data* parent;
    set<Data*, less<Data*> > children;
    map<string,string> attributes;
};
```

This one little generic data structure could represent a hierarchy of anything: locations, automobile components, people, historical events, an investment portfolio, etc. You can round out the suite of classes for DETAIL FILTERING to selectively view different pieces of the hierarchy. I'm not suggesting that you should describe all data with this one structure. It wouldn't be terribly efficient, and you have basically pushed all the type checking into the application or framework. But, using these patterns together forms a very generic foundation for representing complex hierarchical systems. If you are stumped about the best way to represent this kind of data, perhaps using these patterns together is a good starting point. Always err on the side of being too general, as opposed to being too specific.

Step 2.   Map framework classes to roles.

Decide on the names of classes in the framework that will play the roles in the patterns. Also, name data members and member functions that play roles in patterns. You don't have to show a mapping between class members in the pattern and their counterparts in the framework if they have the same names. Show the roles in a table that has the following format:

Pattern Used	Role	Role Played By
PATTERN NAME	*RoleName*	NameInFramework

Step 3.   Introduce new classes.

There will probably be entities in the domain that have not been accounted for in the roles of patterns deemed to be applicable for the framework. Now the creative process begins, and I don't have any sure-fire technique for you to round out the remaining classes that will comprise the framework. There is a tendency to be a bit overanxious to discover new classes, so proceed conservatively.

Study the terms in the glossary of the domain/facet description first. Then, read each characteristic and separate out those that are not yet covered by a role. Seek out the most general, simple, and fundamental concepts that emerge from the domain/facet analysis. They are often the abstract classes. Some of the most important classes in a framework are those that seem so trivial and general that you may be tempted to just ignore them. When you do discover a new class, at this point, don't worry too much about what its member functions and data members are.

Don't labor too hard on this step. If you missed a really important role, it will emerge before long.

Step 4.   Decide how the framework will be extended.

During this step, you are expected to explain how a user will extend the framework. In order to intelligently do this, you need to consider the various techniques that can be used to implement abstract classes. Stroustrup describes an abstract class as one that has one or more pure virtual member functions [ANNOTC++92]. This description is too limiting for framework development. In the context of a framework design, an *abstract class* is one that is missing some implementation or a piece of the application-level view of the entity that it represents. By this definition, there are a variety of techniques for designing abstract classes. Remember, abstract classes are what makes a framework, a framework, as opposed to a component or an application. So, if you truly want to be a proficient framework designer, you must become proficient in applying these techniques.

The various techniques that should be considered for designing an abstract class are:

- Pure virtual members functions
- Delegation
- Virtual functions with implementations that can't be executed
- Member functions left out entirely
- "Object splitting"
- Some combination of the above

Let's briefly discuss the mechanics of each technique.

Pure virtual member functions are used if you want a framework user to derive a class from an abstract class provided with the framework. Pure virtual member functions are those that appear in a C++ class declaration with a suffix of "=0;". For example, a pure virtual member function called "foo" that returns void and takes no arguments is declared like this:

```
virtual void foo() = 0;
```

A class with one or more pure virtual member functions cannot be instantiated. Someone must derive a class and provide implementations for these functions, which will be invoked by the framework at places where more specific behavior is required. A pure virtual member function is normally protected, since it is usually called directly by the abstract class implementation.

Suppose that you don't want to force someone to derive a class in order to use your framework. Then, you should consider delegating missing implementation to another object. A delegate function of an unrelated object is called at the point in an abstract class implementation where additional logic is required. C++ templates can be used for this. You can create a template class and make one or more of its member functions into a GENERIC ALGORITHM that calls functions of the template type.

Sometimes, you want to instantiate an abstract class, but you also want to prevent its virtual member functions from being executed. Instead, you only want them executed from an object of a derived class, which overrides the base class implementation. In the abstract class, the implementation body of such functions should simply throw a "NoImplementation" exception. This technique may be the only practical way to apply the PERSISTENT DATA MANAGER pattern. The Workflow Framework in Chapter 10 applies this technique. The Workflow_Manager class is abstract; the user of the framework must provide application-specific logic by deriving from `Workflow_Manager` and providing several virtual member function implementations. But, the persistent shadow object must be an instance of the base class, because it is instantiated from within the base class implementation. So, you can't use pure virtual member functions.

Sometimes it makes sense to provide protected member functions that are not called by any other member functions in the class. When you do this, you simply give guidelines for using them in the implementation of a derived class. You would want to use this technique when you don't have a complete picture of what the public interface of a class is going to allow the user to do, but you know the functions that implement it will need functions like the ones you've provided in the protected section.

Let's talk about "Object Splitting." When you are designing a class that is going to be part of a framework, it contains member functions and data members that are relevant to the framework. But, for the user of the framework, this class may provide an incomplete view of the object. In other words, it may be too abstract to be used, as is, in the application. As the designer of the framework, you should anticipate this and make the class inheritance-friendly, to give the user of the framework the option to derive a class that gets to a level of abstraction that is suitable for the application. But, from the user's perspective, it may not be desirable to derive a new class just so that the framework can be used.[3] There may already be a class in existence that is at a level of abstraction suitable to the application,

---

3. For small frameworks in particular, you don't want to give the user any cause to be hesitant to use your framework and end up reimplementing what you have done.

and the prospective user simply wants to add new features to the application, using the framework. The alternative technique is to "split the object," associating the new piece from the framework with the more application specific part by using a *key* attribute. The application probably already has a unique name or identifier for the object, and by simply having an equivalent data member in the object that represents the framework perspective, you have made it possible to associate the pieces of the object.

What you are actually doing is *joining* two or more collections of objects using a common attribute. There will be one collection that contains the piece of the object required by a framework that operates on the object. That piece contains the minimal data required for the framework to do its job. Other pieces of the object will be in one or more other collections. The application-specific piece will be in one collection, and other facet-related pieces will be in other collections. Domain-specific, application-independent pieces will be in yet another collection. This is how frameworks developed independently are used together.

When an object is split, the relationships among all the pieces are not necessarily established through one key value. The knowledge of how to aggregate the pieces of an object into a complete application-level view will be embedded in the code that ties the pieces together.

For example, consider Honest Joe's Autos again. Below, I've redrawn part of Figure 1-1 to show some of the frameworks that could be used together in that application, along with likely abstract classes representing their respective "pieces" of an automobile abstraction. The Auto Dealership framework that glues all the horizontal frameworks together will have to know what the various pieces of an automobile are and the keys that relate the various pieces. The Inventory framework will view an automobile as an `InventoryItem`. The Accounting framework will view a automobile as an `Invoice` when it is sold. The Payroll framework will view an automobile that is sold as a `Commission`, and the Auto Dealership framework itself will view the automobile by its features and Vehicle Identification Number (VIN), which will be one of the key attributes that the framework will use to bind the pieces together. As you can see, VIN is only one of the keys that binds together all the pieces of an automobile. The model number is also used to associate pieces within the Auto Dealership framework itself.

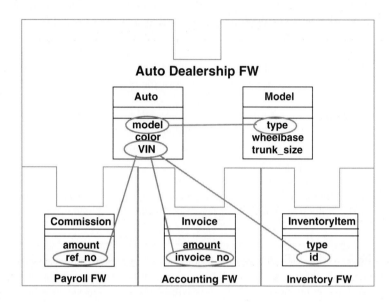

How to decide which combination of abstract class design techniques to use is not definite enough to capture in a set of rules. Sometimes it will be implied by the patterns you are using. Other times, however, you will need to make a judgement call. When you decide on the technique that will be applied for each abstract class, write it down, along with an explanation of how a user of the framework will apply the technique to extend the framework.

Step 5.   Design class interfaces.

Begin the design of class interfaces by writing the public and protected sections of class declarations. Start with skeleton declarations of all the classes that you have identified so far. It is best to create the skeleton starting from a header file template like the one shown below. The template should require the designer to provide all the information you normally find in a manual page. This way, a tool can be built to automatically generate HTML manual pages from header files, eliminating the need to maintain separate manual pages.

Header File Template

```
#ifndef CLASSNAME_H
#define CLASSNAME_H

////////////////////////////////////////////////////////////
// Framework Name: domain or facet name
// File Name:
// Version:
// Creation Date:
// Author:
////////////////////////////////////////////////////////////

// includes
// forward declarations

copy the following for each class in the module

////////////////////////////////////////////////////////////
// Class Name:
// Description:
//
// Pattern: pattern this class participates in
// Role:    class role in pattern
//
////////////////////////////////////////////////////////////


class ClassName {
  public:
      // constructors, destructor
      // operators
      // miscellaneous member functions
  protected:
  private:
};
#endif // CLASSNAME_H
```

Fill in all member function and data members required for the Patterns identified.

Classes don't grow to completion all at once, but rather in bits and pieces as the responsibilities and relationships among objects in the framework evolve. The responsibilities of any given class are subjective because of the close coupling between objects in a framework, so it is quite common to see a class grow and shrink as various divisions of labor are explored. Don't try to completely design one class and then move on to the next. Remember, in a framework, objects depend on each other, so you have to grow them all a little at a time.

I like using operator overloading as a way to give a class interface that comfortable feel. The operators that you would actually overload depend on the nature of the class. For example, classes that represent objects that can be combined and separated are good candidates for the +, −, and = operators. These mathematical operations are semantically consistent with the notions of combining and separating. Any class that can accept a sequence of input makes a good candidate for having the stream operators << and >>. For example, an SQL class or a class that processes a sequence of data would be a good candidate. This is semantically consistent with the use of the stream operator for character streams.

We want an easy way to assimilate framework objects into application code by using a syntax that allows us to treat such objects as if they were built-in types. Consider the case of a class called StockTrade. Sometimes it will look like a const char*, as would be the case when we want a textual description of the details of the trade. Other times we will want it to look like a float, representing the dollar amount of the trade. One way to do this is to overload operator const char*() and operator float(), such that the objects can be mixed transparently with built-in types by relying on the compiler for type promotion to const char* or float, depending on the usage context. Some people don't like this approach, claiming that it makes the class not type-safe and such promotions should be done explicitly by forcing the programmer to invoke a member function. In the only case that I can think of where the context is ambiguous for StockTrade objects, the compiler will complain, and the user can then explicitly cast:

```
StockTrade t(str);
cout << "Trade Details: " << t << endl; // ambiguous
cout << "Trade Value: " << t << endl;    // ambiguous

cout << "Trade Details: " << (const char*)t << endl; // fine
cout << "Trade Value: " << float(t) << endl;          // fine
```

As a programmer, the reason I prefer a convention that favors this approach is because I can start to use classes without always having to refer to manual pages to see if the member function is called value(), data(), or whatever. This becomes very important to productivity as the number of class libraries at your disposal increases. In fact, I would argue that, at some point in the future, not relying on a convention that encourages designers to design classes that "look like" built-in types may become a limiting factor in the proliferation of class libraries of any form. This is one of the primary reasons that the PROTOCOL pattern is so important.

When it is appropriate, use member function names that match those used in STL. For example, if you are providing a class that has containerlike properties and you are going to provide a member function that returns the number of elements in that container, call it size(), which is what all STL containers call the member function that does that.

At some point, you will want to convert your header file declarations into class diagrams to convey the design to others, but don't waste your time using a CASE tool to draw class diagrams and then generate C++ header files from them. This is a flawed approach because the graphical notation is far less expressive and, consequently, more ambiguous, than C++. The process of designing software requires you to think through a lot of details before you can intelligently draw a class diagram with supporting rationale. This detail and rationale are best expressed directly as C++ class declarations, augmented liberally with comments. Class diagrams that are unconfirmed by complete C++ header files are virtually worthless.

If you are really lucky, you have found a CASE tool that can draw diagrams from header files. CASE tool vendors really missed the mark on providing this capability, which, in my view, is one of the most valuable features they could provide. CASE tools to be used by experienced software developers should be code-centric and should focus primarily on extracting visual representations from code.

Step 6. Design primary usage scenarios.

You should now turn your attention to the dynamic aspects of the design, by considering the primary usage scenarios of the framework. A usage scenario is a sequence of calls to member functions of objects comprising a framework. You must design the set of scenarios that provide coverage of all the requirements. Object Interaction Diagrams (OIDs) should be used to express the scenarios (see Appendix B for notation). Only worry about "Sunny Day"[4] scenarios at this point.

If there are patterns used that have an OID in the Collaboration section of the pattern description, you should see the scenario superimposed on the OIDs associated with the framework. In fact, it makes sense to copy and paste such OIDs and use them as a starting point.

Step 7. Rework classes declarations.

When designing the primary usage scenarios, you will, inevitably, discover more data members and member functions. You will also come to understand more fully what the signatures of the member functions should look like. Go back to your header files and rework them such that they can support the primary usage scenarios.

Step 8. Apply the design rules.

Go through each class declaration and make sure that there is compliance with all the design rules presented in section 6.3.

---

4. By "Sunny Day," I mean that no error conditions are encountered.

Step 9.   Work through an example usage.

It's time to go through an intellectual test of your framework design by going back to the original problem that inspired the domain analysis resulting in the requirements for the framework. Determine how you would extend this framework to solve that problem. Ask yourself where the problem-specific extractions "hook in" to the framework. Does the design seem to support the original problem? If it does, move on. If it doesn't, go back and rework as necessary.

Step 10.   Document the design.

It is very important to note that a design is presented in an order that may be dramatically different from the order in which it was conceived. CASE tools, as I pointed out earlier, have really misled people about this. When you formulate a design, you must mentally explore many details through a sometimes lengthy stream of consciousness. It is only after you emerge from this that a high-level view consisting of diagrams and concise role descriptions can be presented. When a design is presented, on the other hand, you first convey a high-level view of it and then drill down into the rationale behind the view.

A framework design is documented by use of the template on the following page.

Framework Name
The name of the domain or facet that the framework addresses.

Framework Type
Horizontal or vertical.

Requirements
A reference to the domain/facet analysis document, or a hypertext link to it.

Structure
Class Diagram, and perhaps an Object Diagram, showing static relationships among classes participating in the pattern. See Appendix B for notation to use. There should also be a table that shows the patterns used in this framework and the roles that are played by classes in this framework.

Participants
The classes and other software entities participating in the framework, along with their responsibilities. A participant's responsibilities may already be partially defined by the roles that it plays in the patterns used by the framework.

Collaborations
How the participants collaborate to support the framework requirements. Object Interaction Diagrams for the primary usage scenarios are put in this section.

Design Details
Presenting the public and protected sections of class declarations and a detailed commentary about the declarations.

Requirements Verification
Document how each of the requirements for the framework (identified as characteristics in the domain/facet analysis phase) is supported by the framework. I use the word "supported" as opposed to "satisfied" because a framework by its very nature does not implement a complete solution, but it must lend itself well to the completion of applications in the domain or facet for which it was designed. When I say "lend itself well," I mean it must make it easier for you to complete the application than to do it from scratch.

Consequences
List design trade-offs and side effects of using this framework.

Sample Code and Usage
Illustrate how you would extend and apply the framework for the problem that initially inspired the domain/facet analysis resulting in the framework requirements.

Known Uses
Examples of real problems that could be dealt with by use of this framework.

Dependencies
List the pieces of the infrastructure, generic algorithms, components, and, in the case of a vertical framework, the horizontal frameworks used.

Step 11.   Apply and document design metrics.

Apply the design-level metrics from Chapter 7 and include them as an appendix to the design documentation. This information will grow in usefulness as your organization establishes a benchmark of goodness based on the metrics.

Step 12.   Hold a design review.

The next step in the development of your framework requires you to do something a bit uncomfortable: present your design to a lot of strangers. I attended a stress management seminar a few years ago, and the guy teaching it had some rather strange ideas. He told us about an exercise he used to engage in whenever he wanted to figure out the parts of his body that are most affected in stressful situations. He said he would take off all his clothes and walk into a room full of people. The parts of his body that turned the reddest were those most affected by stress. Now, I'm not suggesting that you present your design to a bunch of strangers naked, but the story does provide an analogy. The only way to flush out weaknesses in your design is to completely expose it to people.

When we present designs, we tend to present only superficial diagrams. You need to give reviewers all the products of design, as well as all relevant domain and facet analysis documentation. Reviewers should be people who are not afraid to give opinions. In fact, give the design package to people who have turf to protect and may feel threatened by the notion of having their code replaced by something that is reusable. Those are the folks that are going to try their darndest to "make you flush." These people should be from a lot of different worlds, and you should go through examples of how you would extend the framework to suit their needs.

It is very likely that people will feel that your framework should be more detailed. People are just not comfortable with the idea of abstract classes. They want concrete ideas to latch on to. If someone thinks that your framework should include more detail and you don't feel it is appropriate, you should state that the framework is not intended to address that level of detail. Remember, you are much better off being a little too general than a little too specific, because a detail can always be added later, but it cannot be easily removed later.

If you are actually going to make a presentation of your design to a live audience, send out all the design documentation well in advance. Make sure you provide the reviewers with ample time to digest the material before the presentation.

I personally feel that one-on-one discussions with reviewers are the most productive way to conduct design reviews. I understand, however, that some corporate cultures still insist on getting a lot of people together to discuss anything.

Step 13.   Incorporate comments from the review.

Incorporate comments and redistribute the design document. If you are having difficulty reconciling all the input received from one-on-one discussions, then you should sit down with all the reviewers having counter viewpoints.

8.2 Implementing a Framework

Step 1.   Document source code packaging strategy.

Your source code packaging strategy should be documented. Generally, a source code *module* consists of one header file and one source file. The header file will contain the declaration of one primary class and perhaps some helper classes. The source file will contain the implementations of all the member functions of all the classes declared in the associated header file. The two files comprising a module should be named with the same prefix. The prefix name should be the same as that of the module's primary class.

There are usually some frameworkwide `typedefs`, `enums`, and utility functions that don't really belong with a specific framework class. These types of things should be put in a separate utilities module.

Finally, provide a header file that includes all the other header files associated with the framework. Its name prefix should be the name of the framework.[5] So, for example, the XYZ framework will have a header file called XYZ.h. This simplifies life for the user of the framework, who now only needs to include this one header file.

Step 2.   Set up a source code control environment.

If you haven't done so already, set up your source code control. Initialize the controlled header files with those produced during design. Don't worry about initializing controlled source files yet.

---

5. Modified to conform to naming conventions if more than one word.

Step 3.   Pseudocode member function implementations.

Create a source file for each header file, starting with a source code template that looks
something like this:

Source File Template

```
////////////////////////////////////////////////////////////////
// File Name:
// Version:
// Creation Date:
// Author:
////////////////////////////////////////////////////////////////

Each member function in the source file should have a prologue like
the following.

////////////////////////////////////////////////////////////////
//
// Class:    Function:
//
// Implementation Notes:
//
// Modifications: (provide list of MRs affecting this function)
//
////////////////////////////////////////////////////////////////
```

Every developer has his or her own approach to coding. To make sure that a design fits
together as I had envisioned, I usually pseudocode all the member functions first. I do this
as follows:

  a. I copy class declarations from header files and paste them into the appropriate
      source files.

  b. I use the copied declarations to create skeleton member function bodies for all
      functions of all classes.

  c. I go through each function, rapidly jotting down comments indicating the
      sequence of actions that transpire in the functions. Sometimes I just write the
      code, if it is easier to express an action.

When I've done this, I'll have a bunch of source files that contain function bodies looking something like this:

```
void
MyClass:Foo(int i)
{
    if(i > 100)
    {
        // throw exception
    }

    // Do such and such

    // Check the value of blah

    // If blah okay, then do such and such
}
```

Step 4.   Set up a build environment.

In a large company, a good infrastructure group should do this for you. If you are in a small company, however, learn as much as you can about the environment you have chosen, set it up, and then proceed. Don't make the mistake of rushing to set up the environment, just learning the minimum you can to compile, and then jumping right into coding. It is in the nature of programmers to do this, and when they do, they become so engrossed in coding that they may not even realize that they are using the environment very inefficiently.

Step 5.   Code and compile the member function bodies.

Go back to each function body and put in all the C++. At this point, you will potentially be working with the CORBA C++ API, ODMG-93, STL, or the interfaces of other components and horizontal frameworks that this framework depends on. How much you code before you try compiling is, of course, a matter of personal style. I find the most productive way to code is to try to compile after each encounter with a new interface, just to make sure that I am using it correctly. Anything having to do with a C++ template I experiment with by immediately compiling, because of the preconditions that are generally associated and the sometimes off-the-wall errors that you can get by not meeting preconditions. The STL_Lint program in Appendix A was written exclusively to deal with these types of problems. After becoming comfortable with a particular coding idiom, you don't have to compile as frequently.

As you are going through the coding, you will inevitably need to add more private member functions and data members. Because these additions are of no consequence to the user of the framework, you should not feel obliged to go back and change the design documentation. If you find, however, that the implementation just isn't going to work without a change to the public or protected interface of a particular class, you most certainly must go back and reflect the design change in the design documentation. Depending on how dramatic the change is, you may want to consider having your design reviewed again before proceeding.

After you get a module to compile, initialize the controlled source file and save new versions of header files that have changed.

Step 6.   Prepare manual pages.

There should be manual pages for all classes that will be used by the end-user application. There should also be manual pages for each abstract class in a framework. A manual page should contain all the information shown in the following manual page template.

Manual Page Template

Framework Name
The name of the domain or facet of which the class is a part.

Primary Class Name (i.e., module name)

Primary Class Type/s
Abstract, concrete, interface, persistent.

Role(s)
Pattern Name: Role:

Synopsis of *Class*.h
Show only the public and protected sections of classes. In the case of an interface, show the IDL, followed by the C++ mapping.

Description
Provide general commentary about the class and how to use it and, in the case of an abstract class, how to complete its implementation.

For each public and protected member function, present 1) preconditions, 2) postconditions, 3) the meaning of each argument and the return code, and 4) exceptions that may be thrown during member function activation.

Regarding the format of preconditions and postconditions: they can be stated in English prose or a formal specification language, depending on the policy of your organization. The more formal, the more precisely understood the behavior expected from the function will be, and, consequently, it is more likely that the function can be tested by generated code. If English prose is used, on the other hand, it is more likely that the purpose of the function is ambiguous, but it is far easier to write and read the preconditions and postconditions. I have yet to see a framework where the member functions were formally specified, but this will have to change to advance the framework industry.

Example Code Fragments

Dependencies
List the generic algorithms, components, and, in the case of a vertical framework, the horizontal frameworks used by this module.

Make it part of your build process to regenerate manual pages from source code every time a header file is modified. That way, they are always current and you don't have to keep manual pages under change control.

8.3 Testing a Framework

Software quality and programmer productivity would be higher if we approached the design of our test systems with the same diligence that we approach the design of the applications being tested. As an industry, we are still very sloppy and unscientific about how we test any type of software. Testing frameworks is harder than testing traditional software, and how you actually test them in a scientific fashion is something I am still trying to learn. What I can tell you is that it is a very "white box" affair, because you need to be intimately aware of how the framework you are testing actually works and must extend it before you have something that is even testable.

I view framework testing as having two sequential phases. First, you attempt to test as many individual classes as you can. This is called *unit testing*. Then you test the entire framework. In the following sections, I will offer some suggestions on how to perform these two test phases.

8.3.1 Unit Testing Classes

Unit testing a class means testing it in isolation. Ideally, you'd like to be able to create an automated regression testing environment for classes in a library, such that you could make a change to a class, push a button, and the specifications of all classes would be verified. Alas, this dream has escaped me except in one case when I was successful at creating such an environment for a foundation class library (i.e., string, list, set, etc.), where the classes were essentially autonomous. It is much more difficult for a framework that consists of abstract classes with dependencies on each other.

Here's an idea for automating the unit test phase. First, modify the header file template to include the following:

```
class ___ {
public:
    virtual void test(string&);
};

#ifdef TEST__
inline
void ___::test(string& s)
{
    s = "NI"; // not implemented
}
#else inline
void ___::test(string& s)
{ s = "NA"; // not available
}
#endif // TEST__
```

What you are doing is requiring class designers to provide a `test()` member function to unit-test the class of which it is a member. The `test()` function is expected to populate the string s with the results of the test. This string must be examined manually the first time to verify that the class behaves as expected. This result string will then be used as a baseline against which future results will be compared whenever the classes are recompiled.

A regression test program could then be generated by a little tool. This test program could be compiled and run as part of the build process. The generated program could look something like the following, assuming you want to test a class called `Class1` and a class called `Class2`.

```cpp
#include "Class1.h"
#include "Class2.h"
#include <string.h>

template <class TYPE>
void test(const char* typeName, const string& testResultsDir,
ofstream& logStrm)
{
    string goodResults;
    string currentResults;
    string goodResultFilename(testResultsDir);
    goodResultFilename += "/";
    goodResultFilename += typeName;
    goodResultFilename += ".good";
    ifstream goodStrm;
    goodStrm.open(goodResultFilename,ios::in);
    if(!goodStrm)
    {
        logStrm << "No good results exist for " << typeName << endl;
    }
    else
    {
        const int bufLen = 512;
        char buf[bufLen];
        while(goodStrm >> setw(bufLen) >> buf)
        {
            goodResults += buf;
        }
        goodStrm.close();
    }
    TYPE c;
    c.test(currentResults);
```

```
    if(goodResults.size() == 0)  // first time test run.
      {
              if(currentResults == "NI")
              {
                  logStrm << "Test not yet implemented for "
                  << typeName << endl;
              }
              else if(currentResults == "NA")
              {
                  logStrm << typeName <<
                  "not compiled with TEST__ flag" << endl;
              }
              else
              {
                  ofstream initStrm(goodResultFile,ios::out);
                  if(!initStrm)
                  {
                      logStrm << "Can't initialize " <<
                      goodResultFile << endl;
                  }
                  else
                  {
                       initStrm << currentResults << ends;
                       logStrm << typeName <<
                       " results initialized" << endl;
                  }
              }
      }
    else if(currentResults != goodResults)
    {
              string badFilename(testResultsDir);
              badFilename += "/";
              badFilename += typeName;
              badFilename += ".bad";
              ofstream badStrm(badFile,ios::out);
              badStrm << currentResults << ends;
              logStrm << typeName << " test failed. " << endl;
              logStrm << "Check differences between " << typeName;
              logStrm << ".good and " << typeName << ".bad in ";
              logStrm << testResultsDir << "." << endl;
    }
    else
    {
          logStrm << typeName << " test was successful." << endl;
    }
}
```

```
    main()
    {
        string testResultsDir(getenv("TESTRESULTSDIR"));
        string logFile = testResultsDir + "/log";
        ofstream logStrm(logFile,ios::out);
        test<Class1>("Class1", testResultsDir, logStrm);
        test<Class2>("Class2", testResultsDir, logStrm); :
    }
```

If the generated program does not compile, you've found a violator of the convention, identified by a compiler error that will look something like this:

"ClassX._test() - illegal member function"

You will also discover files whose names don't conform to the naming convention that states the module name should match that of the class it implements. You'll get compiler errors like:

"ClassX - no such type"

Packaging the test with the class serves another purpose. It serves as 1) the formal specification of how to use the class interface and 2) a built-in tutorial. This source code should always be provided to the user for these reasons. If the user will not have access to the source of the data members, then the module could be broken up into Foo.h, Foo.C, and FooTest.C.

There are a few problems with this technique. First, this technique will not work for abstract classes. Second, very often in a framework, there is too much coupling between classes to do this, or the class depends on outside entities like a database, so an API must exist to configure the database as expected from within the test function. Also, the test will hang if it presents a GUI that a user is expected to do something with.

8.3.2 Testing an Entire Framework

Testing an entire framework is a two-step process:

1. Extend the framework for the problem that inspired its inception.
2. Come up with a set of test cases based on Sunny Day and Rainy Day scenarios.

You already have the Sunny Day scenarios documented in a set of OIDs. Now you have to sit down and come up with OIDs for scenarios where things go awry (i.e., are Rainy Day). Make sure that you exercise all exceptions defined for all classes comprising the framework.

Even after you test the framework in this way, you are not really sure if it is reusable. Only after a few more problems in the same domain use the framework can you say that it has been tested for reusability.

8.3.3 Debugging

Debugging has always been an art form. I guess you could probably get away with defining it as a two-step process: 1) you find out where the code is broken; 2) you fix it. The "binary search" technique is applied to accomplish step 1, whether you are using a symbolic debugger to set breakpoints or you are embedding `printfs` in the code and watching for the point where they stop coming out. The truth of the matter is that today most debugging is usually done in your head, whereas it used to be done on your computer—because today, more bugs are the result of logic errors, as opposed to mechanical ones. A few years ago, whenever I got a core dump, nine times out of ten it was because I was trying to put N elements into an array of size N-1. Container classes virtually eliminated that type of bug. The ones that I encounter these days are far fewer in number but are generally harder to debug.

8.4 Preparing User Documentation

User documentation encompasses the analysis and design documentation already written. This must, however, be supplemented with a *Programmer's Guide* that shows programmers how to extend the framework for their particular application and how to use the extended framework. This is distinctly different from the traditional view of a programmer's guide.

CHAPTER 9
Framework Development Strategies

Even if a framework is developed and used to solve one customer's problem and is never reused in another application, chances are good that the extra effort required to develop it will be paid back. Framework-based development, however, cannot reach its full potential as a mechanism for software reuse unless strategies are devised at a variety of levels. For a framework industry to emerge on a grand scale, the potential producers must form a strategy together. For firms that will be both producers and consumers of frameworks, the development organization must be structured a certain way. Current practices employed by application development teams must also be altered in order to take advantage of frameworks. In this chapter, I offer suggestions for formulating strategies at the levels of industry, development organizations, and individual application development teams.

9.1 Creating a Framework Industry

There are a few things that must happen before a framework industry can thrive:

- There must be a public forum for educating potential producers and consumers of frameworks.
- There must be a consortium consisting of potential users and producers. This consortium would develop standards for framework documentation, design, and categorization. There must also be standards for how frameworks will interface with each other, and these standards must be maintained in a public place.

- There should be *one* publicly accessible catalog containing consortium-certified frameworks that are available. The catalog should include browsing tools that would enable development teams to quickly identify frameworks that are potentially useful for their applications. In the long term, an electronic "framework supermarket" would be the ideal, where you could browse for, test drive, purchase, and retrieve all of your frameworks from one Internet site.

9.2 Reengineering the Development Organization

Many development organizations were not designed to take advantage of the Object paradigm. I've lived through multiple development organization "reengineering"[1] efforts and have still not seen a structure and a culture emerge that is conducive to the production of frameworks that are truly valued as corporate assets. After studying this for a few years now, I have a few suggestions for those who are reengineering a development organization.

9.2.1   Why Reuse Does Not Happen

Let's first discuss some of the problems that hinder development and use of frameworks, and reusable software in general. They include the following:

- The "Not Invented Here" (NIH)[2] syndrome prevails.
- Reuse occurs largely by accident.
- Incentives are oriented toward short-term results.
- Higher-level design skills are not cultivated.

These problems can potentially be alleviated with a properly structured development organization and culture.

The NIH syndrome has been blamed for years as the primary reason that development teams rebuild from scratch instead of starting with software that is already written. It doesn't appear to be as much of a problem as it used to be. Development resources are more scarce, and deadlines are tighter. Anything that can be done to leverage development is considered. There is one exception to this, however. Developers often have a deep distrust for reusable software that is produced in-house. A software package produced by a

---

1. This used to be called "reorganization," but since "reengineering" seems to be the fashionable term these days, I'll just go with the flow.

2. Phenomenon occurring in software development when developers don't want to use software that they have not written themselves.

cost center and packaged for use within the same company is generally not considered, by developers, as viable as one that is produced by an outside vendor. Part of it is packaging; it's not as glitzy. Part of it is poor internal marketing, support, and education. Part of it is that the products are sometimes not as good, because the environment in which they were produced lacked the entrepreneurial spirit needed to produce something that the customer is awe-stricken by. If you were to survey developers, I think that you would find these perceptions to be the root causes of the NIH syndrome.

Consider the second problem: reuse occurs largely by accident. I came to appreciate this firsthand when I was developing a framework for a project in a very large development organization. The framework implemented the BLACKBOARD pattern, which is commonly applied in the development of expert systems. Realizing that this had potential for reuse on other projects, I wrote and distributed a rather lengthy document describing the framework and what it could do. I even wrote an article for a newsletter that was distributed to all development managers. I received about 30 inquiries, but the framework was only distributed to one group outside of the project for which it was originally developed. Why? Part of the reason may have been the NIH problem that I just talked about. I couldn't offer any support, because I was dedicated full-time to delivering a system to one particular customer. But, I believe the primary reason was because my attempt at proliferating the use of the framework was an ad hoc, grass-roots effort. The 30 inquiries that I got were from people that just happened to read my article or paper. What were the odds that a new project that could potentially use the framework was starting right at the point when my article and paper were being distributed? Not very high, I suspect. Okay, maybe sometime down the road a project would start that could use it. But, how will project members find out about it then? They could query the database of corporate technical papers, but what is the likelihood that they will use keywords that will locate my document? There was no reuse process; it could only occur by accident!

The third problem is that there is rarely incentive for staff developers to build frameworks. Frameworks are built as an integral part of the development of end-user applications. This pushes out the first delivery date, because it's hard to develop a framework. The customer probably doesn't want to hear that you are going to build a framework first for a long-term payback or for the potential benefit it may have to other projects in the future. They don't care; they want their system as soon as possible! You are going to be judged and rewarded according to how quickly you deliver.

In the rare event that you do get the opportunity to build a framework, you are then faced with the same problem that I had with the BLACKBOARD framework: there is no incentive to support it and probably no support group to hand it off to. In my case, I quickly lost interest in seeing others use it, especially since it meant I would have more work and would not be rewarded for doing it.

The last problem mentioned that hinders the development of frameworks is related to incentives: higher-level design skills are not cultivated in many development organizations, because there is such an emphasis on short-term deliverables. If you are a development manager with an organization that has been operating in "crunch mode"[3] for some time, you'll find that you have a development staff skilled at buying, recycling, or stealing less than adequate solutions and cleverly hacking them to solve a particular problem by some unrealistic deadline. To get a feel for how this situation could eventually lead to the demise of the organization, consider Figure 9-1.

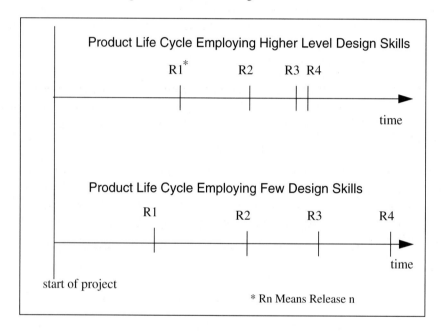

FIGURE 9-1.

Organizations that elevate the skill set of their developers and give them a long-term focus will see innovations emerge, often in the form of frameworks. This will ultimately increase the organization's ability to deliver new features faster and with fewer resources. For an organization that does not take this approach, each new release becomes a major rewrite or a set of bug fixes. Such an organization may soon be unable to keep up with innovative competitors.

The crunch mode phenomenon has always been one that I have either seen in other groups or one whose precipice I have seen in a project that I was on (but cool heads prevailed before it was too late). Recently, I worked in a group that had gone through a rather long

---

3. Understaffed, complex applications, and very tight deadlines.

stretch of crunch mode before I arrived. When I joined, I was asked to add new features to the application that they had built and deployed. As I descended into the belly of the beast, I quickly realized that my design skills were of secondary importance. What I found as I started to study out the system was a patchwork of ANSI C, C++, K&R C, Perl, FrameMaker®, Shell scripts, stored procedures, freeware, in-house libraries, and off-the-shelf packages. There was also no MR system to speak of, and the compiler they were using was five years behind. The patchwork nature was readily apparent to the user because there was a different look-and-feel to every screen that they had to interact with. Users were calling the development team members constantly. The team members spent much of their time trying to keep the system up or repair it through sheer witchcraft. A little "eye of newt" and "wing of bat" and the system might continue for another day. There was no security, no consistent error reporting strategy, no system shutdown procedure, no error recovery strategy, and no installation procedure. There was no time for innovation and moving forward, only trying to prevent things from going backward! I added the features that they wanted and then left. I just spoke to someone recently who is still involved with the project. They are replacing the whole application with an off-the-shelf product.

Before offering suggestions that may lessen or correct some of these problems, let's look a little more deeply at the structure of a typical development organization (see Figure 9-2).

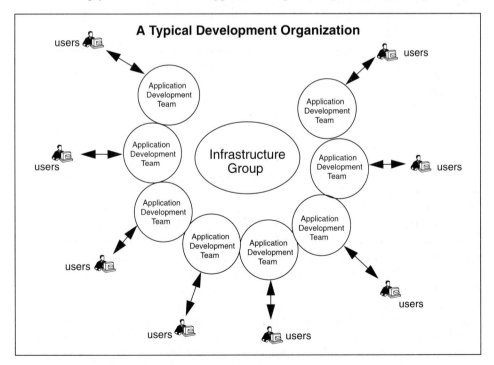

FIGURE 9-2.

On the front line are the application development teams. We just discussed the havoc that short-term focus and demanding customers often have on the ability of such groups to increase productivity through innovation. Companies are starting to realize this and have put infrastructure groups in place to play the role of innovators. In fact, I've worked in three such groups for two different companies in two different industries. Unfortunately, none were very effective during the time I was there. They had great talent, but it was retracted into an isolated environment where the group members hypothesized about the needs of the business. The problem was that they were too far removed from the day-to-day operations of the business.

9.2.2   Organizing for Reuse

Now let's talk about possible solutions to these problems, manifesting themselves in the structure and policies of the development organization. Before I offer the suggestions, I should mention that I understand that the changes I propose may be difficult to achieve and can't be done overnight. I also don't have any proof that my suggestions will work, because I've never actually seen an organization that operates as I envision. I have, however, seen evidence of improved situations in tiny pockets of organizations, and that is the inspiration for my ideas.

I think that there are two key goals that must be sought as we move away from the type of organizational structure shown in Figure 9-2. First, the infrastructure group needs to be closer to the business. Second, there needs to be an injection of entrepreneurial incentives into the organization. With these goals in mind, I submit that the structure shown in Figure 9-3 is a good one to aspire to for applying framework-based development to the maximum benefit of the firm. As you can see, the idea is to actually have infrastructure group members work on application development teams.

Although very few processes these days are strictly sequential, certain aspects of the job of an infrastructure group member working on an application development team are chronological, as shown in Figure 9-4. If the tasks shown in this flowchart are not performed at least in an order similar to this, the value added by the infrastructure group will be diminished.

Let's now discuss the second goal that we want to achieve when creating a new development organization: injection of entrepreneurial incentives. Companies are making progress in this area for application team members, especially in the financial industry. The bonuses of the team members are becoming more commensurate with the profits of the business area that they support. How do you inject entrepreneurial incentives into an infrastructure group, which is generally funded with some form of tax put on all of the application groups? Every time a framework is reused internally, perhaps there should be a royalty of some kind paid to its marketer and designer. Additionally, if some frameworks can compete with off-the-shelf products and it is not in conflict with the firm's main business, perhaps the infrastructure group should be allowed to seek additional income by marketing the frameworks on the open market, again with royalties going to the original developers. I know of one very large financial institution that has done this with a trading system framework. Imagine that, banks getting into the third-party software business.

In an organization that is structured as I suggest, people with different reporting structures and distinct deliverables of varying time horizons work together on one problem. This is a radically different approach to software development and, I believe, one whose time has come.

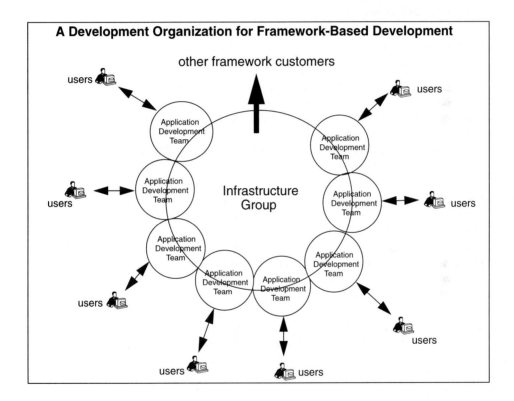

FIGURE 9-3.

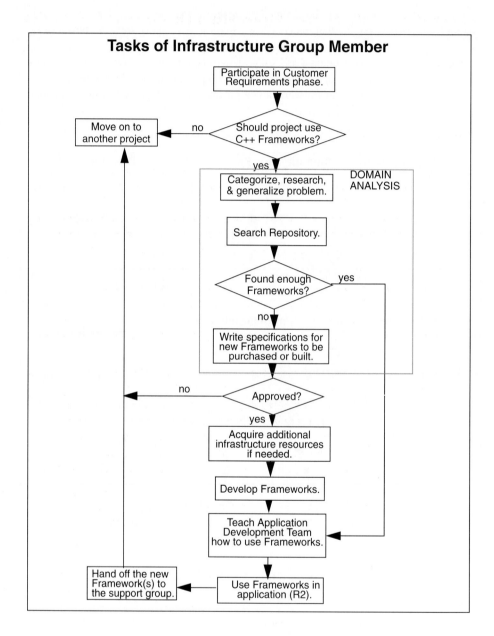

Tasks of Infrastructure Group Member

Participate in Customer Requirements phase.

Should project use C++ Frameworks? — no → Move on to another project

yes

DOMAIN ANALYSIS

Categorize, research, & generalize problem.

Search Repository.

Found enough Frameworks? — yes

no

Write specifications for new Frameworks to be purchased or built.

Approved? — no

yes

Acquire additional infrastructure resources if needed.

Develop Frameworks.

Teach Application Development Team how to use Frameworks.

Use Frameworks in application (R2).

Hand off the new Framework(s) to the support group.

FIGURE 9-4.

9.3 Putting Together an Application Development Team

I have found that the most productive teams are small (four to six people). If a project is too large for four to six people, part of the development strategy should be to partition the job such that you have semiautonomous teams of four to six people.

Each team has the following roles to fill:

- **Release 1 Lead.** This person is responsible for quickly delivering a pilot system (i.e., Release 1) to the customer. He or she is generally business-oriented and has some development background. This person is the primary customer contact for the group and leads the requirements effort. This person should also have a personal deliverable for the first release and direct the efforts of others who have deliverables for the first release. It is very important that this person have a deliverable, because it will keep the person sensitive to the problems of the developers. I have seen project managers that could not manage customer expectations and alienated the development team because they forgot how difficult it can be to produce something.

- **Release 2 Lead** (dual role played by framework developer from infrastructure group). This person is generally an experienced developer from the infrastructure group who is responsible for the direction and development of the long-term solutions for the application (this may require other resources from the infrastructure group). The person also leads the domain analysis effort.

- **Developer(s).** One or two persons, generally junior or mid-level developers who have deliverables in both Release 1 and Release 2. In Release 1, developers will use rapid application development environments to quickly produce pilot features delegated by the Release 1 Lead. In the second release, the developer(s) will be mentored by the Release 2 Lead to deliver features, using frameworks. As developers mature, they should be nurtured into either a Release 1 Lead or a Release 2 Lead position, depending on their interests and talents (i.e., business oriented or technology oriented).

- **Quality Assurance Person.** This person is responsible for the development environment for the group (i.e., build-environment setup, system builds, MR administration, configuration management). He or she is also responsible for integration testing (i.e., testing the interfaces between features turned over by different developers).

- **System Tester.** This person is responsible for verifying that user requirements are satisfied by the application and is also responsible for testing the documentation for clarity, accuracy, and completeness. The person filling this role must understand the business need being filled by the application.

- **Tool Developer.** Every team needs a resident, part-time toolbuilder. It will be inevitable that at some point in a project you have to build some tools to automate tasks that just don't make sense to do manually (e.g., data translation, test generation, automated documentation of manual pages from source). The ideal tool person is someone who is, or is willing to become, proficient at a scripting language like Perl.

9.4 Putting Together an Infrastructure Group

The size of the infrastructure group will vary with the size of the development organization, but as a rule of thumb, there should be the same number or more people in the group as there are application development teams. This means that most application development teams can have at least one infrastructure person dedicated to them. The following are some guidelines for the roles to be played by members of the infrastructure group.

- **Framework Developers** (dual role of Release 2 Lead on Application Development Team). I believe that the bedrock of a framework developer's skill set is 1) ability to generalize, 2) ability to think abstractly, 3) design skills, and 4) proficiency at using one enduring and widely used object-oriented programming language (e.g., C++). I think that framework developers should probably be ambidextrous when it comes to operating systems. There are other skills that are essential. Framework developers must have excellent communication skills (writing and verbal) and must be able to discuss and understand the firm's business.

- **Software Librarian(s) and Quality Assurance.** These people (or person) must be comfortable with the company's repository mechanisms, which will most likely be Web-based. They must know and enforce the policies for acceptance and update of frameworks in the repository and have excellent organizational skills so that frameworks are categorized properly. The Software Librarian(s) is also responsible for the development environment for the group.

- **In-House Framework Support.** The person filling this role maintains and enhances internally developed frameworks. This role also includes educating people in the firm on how to use the frameworks. The people in this role will generally be of an intermediate skill level. They must keep users informed about enhancements to in-house frameworks and assist them in upgrading to new releases. Enhancements made to any framework should be approved by its original designer to preserve its integrity and intended character. Enhancements will almost always be required until the framework has been deployed in a few applications, because the design of a framework will inevitably have a bias toward the initial application for which it was developed.

- **Third-Party Software Support**. The person in this role purchases, installs, and provides in-house support of third-party products used throughout the firm. A person in this role is also responsible for making sure that all application groups are using the same releases of third-party products.

- **Manager.** This person is the arbitrator, application group liaison, assigner of framework developers to application groups, approver of new framework development, and approver of site licenses for third-party products to be used throughout the firm (e.g., compilers, debuggers, GUI toolkits).

- **Software Historian.** This person is responsible for collecting and maintaining a database of important statistics and metrics pertaining to productivity and software quality. As we will discuss shortly, this information is crucial for intelligent planning and cost justification.

- **Software Security Analyst.** This person is responsible for assessing the security of all software developed in-house and purchased from an outside source. The importance of the role cannot be overstated. The fate of entire companies depends on execution of software that is virus-free and does not have vulnerabilities that allow intruders to cause damage to the firm's operation.

- **Framework Marketer.** This person tries to find other markets, outside the firm, for frameworks produced by the Infrastructure Group. This is an optional role.

9.5 Evaluating an Off-the-Shelf Framework

I have been asked several times to evaluate frameworks for use throughout large development organizations. I can tell you the criteria upon which I base my recommendations. Since intelligent selection of frameworks must always come from the recommendation of technical people, this may provide a good starting point for a framework marketing strategy. The following are some of the "boilerplate" criteria that I use when evaluating a framework.

- **Portability.** The framework should be portable to all operating systems used or planned to be used in the development organization.

- **Software security.** The framework vendor should be willing to guarantee against viruses and vulnerabilities in the framework code.

- **Fiscal health of vendor.** The framework vendor should meet minimum standards of fiscal health. The company should be profitable or exhibit a growth trend toward becoming profitable. The vendor should have positive earnings growth.

- **Product direction of vendor.** The framework should either be compliant with, or be on track to soon be compliant with, emerging standards (e.g., CORBA, ODMG-93, C++ STL). This will minimize vendor dependence.

- **Reliability and performance.** The evaluator should have a set of test cases that can be applied to measure the reliability and performance of one framework versus another in the same category.

- **Technical support.** A good technical support organization responds promptly to a customer's problem. Promptness can be assessed and documented during a product evaluation, to some degree. Depending on the nature of the tool and its mission criticality, you may require a guaranteed response time. This should be discussed with the vendor during the evaluation period. A good technical support organization should also be proactive. For example, when distributing a new release of a product, good support organizations call the customer to make sure that there are no problems installing and using the new release. Another characteristic of a good support organization relates to how it resolves a customer's problem. Good organizations do not throw a solution "over the wall" to a customer, hoping it works. They provide a solution and remain in contact until that customer is satisfied. Lastly, good technical support organizations always track a customer problem with some form of system that assigns the customer a reference number to be associated with the problem.

- **Quality and thoroughness of documentation.** The documentation provided with a toolkit should be complete and correct. It should be indexed in such a way that any class, free function, or command can be found immediately. In the case of class libraries, the usage of all classes and how they interact should be explained in text and demonstrated with a generous number of annotated code fragments. Class diagrams, object diagrams, and scenario depictions should provided. The documentation should be provided on line and in hardcopy.

- **Price.** Price is only a factor when comparing two or more frameworks with equivalent functionality. For example, there are many inexpensive GUI toolkits available (a few hundred dollars), but the toolkits that cost more by an order of magnitude generally provide an order of magnitude more in feature content. The level of need must be documented for each tool category before price can be factored into an evaluation.

9.6 The Economics of In-house Framework Development

This section focuses on the economics of building a framework for strictly in-house use. I refer entrepreneurs to marketing consultants to predict the amount of money that they will make on their framework.

Whether you are trying to convince your manager to buy a framework or allow you to build one, you should be prepared to justify the cost. In this section, I offer some suggestions on how to do this. First, we discuss the circumstances where it is likely that building a framework is a good idea, economically speaking. Second, we discuss how to quantify the value that a framework provides to the firm in which it was created. Last, we discuss how to determine the break-even point for a framework developed in-house.

When does it make economic sense to consider building a framework? Well, the short answer is: when you can't buy it and the cost of its development is less than the costs that would be incurred over the life of that framework were it not to be developed.[4] Before trying to quantify this, there are some heuristics that decision-makers should apply.

---

4. This oversimplifies things a bit, because it focuses only on costs. It does not take into account additional profits that can be made because of the faster time to market that can be achieved after the framework is developed.

RULE 1: A horizontal framework that takes longer than one year to build with three or more developers will probably not be justifiable to build for strictly in-house use.

The rationale behind this rule is the following. If the framework is horizontal, then there is a large market for it. If there is a large market for it, in a year you will probably be able to buy such a framework off-the-shelf. The cost of buying it off-the-shelf will be far less than if you were to build it yourself, because the vendor's development costs will be spread across its customer base.

RULE 2: Developing a small vertical framework (i.e., 12 staff-months or less) that can't be bought is probably justifiable if the initial application for which it is proposed is 1) going to have many new features added to it in the future or 2) similar in nature to other applications developed in-house.

If you can't currently buy a vertical framework for which there is a perceived need and the framework is fairly small, it is unlikely that someone is out there building one. The more vertical, the less likely, not only because the market for such a framework is smaller, but because the domain expertise required to build it is harder to find.

If the initial application for a framework is expected to have many new features added, the cost of developing the framework may be justified by this one application alone. Because new feature releases often require adding to, and/or rewriting substantial portions of, an application, you may very well find that framework-equivalent functionality is being developed over and over again. If the cost to redevelop framework-equivalent pieces for the new releases exceeds the cost of developing the framework, it is only logical to build the framework.

RULE 3: A small vertical framework (i.e., 12 staff-months or less) that is being proposed for development as part of a large application (60+ staff-months) will probably not delay delivery of that application.

To understand the logic behind this rule, consider Figure 9-5. It is well known that the productivity of software teams decreases with the size of the application because of the increased number of interfaces, the additional coordination required among team members, additional testing, etc. It has also been stated that it takes longer to develop a framework than a custom solution because the generalization process takes time. However, development of a small framework (FW A in Figure 9-5) can be broken off as a separate development effort from the application (APP A in Figure 9-5) in which it will be used. As a result, it does not have the additional productivity decreases associated with the large application. Consequently, the productivity of the framework developer may be better than that of the application team overall. This implies that if an application is large, developing a small framework to use in this application is probably not going to push out its delivery date.

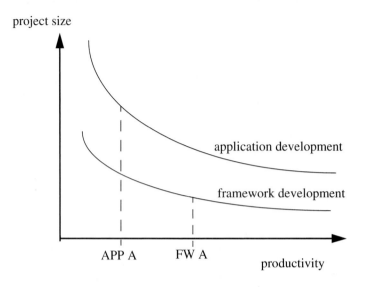

FIGURE 9-5.

This concludes the heuristics section. Let's move on to something a little more number oriented. I've learned over the years that a manager will always feel better about a decision if you can provide supporting numbers, even if underlying assumptions upon which they are based are subjective.

To quantify the cost-benefit of a proposed framework is a tough thing to do because it requires predicting things that are not very predictable. There is, however, an estimating technique that can be applied in a mature development organization that has a large base of legacy systems and a fairly stable business model. This technique, which consists of three steps, is the focus of the rest of this section.

What you can do is try to quantify the "historical value" that a framework would have if it was currently deployed throughout the organization. The value is equal to the money that the company has spent to put redundant software in place that does what the framework would do. This is presumably a measure of the minimum that such a framework would have been worth to the company if it were available before the existing software base was installed.[5]

---

5. We will not take into account an inflation premium and therefore this is not a true, present-value calculation.

The formula for calculating the historical value of a proposed framework is:

Step 1:
$$\text{historical value} = \sum_{x=1}^{n} C_x \times P_x$$

where

n = number of applications deployed throughout the firm

P_x = % of application x source that could be replaced by framework

C_x = cost to develop application x

The historical value will be maximized in organizations having a similar application by using vertical frameworks, because P_x will generally be higher. For organizations having many dissimilar applications, horizontal frameworks may yield a higher historical value because there are more value components.

As you can see by the equation, fairly accurate records of the labor spent on software development need to be kept. The real legwork associated with determining a reasonable estimate of historical value, however, is going to be in coming up with the percentage of each application's source code that could be replaced with the framework.[6] I want to point out that the beauty of this equation is that you can come up with a value, even if all your applications are currently written in COBOL. The percentage variables (P_x) are based on features, not a specific programming language. I wouldn't go nuts about getting accurate percentage numbers; you can't be accurate without a fully designed framework. If we are talking about a huge application that is solving problems for an aspect of the business that is far removed from the domain for which the framework is intended, assume 0 percent and move on to the next. If the company has a bunch of applications that are very similar, estimate the percentage for one of them and assume the same percentage for the rest.

Now you should try to estimate the cost of building a framework. From this estimated cost and the historical value of the framework, you can forecast when the framework will pay back the cost of its development, based on the future plans of the organization.

---

6. If an application is written in more than one language, you will have to normalize this percentage by using a technique like Function Point Analysis [see JONES91]. I also want to point out that this technique assumes a uniform NCSL/month productivity.

The formula for estimating the cost of developing a framework is:

Step 2: $$\text{framework cost} = L_d \times N_d \times Months$$

where

L_d = monthly labor cost per developer

N_d = number of developers dedicated

$Months$ = estimated number of months to develop framework

Once you have estimated the historical value of a framework and the estimated cost to build that framework, you can then predict how long it will be before the framework development costs are recovered, based on the plans of the development organization. The plans may include replacing legacy applications or building new ones. If the legacy applications will be replaced by systems that solve similar business needs, it seems reasonable to assume that the framework can be used to build a comparable portion, as was estimated in the historical value calculation. If new systems are being planned that can use the framework and they are similar in nature to those that already exist, this also seems like a reasonable assumption. The break-even point is the number of applications that must use the framework before the sum of the labor costs saved on the applications is greater than or equal to the framework cost. First, calculate the average cost per application spent on developing the features provided by the framework in past applications. If the total number of applications is n, then:

$$\text{historical average} = (HistoricalValue) \div n$$

Strangely enough, this average cost may end up being higher than the cost of developing the framework. Why? Well, remember what we said about Rule 2? With each new release of an application, you may have had to rebuild framework functionality. If the organization has a tradition of re-releasing applications many times, the average cost to develop framework-equivalent features in each application could, therefore, end up being higher than the cost of developing the framework itself.

Finally, an estimate of the number of applications that must use the framework before it pays for itself is given below. Ideally, this value would be less than 1.

Step 3: $$\text{BEP} = \text{framework cost} \div \text{historical average}$$

9.7 Setting Up the Ideal Development Environment

If you have the opportunity to start a new project and set up a development environment from scratch, you are very lucky. There are now some excellent off-the-shelf tools available upon which you can create what I'll call "the ideal development environment." If you are already in the middle of a project, you should strive to move toward such an environment. The problem is, you really need everyone on the project to stop and retool. Trying to change a development environment while development is fully engaged is like trying to change your oil while driving down a highway. Many projects that I have been on should have just stopped what they were doing, gotten a good environment in place, and then picked up from where they left off. But, as we've discussed earlier, customers and high-level managers often cannot appreciate why this is important.

In my view, the ideal development environment is platform independent. It also has integrated Modification Request (MR) tracking, source code control, manufacturing, and automated regression test tools. It also supports the notion of a translucent file system. Wow, what a mouthful! Is this realistic? Sure it is and may, in fact, provide you with the competitive edge, but it takes time and money to set up correctly. Let's briefly review each of these features and explain why they are important and how they can be integrated.

Platform independence is becoming increasingly important for the development environment, for two reasons. First, the software that is developed on them more than likely needs to be portable, and there is no worse headache than trying to support such software in multiple development environments. It can take more time to switch between development environments on different platforms than to actually port the code. Second, development teams themselves are very mobile these days. You want to be able to get a module out for edit, put it on your laptop, and bring it to the Caribbean with you.

Any experienced developer knows that you can't easily manage a medium-to-large software project without an MR system, and you need to be able to trace the solution to an MR back to the source code. The only way to realistically hope to do this is by using tools that integrate MRs with versions of source files. Further, new releases of a product should be based on bug fixes and features corresponding to specific MRs. So, the manufacturing process must also be integrated such that the build person can specify a build that contains certain fixes and features.

Next, manual regression testing is almost as good as no testing, because once a developer is in the throes of development, it's just no fun to retest the same thing over and over again. If there are full-time testers, they, too, will have their hands full with new bugs without having to worry about going back to old ones to make sure that they still work. So there needs to be tools that automatically regression-test each build. How many times have you been working on a project and a user says: "Hey! I thought you guys fixed that!"? You scratch your head and say, "Yeah! I thought we did too!" You then have no idea when this problem reintroduced itself and what recent changes may have caused it to resurface. Automated regression test tools prevent this embarrassing phenomenon.

Last, you would like a translucent file system. A translucent file system enables you to build locally, having only those files that you are working on populated in your working directory. When a build is run locally, the translucent file system is smart enough to go back and find the latest versions of the other files required for the build. This helps you avoid compiling with obsolete or hacked versions of the modules that you are not directly working on.

9.8 The Project Plan for Developing a Framework

Projects are managed with varying degrees of formality. I've seen projects that have absolutely no project plans, including deadlines. These projects, strangely, appear to be those most coveted by developers. I have seen projects where the only element of the project plan was a delivery date. I've been on projects like this that were very successful. The catch is that the development team consisted of a small group of highly skilled people, who knew exactly what their roles were from previous experiences, being managed by a trusting manager. So, in essence, there was an implicit project plan, I suppose. Generally, a project with more than a few people always fails to deliver when the only project plan they have is a delivery date. The pattern is always the same. The project goes smooth as silk in the early stages (because no one is actually doing anything). Then, as the delivery date begins to draw near, the project spirals into bedlam. I would strongly suggest a real project plan be prepared at the outset for most projects.

A project plan for framework-based development, in an organization like the one that I just suggested, is quite different from one used in the olden days of the waterfall model. Project plans for OO development in general make managers very uncomfortable because there are a significant number of what I'll call "fuzzy milestones" before anything that a user can see is produced; the generalization process takes time to do correctly and many activities occur in parallel.

To come up with a reasonable project plan for the development of a framework, you first have to identify the tasks involved in developing a framework. I give my rendition in Figure 9-6. Notice that I have shown the activities of the application development team that is going to be the first to apply the framework.

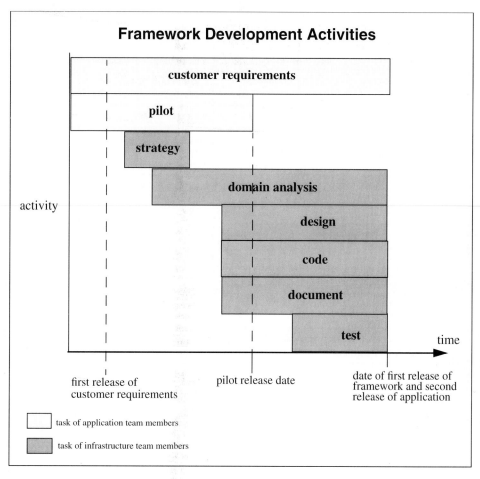

FIGURE 9-6.

Strategy is the first activity in framework development. This includes tasks like determining if you should try to develop a framework, evaluating off-the-shelf frameworks, and developing a project plan. The second activity is domain analysis, which is different from other types of system analysis in that there is not an emphasis on characterizing one specific problem, but identifying a class of problems generalized from a specific one (i.e., that described in the customer requirements). You then engage in massive parallel processing of continued domain analysis, designing of classes, coding them, and documenting them. When there is enough substance to the framework code to start to test it, you then try to do so by implementing problem-specific code and using it to test the framework. When the framework is tested, the first application built on it is essentially complete as well.

Based on the tasks discussed so far, I offer, in Table 9-1, a template for constructing a framework development project plan.

TABLE 9-1.   Framework Development Project Plan

Milestone #[a]	Description	Responsible Person(s)	Depends On
1	Release customer requirements (release 1).	Customer, Release 1 Lead	
2	Domain Analysis—Specify frameworks to be built.	Release 2 Lead	1
3	Approve building of frameworks.	Infrastructure Group Manager	2
4	Assess staffing needs and prepare schedule for remainder of milestones in this plan.	Release 2 Lead	3
5	Approve staffing needs and schedule.	Infrastructure Group Manager	4
6	Assign roles.	Infrastructure Group Manager and Release 2 Lead	5
7	Prepare development environment.	Infrastructure Quality Assurance	3
8	High-level design (header files, public interfaces).	Release 2 Lead	7
9	Draft high-level design document (class diagrams, scenario diagrams, and text).	Release 2 Lead	8
10	Code.	Release 2 Lead and other developers	9
11	Draft manual pages.	Release 2 Lead and other developers	9
12	Unit-test.	Release 2 Lead and other developers	9
13	Teach Application Group how to use framework.	Release 2 Lead	12
14	Develop application-specific classes.	Application Development Team	13
15	Deliver Release 2 to customer.	Release 2 Lead and Application Developers	14
16	Finalize domain analysis, design document, and manual pages.	Release 2 Lead	15
17	Hand off framework to Support.	Release 2 Lead and in-house Framework Support	16

a. It is assumed that conventions, guidelines, and procedures not explicitly mentioned as milestones are already in place.

9.9 Red Flags

Every well-run project has people that see signs of problems before they get out of hand. Sometimes the problems can be prevented, and sometimes they can't. The warning signs aren't like callbacks; someone usually has to be polling for them. I believe that it is the obligation of good developers to bring the potential for problems to their manager's attention. Table 9-2 contains warning signs that require red flags to be raised.

TABLE 9-2.   Signs of Project Trouble

Description of Red Flag	Likely Reasons	Actions To Be Taken
People start to blame each other for problems.	Roles not well defined, deadlines too tight, personality problems.	Clearly define roles, rework schedule, get group together socially, warn troublemakers that they must playing nicely; if they don't, either move them into a role that requires no interaction or get rid of them. Nothing destroys a project faster than one difficult person. Don't throw more people at the problem!
You find yourself starting to compromise your standards.	Schedule pressures, an overwhelming amount of legacy code to maintain.	Inform your manager of specific instances where your standards are being compromised and the implications. Pick out a small piece of the system where you can start to regain control.
Management is deciding how long it should take to complete a project, and their decision is just unrealistic.	Too many projects, too few people, ignorant managers.	Immediately explain to management the flaw in their estimates. If they are not going to be realistic, leave.

PART 3
Example Frameworks

CHAPTER 10
A Horizontal Framework for Workflow

I've seen companies spend many millions of dollars building workflow applications; some with more than 50 people developing them. Of the ones I've seen, few have been viewed as successful. It's really pretty astonishing when you think about it. How could it be so hard? Well, I think a good part of the reason is that these systems were designed with a specific workflow hardcoded into the software. Inevitably the nature of workflow changes, and when it does, the software is hacked up to accommodate. Tell me if this sounds familiar.

A small well-meaning team of developers and systems engineers/analysts is formed to develop a repair ticketing system. An initial set of requirements is baselined, and the developers quickly go off and write the code to implement the system. They test it themselves, or perhaps there is a tester or two to help them. The system goes out the door, and the customer says, "It's okay, but we forgot to tell you we need a variation of this kind of ticket, which actually gets handled a little differently." The developers copy and paste some of their code, perhaps adding a couple extra `if()` statements in their main processing loop. They test that new feature and turn it over to the customer, forgetting to regression-test the other features previously tested and, of course, never updating the requirements document. The customer likes that new feature, but now the original ones don't quite work right anymore, and because new users are coming on line, there are now more requests for new features and modifications to existing ones.

The copying and pasting continues, as do the number of test cases and the realization that the requirements are a tad out of date. So, the managers hire more systems engineers and testers to help them meet their now slipping deadlines. Just about now, some of the developers are burned out and disgusted with the project, so they leave. Of course, there are no comments in the code, so those that take over have no clue what it does. When a new feature request comes in, the new developers are afraid to change what is there, so they just write code from scratch and perform the software equivalent of heart bypass surgery. The code size is starting to grow exponentially. The Modification Request (MR) Review Board is now formed and spends many hours in meetings each week trying to decide which of the hundreds of MRs to fix, perhaps opting to just give up on the ones that have been under review for the last six months. Finally, the demise is seen as inevitable by all on and outside the project, as its budget begins to shrink, and a new replacement system is planned.

I'm certainly not going to claim that framework-based development will prevent all the mistakes that were made on this hypothetical project, but it could make some of them less likely to occur. The crack in the dike occurred when the development started. Instead of just taking the current set of requirements and running with them, the development team should have approached the problem by first performing a domain analysis and specifying a generic "repair ticketing" framework, one of the facets of which was "workflow." They then would have bought or built the horizontal frameworks, one of which handled workflow. Then, they would have built the ticketing framework on top. Last, they would have developed the application on top of the ticketing framework. If they had done this, they would not have been as vulnerable to being caught off guard when the first new feature request came in. They would have better anticipated it because they had a better understanding of the domain and the workflow facet, and they would have built software that was designed to be extended and modified instead of copied, pasted, and hacked. And, if they did this correctly, the original team may have been able to stay in control of the situation.

In this chapter, I present the analysis, design, and part of the implementation of a framework that deals with the workflow facet that is common to applications in different domains. A good portion of the development procedures are demonstrated, but I will not show a formal test plan or programmer's guide. The emphasis will be on analysis, design, and implementation techniques.

10.1 Facet Analysis: Workflow

The facet analysis phase is initiated in response to a domain analysis. In Chapter 5, we identified a workflow facet in the operation of a mail order business, but very few of its characteristics were specified. If we were to continue with the intention of actually building a mail order system, one of the things we should do is more thoroughly analyze this facet. That is what we are going to do in this section, following the procedures discussed in Chapter 5.

The first step of the analysis involves studying other applications that have a workflow facet. I'll start by briefly discussing the applicability of workflow to an application that I was involved with for an investment bank, which supported the processing of fixed-income derivatives contracts. I will also discuss how workflow applies to other types of applications that may seemingly have no use for a workflow framework. After I've done this, I'll claim we have verified that this is, in fact, a facet that spans multiple domains and that we have a decent grasp of what characteristics are part of a generic workflow model.

10.1.1 Background Discussion

I spent some time supporting and enhancing a workflow application that facilitated the processing of fixed-income derivatives contracts, called "swaps." Swaps are basically agreements between two parties, usually financial institutions, to loan each other the same amount of money, usually many millions of dollars. One party generally agrees to pay a fixed interest rate, and the other agrees to pay a floating interest rate. Without getting into details about why two parties would want to do this, suffice it to say that it helps parties with different tolerances for changes in interest rates assume levels of risk that they are more comfortable with.

These swaps can have many different variations and require complicated legal documentation. This documentation goes through quite a few stages of review and modification before it is considered legal. First a deal is made. Then the terms have to be worked out in detail by passing the documentation back and forth between the parties. When changes in wording are proposed, the proposals are automatically faxed to the counter-party for review, then eventually faxed back with the comments. After the exact wording is worked out, final signatures are put on the contracts and they are passed off to the back office so that the terms can be executed.

The people involved in this workflow have a nice little GUI that shows a grid containing the swaps being negotiated, the people assigned to work on each, and the current state of the swap. Some state changes are manually performed by dragging and dropping a swap from one state to another in the GUI. Other changes occur automatically when a person enters a specific piece of information into a contract or a fax is automatically received.

That summarizes one example of workflow that is very human intensive and has a document-centric view of work.

So far, we have talked about workflow mostly in the context of human activity, and, in fact, that's where the companies that I've worked for have built systems—to accommodate human activity. When most people think of workflow, they also envision documentation being passed from one person to the next, as would be the case for a ticketing system, mortgage processing, insurance claim processing, or contract processing. But, the essence of a workflow model is nothing more than a specialized state machine. Humans and documentation are irrelevant to this core model.

Control systems are also examples of systems that may involve a workflow model: a power plant, an automated factory, your dishwasher (i.e., fill, wash, rinse, dry). Consider the space shuttle: "prepare for lift-off," "count down… 10, 9, 8, 7, 6, 5, 4, 3," "ignition," "2, 1," "lift-off." Yes, there are people involved in this sequence of tasks, but a launch sequence obviously requires complex orchestration of software tasks during the countdown— starting systems and verifying that they are functioning properly. This is workflow. The key thing to remember is that the workers may be people using a GUI, or an autonomous software process. The actual work order can be anything, from a request to approve a loan, to checking the status of a hardware register. Details about the nature of workers and work are not part of a core workflow model, which is what we are concerned with here. And now, let's proceed with the facet analysis by presenting the glossary of terms in this facet, followed by the list of workflow characteristics.

10.1.2 Glossary

task – processing that completes some portion of a service.

work order – request for a service to be performed.

worker – entity that is responsible for engaging in a specific type of task.

workflow – the act of performing a sequence of tasks to deliver a service.

workflow manager – entity that is responsible for assigning work orders to workers and passing such orders through the workflow.

workflow specification – description of the types of tasks that need to be performed and the order in which they must be performed in order to deliver a complete service.

10.1.3 Workflow Characteristics

1. A work order shall have a unique identifier.
2. Some work orders could be given a high priority.
3. Work orders shall be assigned to workers, based on any number of algorithms, including manual selection requiring an individual's judgment, FIFO selection, or any other algorithm that is specific to the problem domain.
4. A workflow specification shall allow for conditional execution of certain tasks and shall specify termination conditions.
5. It shall be possible to specify a workflow where multiple tasks can process the same work order simultaneously. There shall be a mechanism for synchronizing such tasks. Synchronization involves waiting for multiple tasks to complete before continuing the work order down the workflow route.
6. Multiple workers shall be able to perform the same type of task.

7. Upon completing a particular task, a worker shall notify the workflow manager.

8. It shall also be possible for workers to share one queue of incoming orders.

9. Workers shall request work when they become available to perform their given task.

10. Shall efficiently support a model of perpetual work, which presumes that workers are never idle.[1]

11. Shall efficiently support a model of bursty work, which presumes that workers will have idle periods. The worker shall be able to poll for new work or act in the capacity of observer to receive notification that there may be new work.

12. A work order shall be completed within a certain amount of time; otherwise, an alarm condition shall be raised. A task shall be completed within a certain amount of time; otherwise, an alarm condition shall be raised.

10.2 Design of the Workflow Framework

As you will see, this framework is heavily weighted with persistent classes, so its interface depends on the ODMG-93 API. I wanted to give the Workflow Framework its own `namespace`. Unfortunately, at the time of this writing `namespaces` were not officially supported by ODMG-93, although there was a statement of intent in the latest specification (see [ODMG93], pg 92). The names of the classes are such that it will be a trivial exercise to convert to a `namespace` called "Workflow" when this language feature is officially sanctioned and subsequently supported by object database vendors. I took the same approach as the OMG on this issue by saying that, in lieu of using `namespaces`, it is okay to prefix all class names with what would be the `namespace` name, followed by an underbar (_).

Starting on the following page, I formally present the design of the framework, using the design documentation template specified in Chapter 8.

---

1. This is the model of a very efficient, high-volume telemarketing operation or customer service hotline. Ideally, this would be the model of any operation, wouldn't it? If there are gaps of time when workers don't have work, then maybe you aren't allocating your work staff properly, or worse yet, you don't have any business.

Framework Name   Workflow

Framework Type   Horizontal

Requirements   Presented in section 10.1

Structure

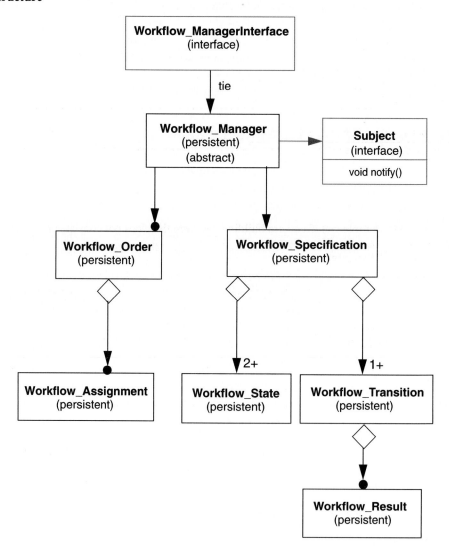

FIGURE 10-1.

Pattern Used	Role	Role Played By
CORBA-FRIENDLY CLASS	*Server*	Workflow_ManagerInterface
CORBA-FRIENDLY CLASS	*Server_i*	Workflow_Manager
INTERPRETER	*Interpreter*	Workflow_Specification
INTERPRETER	*Output*	Workflow_State
INTERPRETER	*Output*	Workflow_Transition
OBSERVER	*Subject*	Subject
OBSERVER	*Subject::notify()*	Subject::notify()
PERSISTENT DATA MANAGER	*DataManager*	Workflow_Manager
PERSISTENT DATA MANAGER	*Data*	Workflow_Order
SPECIFICATION-ENGINE	*Specification*	Workflow_Specification
SPECIFICATION-ENGINE	*Engine*	Workflow_Manager

Participants

- `Workflow_ManagerInterface`
  - May be relevant if you are building a system that does not consist entirely of C++ worker clients. The `Workflow_Manager` class was designed to be CORBA-FRIENDLY. It can be tied into this interface, so that the essential functions needed for entering an order and passing it through a workflow can be accessed via an ORB. So, you can use this framework with a Java client, for example. Unfortunately, you will not be able to access all the public member functions this way, because there is simply no way to promote the C++ types that are mapped to IDL to some of the ODMG-93 argument types, like `d_List`.

- `Subject`
  - Can be used for notification of changes in the state of work orders, should a particular application need this feature. Notice that the framework only participates in the OBSERVER pattern in the sense that it assumes the existence of a `Subject` interface that it can notify. The application will be responsible for providing classes to play the remaining roles in the OBSERVER pattern, which are well documented in the pattern description.

- `Workflow_Assignment`
  - Used to capture a worker's involvement with a particular work order.

- `Workflow_Manager`
  - Responsible for assigning work orders to workers and passing such orders through the workflow.

- `Workflow_Result`
  - Captures the results a worker returns when finished with a task involving a work order.

- `Workflow_Specification`
  - Description of the types of tasks that need to be performed and the order in which they must be performed to deliver a complete service.

- `Workflow_State`
  - Captures the state of a `Work_Order` in terms of the tasks that currently need to be performed on that order. An aggregation of `Workflow_State` objects comprises part of a `Workflow_Specification`.

- `Workflow_Transition`
  - Specifies the conditions that would result in moving a work order from one state to another. The conditions are based on results returned from workers when they have finished a work order. An aggregation of `Workflow_Transition` objects comprises part of a `Workflow_Specification`.

Collaborations

There are three primary usage scenarios:

1. Setting up a workflow specification (Figure 10-2)
2. Entering an order into a workflow (Figure 10-3)
3. Passing an order through a workflow (Figure 10-4)

Setting up a Workflow Specification[1]

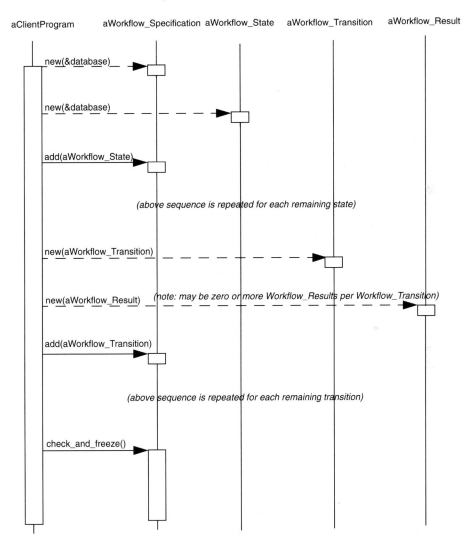

| aClientProgram | aWorkflow_Specification | aWorkflow_State | aWorkflow_Transition | aWorkflow_Result |

new(&database)

new(&database)

add(aWorkflow_State)

(above sequence is repeated for each remaining state)

new(aWorkflow_Transition)

new(aWorkflow_Result)   *(note: may be zero or more Workflow_Results per Workflow_Transition)*

add(aWorkflow_Transition)

(above sequence is repeated for each remaining transition)

check_and_freeze()

1. The program setting up the workflow in this way is responsible for beginning a database transaction before the scenario starts and committing it when the scenario is complete.

FIGURE 10-2.

Entering an Order into the Workflow

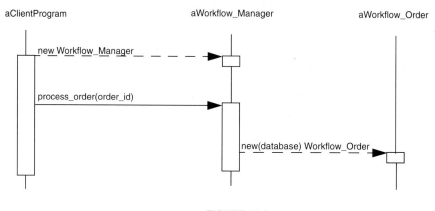

FIGURE 10-3.

Passing an Order Through a Workflow

(The following is repeated for an order for each transition it must go through)

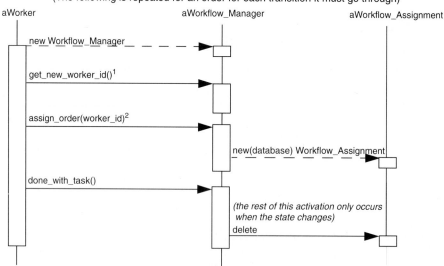

1. This only needs to be called if the worker does not yet have an ID.
2. Assume we are in manager-driven mode, so first version of assign_order is called.

FIGURE 10-4.

Design Details

Turning our attention to `Workflow.h` (Listing 10-1): you can see that the classes `Workflow_State` **1** , `Workflow_Result` **2** , and `Workflow_Transition` **3** are just data structures (see Listing 10-1.a.). They are used to specify how work orders should flow for a particular application.

```
    // Workflow.h

1  struct Workflow_State {
        Workflow_State();
        d_String            name;
        d_Set<d_String>     tasks;
        d_Interval          acceptable_duration;
    };

2  struct Workflow_Result {
        Workflow_Result();
        Workflow_Result(const d_String& task, const d_String& result);
        d_String    task;
        d_String    result;
    };

3  struct Workflow_Transition {
        Workflow_Transition();
        Workflow_Transition(const d_String& current_state,
            const d_String& next_state);
        d_String    current_state;
        d_String    next_state;
        d_List<d_Ref<Workflow_Result> > event;
    };
```

LISTING 10-1.a.

A `Workflow_State` is defined by the tasks that are simultaneously being performed on an order while it is in that state. Every state also has an acceptable duration of time, within which all of these tasks must be completed. `Workflow_Result` is just a helper class used by `Workflow_Transition`. It specifies an association between a task and the results of performing that task, which are assumed to be expressible in a string. A `Workflow_Transition` specifies the `event` that must occur to transition an order from a specific `current_state` to a specific `next_state`. A specific set of results returned by workers when tasks are completed comprise the `event`. If no `event` is specified, there will be an unconditional transition to `next_state` whenever all of the tasks associated with the `current_state` are complete. In other words, the results of the tasks are ignored.

The following is an example of a workflow transition: an order moved from the state "unpaid" to "paid" when someone "processing payments" "received payment" for the order. In this example, `current_state` is "unpaid," `next_state` is "paid," the one and only `task` for the `current_state` is "processing payments," and the `event` that will move the order to the "paid" state is when the person processing the payments returns a "received payment" indication (i.e., `result`).

The declaration of `Workflow_Specification` is shown in Listing 10-1.b. There can be one and only one such object in a particular database. The object must be named "Workflow_Specification." All `Workflow_Manager` objects will be looking for this object in the database they are assigned to use. This drives consistent behavior for all `Workflow_Managers` using the same database and prevents improper usage of the framework, which was designed with the intention that there will be only one workflow per database.

The class has two constructors. The first one **4** is used if you want to add states and transitions programmatically after construction. If the first constructor is used, you are expected to make a sequence of calls to add states and transitions **6** **7** , followed by a call that checks the validity of the specification and then freezes it if it is valid **8** . Among the things that `check_and_freeze` verifies is that there is at least one possible set of transitions from the starting state to the ending state. If the specification is not legal, an exception will be thrown.

The second constructor **5** should be used if you want to add all states and transitions to the specification at the time of instantiation. This constructor has a built-in INTERPRETER. It is designed to interpret a grammar that allows a user to specify workflow states and transitions between them. The one and only argument to the constructor is an ASCII string (i.e. *Input*) that is assumed to conform to this grammar. This constructor will be beneficial in situations when a number of simultaneous workflows are associated with a business, and/or the workflow specification changes quite frequently, and it is undesirable to have to recompile code for every change. You can simply keep the string in a file. Be forewarned, however, that specifications cannot be indiscriminately changed. The framework is not designed to support the evolution of a specification.

If the second constructor is used, the state of the object will be frozen at the time of construction. You have to remove the object and start over again if workflow behavior is to be modified. This design prevents a specification from changing after a `Workflow_Manager` has already started to use it, which could have unknown consequences to orders already in a workflow.

```
    // Workflow.h - continued

  class Workflow_Specification {
      friend class Workflow_Manager;
    public:

      // exception classes
      class InvalidStartingState {};
      class InvalidEndingState {};
      class InvalidState {};
      class InvalidEvent {};
      class DuplicateState {};
      class SpecAlreadyFrozen {};
      class NoPersistentShadow {};
      class InvalidSpecification {};

(4)   Workflow_Specification(const d_String& starting_state,
          const d_String& ending_state,
          const d_Interval& acceptable_duration);

(5)   Workflow_Specification(const d_String& ascii_spec);

(6)   void add(const d_Ref<Workflow_State>&);
(7)   void add(const d_Ref<Workflow_Transition>&);
(8)   void check_and_freeze();

    protected:
      const char* _next_possible_state(const d_String&) const;
      d_Ref<Workflow_State> _get_state(const d_String&) const;

      // persistent
      int frozen;
      d_List<d_Ref<Workflow_State> >  states;
      d_List<d_Ref<Workflow_Transition> >  transitions;
      d_String    starting_state;
      d_String    ending_state;
      d_Interval  acceptable_duration;
  };
```

LISTING 10-1.b.

The `Workflow_Assignment` (9) and `Workflow_Order` (10) classes are shown in
Listing 10-1.c. As you saw in Figure 10-1, they are used by the `Workflow_Manager`
class, along with `Workflow_Specification`. A `Workflow_Assignment` object
is instantiated at the point when a worker is assigned a specific order on which to perform
his/her/its task. It is deleted at the point when the order transitions into a different state. In
between, these objects are used by the `Workflow_Manager` to keep track of the
progress of an order and to use their contents to determine when a transition should occur.

Notice the done data member of Workflow_Assignment. This is a flag that is needed because a worker is not required to return a result, so you have no other way to tell if such a worker is finished with a task.

The Workflow_Order class is the abstraction of a work order. In other words, it contains only information about an order that is significant to workflow. This includes information that is invariant for the life of an order, like id, for example. It also includes dynamic information, like the last time the order changed state, the name of its current state, and the current Workflow_Assignments associated with the order.

```
    // Workflow.h - continued

 9  struct Workflow_Assignment {
        Workflow_Assignment();
        d_String   task;
        d_String   worker_id;
        d_String   result;
        int        done;
    };

10  struct Workflow_Order {
        Workflow_Order(const d_String& id,int urgent = 0);
        int          urgent;
        d_String     id;
        d_String     current_state;
        d_Timestamp  when_created;
        d_Timestamp  last_state_change;
        d_List<d_Ref<Workflow_Assignment> >   current_assignments;
    };
```

LISTING 10-1.c.

And now we get to the main workhorse of workflow: Workflow_Manager (see Listing 10-1.d and 10-1.e). This class contains the algorithms that handle assignment of work orders and transitioning them through their states. It is the *Engine* of the SPECIFICATION-ENGINE pattern employed as the primary structural pattern of the framework.

The Workflow_Manager class has one public constructor **11** . Its first argument is the name of the database that the object is expected to work with. As I mentioned earlier, there must be a frozen Workflow_Specification object named "Workflow_Specification" in this database; otherwise, a NoWorkflowSpecification exception will be thrown.

The manager_driven argument puts the Workflow_Manager object in either a manager-driven mode or a worker-driven mode, depending on whether you want the Workflow_Manager to select the next work order that a worker is to work on or allow the worker to choose an open order. The `get_orders_waiting` 🔟7️⃣ function gets a list of orders waiting for a task to be performed.

```
    // Workflow.h - continued

    class Workflow_Manager {
      public:
        // exception classes
        class  CantAssignOrder {};
        class  AssignmentViolation {};
        class  CantGetShadow {};
        class  IllegalWorkerId {};
        class  InvalidOrderId {};
        class  OrderStuckInState {};
        class  NoImplementation {};
        class  NoWorkflowSpecification {};
        class  DuplicateOrderId {};

        Workflow_Manager(const d_String& database_name,
                         int manager_driven = 0,
                         const char* notifier = 0);


        // The following five functions are CORBA-Friendly.
        virtual void process_order(const d_String& order_id,
                                   int urgent=0);
        virtual char* get_new_worker_id(const d_String& task);
        virtual char* assign_order(const d_String& worker_id);
        virtual void  assign_order(const d_String& order_id,
                                   const d_String& worker_id);
        virtual void done_with_task(const d_String& order_id,
                                    const d_String& worker_id,
                                    const d_String& task,
                                    const d_String& result);
        void get_orders_waiting(const d_String& task,d_List<d_String>&);
        void get_orders_assigned(const d_String& worker_id,
                                 d_List<d_String>& order_ids) const;


        // returns orders changed in interval
        void get_recent_changes(d_Interval, d_List<d_String>&);
        Workflow_Order get_order(d_String order_id) const; // used by GUI
        virtual void check_for_alarms();

    // declaration of Workflow_Manager continued in next listing block
```

// declaration of Workflow_Manager continued in next listing block

LISTING 10-1.d.

```
   // Workflow.h - continued

   // declaration of Workflow_Manager continued

    protected:
22     Workflow_Manager();
23     virtual char* _new_worker_id() const;
24     virtual void _state_changed(const d_String& order_id,
                                   const d_String& state_name);
       virtual void _notify_observers();
       d_Ref<Workflow_Manager> _get_shadow() const;
       void _get_task(const d_String& worker_id,
                    d_Ref<Workflow_Manager> shadow, d_String& task);
       int _get_open_assignment(const d_String& task,
                             const d_Ref<Workflow_Order>& order);
       int _state_needs_task(const d_String& state_name,
                           const d_String& task);
       int _is_state_complete(const d_Ref<Workflow_Order>& order);
       int _event_satisfied(
            const d_List<d_Ref<Workflow_Result> >& transtn_conditions,
            const d_List<d_Ref<Workflow_Assignment> >& current_conds);
           void _remove_order(const d_String& order_id);

       // transient data elements, will be stored, but not
       // used from shadow.
       d_Ref<Workflow_Specification> spec;
       int          manager_driven;
       d_String     database_name;
       d_Database* database;
       d_String     notifier;    // string of ref to Subject.

       // persistent data elements, kept in shadow,
       // and only accessed from shadow. In transient
       // instance of Workflow_Manager, these members
       // are dummies.
25     d_List<d_Ref<Workflow_Order> > all_orders;
26     d_List<d_String> worker_ids; // mapped by index to tasks
27     d_List<d_String> tasks;
   };
```

LISTING 10-1.e.

The third constructor argument, `notifier`, is a string that can be converted into a reference to a `Subject` (see OBSERVER pattern), designated as the distributer of workflow-related events. This explains the appearance of the `Subject` interface on the class diagram (Figure 10-1). The `Workflow_Manager` will call the `Subject`'s `notify` function whenever a new order is added to the workflow or whenever an order that is already in the workflow changes state. Any object interested in this information can attach to that `Subject` and will have its `update` function called when the `Workflow_Manager` notifies the `Subject`. The implementation of the `Subject` can change with no impact on the implementation of the Workflow Framework. In fact, the implementation of the `Subject` can change while the Workflow Framework is in operation. If a `notifier` is not specified, a perpetual or polling model is assumed.

When an order needs to be put into a workflow, the `process_order` function ⑫ is invoked. At this time, a new `Workflow_Order` object is put in the database, and a reference to it is added to `Workflow_Manager::all_orders` ㉕, which is the extent of all such objects. Unless the `urgent` argument is set to 1, the order is put at the end of this list, which means it will be the last one processed. On the other hand, if `urgent` is set to 1, the order will be put at the head of the list and will be the next one processed. If this strategy is not suitable to a particular domain, the behavior can be overridden, being that this is a virtual function.

It is a worker's responsibility to request work. This is a key concept. The `Workflow_Manager` object is truly a server, waiting for requests from worker clients. The first time a worker enters a workflow, that worker must obtain an ID by calling the `get_new_worker_id` function ⑬, which will select a unique ID for that worker and register the worker as being able to perform the task specified in the argument passed. This function is not completely implemented. The class derived from `Workflow_Manager` must provide an implementation of `_new_worker_id` ㉓ with the ID selection algorithm.

Once a worker has an ID, there are two functions for getting work assigned ⑭ ⑮. If the `Workflow_Manager` being used is manager driven, the worker will not be able to select a work order. In other words, only the first version of `assign` ⑭ can be called, which returns the `id` of the newly assigned order, or a null string if there is no work. If the application tries to call the other ⑮, where an order id is specified as an input argument, an exception is thrown.

When a `Workflow_Manager` is not being used in manager-driven mode, this doesn't imply a free-for-all, where workers can pick whatever they want to work on. It just means that more responsibility is placed on the designers of the client worker programs. For example, consider a typical repair service workflow, where technicians are dispatched to the field to repair equipment. Most of the office tasks involved in the workflow, like generating the trouble ticket and the billing, can be handled by simply doling out work in a FIFO fashion as the workers free up for the next assignment. But, consider the service technicians. When a technician finishes a task, the most efficient way to give him the next assignment is to make it the one that is closest to his current location, perhaps without regard for the sequence in which the service requests are received. In this case, a worker program, which is outside of the workflow framework and knows the details of the application, can query a `Workflow_Manager` for all orders where a service call has not been made, then go to the database containing the details of the orders, including location.

Remember, these details are domain specific (service repair domain) and, therefore, not handled by the framework. After finding the closest open service request, the worker program assigns the associated order to itself.

This "worker-driven" mode is equally applicable to the task of paying bills. Someone is sitting in a billing department, opening payment envelopes from customers. Obviously, the people doing this must tell the `Workflow_Manager` what order they are working on for the "process payment" task. The second `assign_order()` function **15**, used in conjunction with the `get_orders_waiting()` **17** function, satisfies this requirement, placing the remaining logic in the worker program.

All workers are obliged to call `done_with_task` **16** when they are finished processing an order and to pass the results of their processing back to the `Workflow_Manager`, so that it can decide what to do next with the order.

Moving down the public section, you will see a suite of query functions **17** **18** **19** **20** that will be useful for applications that are not entirely manager driven. The `get_order` function would certainly be useful to a GUI client for displaying order information.

The `check_for_alarms` function **21** will check for orders that have been in one state too long or have not gone from a starting state to an ending state within an acceptable duration.

I'm not going to discuss many of the protected functions shown in the declaration, but you will see their implementations a little later. There are a few key points that need to be made about protected data and functions. First, notice the default constructor **22**. This is needed to construct the persistent shadow.

The `_new_worker_id` **23** and `_state_changed` **24** functions must be overridden in a derived class. A function body is provided for each in `Workflow_Manager`, because the framework must be able instantiate a `Workflow_Manager` shadow to store state information. But, if you instantiate and use a `Workflow_Manager` object directly, you would soon get an exception because both of these functions throw a `NoImplementation` exception. I discussed `_new_worker_id` earlier, but what's `_state_changed` supposed to do? It gets called after every state transition. This function is just another hook: potentially an alternative to using a `Subject` for event notification. You can make it do whatever you like, from logging the state transition to actually instantiating a new worker object that would immediately invoke the `Workflow_Manager` and find new work.

Regarding persistent data elements: Remember, all `Workflow_Managers` are actually working with the state of the same persistent shadow. The three data members of the shadow that are shared are the list of all orders **25**, all worker ids **26**, and their associated tasks **27**.

Although the preferred mode of framework usage is to directly instantiate a
`Workflow_Manager` object inside your C++ program, I made the
`Workflow_Manager` class CORBA-FRIENDLY, to the extent that a client can call a
subset of `Workflow_Manager` functions via an ORB, using the
`Workflow_ManagerInterface` interface, which is shown below. All IDL `strings`
will be promoted to `d_String` when the corresponding `Workflow_Manager` function
is called via the tie object. Notice that the overloaded
`Workflow_Manager::assign_order()` functions had to be named differently in
the interface because of IDL limitations. We are not going to discuss this interface any
further in this chapter, focusing instead on using the framework via regular C++ objects.

```
//
// Workflow_ManagerInterface.idl

interface Workflow_ManagerInterface {
  string get_new_worker_id(in string task);
  string assign_order1(in string worker_id);
  void    assign_order2(in string order_id, in string worker_id);
  void    process_order(in string order_id,in short urgent);
  void done_with_task(in string order_id,
                      in string worker_id,
                      in string task,
                      in string result);
};
```

Requirements Verification

	Workflow characteristic	**How the framework supports characteristic**
1	A work order shall have a unique identifier.	`Workflow_Order` has an id field.
2	Some work orders could be given a high priority.	`Workflow_Manager::process_order()` has an argument that designates an order as urgent. Any order entered into a workflow with this argument set is put at the top of the queue.
3	Work orders shall be assigned to workers, based on any number of algorithms, including manual selection requiring an individual's judgment, FIFO selection, or any other algorithm that is specific to the problem domain.	The member functions of `Workflow_Manager` directly support manual selection by a worker or FIFO selection by the `Workflow_Manager`. Other algorithms can be formulated, utilizing the query functions in a non-manager-driven mode or providing different implementations of the `assign_order` functions.

	Workflow characteristic	**How the framework supports characteristic**
4	A workflow specification shall allow for conditional execution of certain tasks and shall specify termination conditions.	By defining multiple `Workflow_Transitions` with the same `current_state` but different `next_state` and `event`, you have specified multiple paths through a workflow and, hence, conditional execution of certain tasks. Termination conditions are specified by having one or more `Workflow_Transitions` with the `next_state` equal to the `ending_state` of the `Workflow_Specification`.
5	It shall be possible to specify a workflow where multiple tasks can process the same work order simultaneously. There shall be a mechanism for synchronizing such tasks. Synchronization involves waiting for multiple tasks to complete before continuing the work order down the workflow route.	`Workflow_Order` contains a list of `current_assignments`, not just one. This makes it possible for multiple tasks to be tracked simultaneously to the same order. Indeed, the algorithms in `Workflow_Manager` assume just that and will not transition an order from one state to another until all currently assigned tasks are done.
6	Multiple workers shall be able to perform the same type of task.	`Workflow_Manager` does not constrain the number of workers allowed to perform the same type of task.
7	Upon completing a particular task, a worker shall notify the workflow manager.	`Workflow_Manager::done_with_task()` is provided as a public member function for this purpose.
8	It shall also be possible for workers to share one queue of incoming orders.	`Workflow_Manager::all_orders` will contain all orders entered into a workflow. All workers in that workflow draw from this indirectly via the `Workflow_Manager::assign_order` functions, so this is actually a shared queue.
9	Workers shall request work when they become available to perform their given task.	`Workflow_Manager::assign_order` functions support this.
10	The framework shall efficiently support a model of perpetual work, which presumes that workers are never idle.	In a model of perpetual work, the presumption is that once a worker gets into a workflow, he/she/it will always have something to work on, so that after one work order has been processed, he/she/it will make a function call to get another piece of work, and off they go without a break. The `Workflow_Manager::assign_order` functions support this.

	Workflow characteristic	How the framework supports characteristic
11	The framework shall efficiently support a model of bursty work, which presumes that workers will have idle periods. The worker shall be able to poll for new work or act in the capacity of observer to receive notification that there may be new work.	In the less than ideal environment, where work load is bursty, you can easily use this framework. For small businesses, you could write the application such that workers poll, which, in the situation where the worker is a human, may not be too inefficient because the polling interval could be on the order of seconds. But these days, most designers cringe at the thought of designing an application that polls. If you have a small operation, I don't see the problem. But I certainly see the potential for problems when we are talking about systems that may have thousands of simultaneous workers. In such cases, you can use the framework's built-in event notification mechanism, which employs the OBSERVER pattern. When a worker runs out of work, he/she/it can simply `attach` to the designated `Subject` and then `detach` and check for new work when its `update` function is called. If there is still no work for the worker, he/she/it can just `attach` and wait again.
12	A work order shall be completed within a certain amount of time: otherwise, an alarm condition shall be raised. A task shall be completed within a certain amount of time: otherwise, an alarm condition shall be raised.	Acceptable durations for both a task and the total length of time it takes an order to get through a workflow can be specified when setting up a `Workflow_Specification`. The `Workflow_Manager::check_for_alarms` function can be called to check for tasks and orders that are taking too long, based on the specification.

Sample Code and Usage

The only two classes in the framework that have algorithmic substance to them are `Workflow_Specification` and `Workflow_Manager`. Of the two, only `Workflow_Manager` is abstract, so the user of this framework need only derive a class from `Workflow_Manager`, provide implementations for two virtual member functions, and then be off and running. `Workflow_Order` is abstract, providing only information that is significant to workflow. Object Splitting should be employed to associate domain-specific information with an order.

In the next section, when we discuss implementation, I will show how to extend this framework for a hypothetical mail order operation.

Known Uses

Insurance claim processing, fixed-income derivatives trading, mail order.

Dependencies

ODMG-93 and CORBA

10.3 Implementation of the Workflow Framework

I am obliged to show you at least some aspects of the implementation of this framework, and I feel the best way to do this is in the context of a specific domain. I will do this by showing how it might by applied in a mail order catalog operation. The first thing we need to do is derive a class from `Workflow_Manager`; I'll call it `Catalog_Workflow_Manager`. This new derived class will provide implementations of the `_new_worker_id` and `_state_changed` functions. We also need to figure out what a workflow might "look" like in a catalog operation.

If you study the domain analysis presented in Chapter 5, you'll see there are actually a couple of different workflows: one on the sales side and one on the inventory management side. The state transition diagram shown in Figure 10-5 approximates the one on the sales side, which is what we will focus on. The names of the states are shown on top of the bubbles. The tasks performed on an order while it is in a given state are shown inside the bubbles. Result strings leading to a transition are shown on a transition arrow, in italics.

Now we are ready to present usage scenarios and the relevant pieces of the framework that implement them. At this point, you are probably as sick of reading code narration as I am of writing it, but I want you to see some of the coding idioms and rules applied in the implementation of a real framework. I have included listings that show much of the code that gets executed for the three primary scenarios that occur when this framework is used: 1) setting up a workflow specification,[2] 2) entering an order into the workflow, and 3) passing an order through the workflow. These three scenarios are depicted in the object interaction diagrams shown in Figure 10-6, Figure 10-7, and Figure 10-8, respectively. These diagrams are supplemented with the numbers of the listings containing the code that gets executed for each request arrow, so you can trace through the code that is executing as the scenario progresses. As you are tracing through the code, notice the tremendous amount of iteration that is done, using `d_Iterator`. I'd be in big trouble trying to implement this framework without it.

---

2. I show this done programmatically as opposed to using the ASCII interpreter.

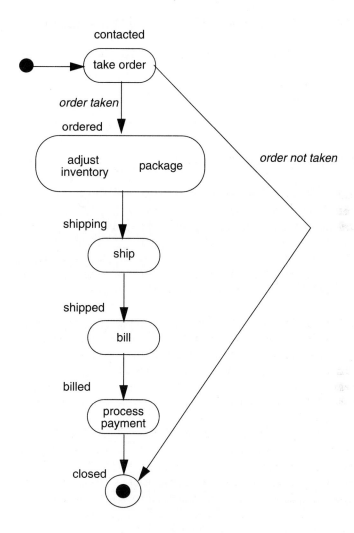

FIGURE 10-5.

Setting up a Workflow Specification[1]

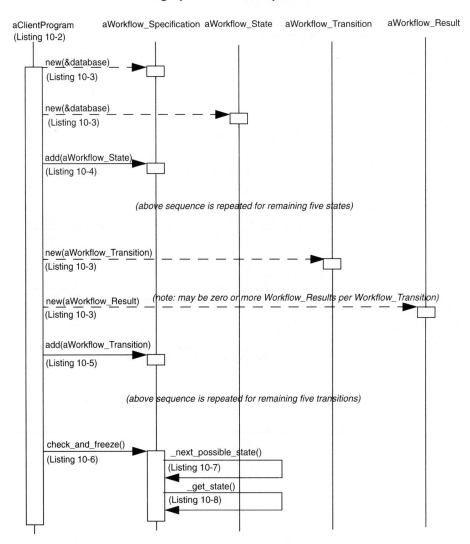

1. The program setting up the workflow in this way is responsible for beginning a database transaction before the scenario starts and committing it when the scenario is complete.

FIGURE 10-6.

Entering an Order into the Workflow

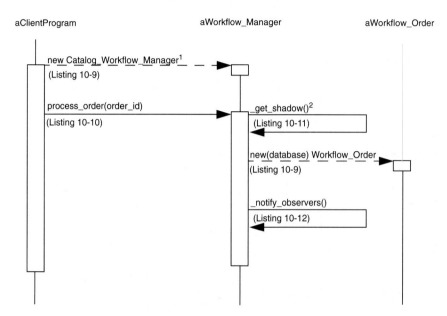

1. Even though a Catalog_Workflow_Manager is instantiated, we are only concerned with the implementation of the base class Workflow_Manager. The scenario will, therefore, focus on the base class perspective.
2. The first time this function is called, the shadow is instantiated by use of the protected default constructor, which doesn't contain any logic.

FIGURE 10-7.

Passing an Order Through the Workflow
(The following is repeated until an order goes from "contacted" to "closed")

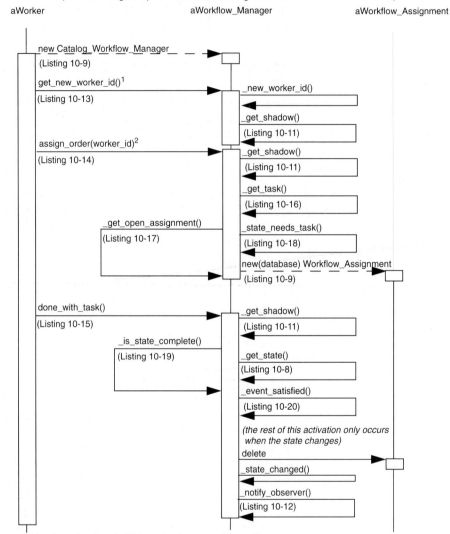

1. This only needs to be called if the worker does not yet have an ID.
2. Assume we are in manager-driven mode, so first version of assign_order is called.

FIGURE 10-8.

```
#include "Workflow.h"
int
main(int argc, char* argv[])
{
// database-specific initialization
d_Database database;
database.open("catalog_workflow");
d_Transaction t;
t.begin();

d_Interval i;
d_Ref<Workflow_Specification> spec =
  new(&database) Workflow_Specification("contacted","closed",i);
database.set_object_name((d_Ref_Any&)spec,"Workflow_Specification");

d_Ref<Workflow_State> state1 = new(&database) Workflow_State;
state1->name = "contacted";
state1->tasks.insert_element("take order");
state1->acceptable_duration = d_Interval(0,1); // one hour
spec->add(state1);

d_Ref<Workflow_State> state2 = new(&database) Workflow_State;
state2->name = "ordered";
state2->tasks.insert_element("adjust inventory");
state2->tasks.insert_element("package");
state2->acceptable_duration = d_Interval(5); // three days
spec->add(state2);

d_Ref<Workflow_State> state3 = new(&database) Workflow_State;
state3->name = "shipping";
state3->tasks.insert_element("ship");
state3->acceptable_duration = d_Interval(1); // one day;
spec->add(state3);

d_Ref<Workflow_State> state4 = new(&database) Workflow_State;
state4->name = "shipped";
state4->tasks.insert_element("bill");
state4->acceptable_duration = d_Interval(1);
spec->add(state4);

d_Ref<Workflow_State> state5 = new(&database) Workflow_State;
state5->name = "billed";
state5->tasks.insert_element("process payment");
state5->acceptable_duration = d_Interval(30); // 30 days
spec->add(state5);
```

LISTING 10-2.a.

```
    d_Ref<Workflow_State> state6 = new(&database) Workflow_State;
    state6->name = "closed";
    spec->add(state6);

    d_Ref<Workflow_Transition> t1 =
        new(&database) Workflow_Transition("contacted","ordered");
    d_Ref<Workflow_Result> r1 =
        new(&database) Workflow_Result("take order","order taken");
    t1->event.insert_element(r1);
    spec->add(t1);

    d_Ref<Workflow_Transition> t2 =
        new(&database) Workflow_Transition("contacted","closed");
    d_Ref<Workflow_Result> r2 =
        new(&database) Workflow_Result("take order","order not taken");
    t2->event.insert_element(r2);
    spec->add(t2);

    // the following are unconditional transitions that take
    // place automatically when all tasks in the state are complete

    d_Ref<Workflow_Transition> t3 =
        new(&database) Workflow_Transition("ordered","shipping");
    spec->add(t3);

    d_Ref<Workflow_Transition> t4 =
        new(&database) Workflow_Transition("shipping","shipped");
    spec->add(t4);

    d_Ref<Workflow_Transition> t5 =
        new(&database) Workflow_Transition("shipped","billed");
    spec->add(t5);

    d_Ref<Workflow_Transition> t6 =
        new(&database) Workflow_Transition("billed","closed");
    spec->add(t6);

    spec->check_and_freeze();

    t.commit();
    database.close();

    // database-specific clean-up

    }
```

LISTING 10-2.b.

```
Workflow_State::Workflow_State()
{
}

Workflow_Result::Workflow_Result()
{
}

Workflow_Result::Workflow_Result(const d_String& t,
        const d_String& r) : task(t), result(r)
{
}

Workflow_Transition::Workflow_Transition()
{
}

Workflow_Transition::Workflow_Transition(const d_String& cs,
        const d_String& ns) : current_state(cs), next_state(ns)
{
}

Workflow_Specification::Workflow_Specification(
        const d_String& s, const d_String& e, const d_Interval& a) :
        starting_state(s), ending_state(e),
        acceptable_duration(a), frozen(0)
{
    if(starting_state.length() == 0)
    {
        cerr << "Invalid Starting State: NULL " << endl;
        throw InvalidStartingState();
    }
    if(ending_state.length() == 0)
    {
        cerr << "Invalid Ending State: NULL " << endl;
        throw InvalidEndingState();
    }
}
```

LISTING 10-3.

```
void
Workflow_Specification::add(const d_Ref<Workflow_State>& new_state)
{
    if(frozen)
    {
        cerr << "Spec Already Frozen" << endl;
        throw SpecAlreadyFrozen();
    }

    for(int i = 0; i < states.cardinality() ; i++)
    {
        if(states[i]->name == new_state->name)
        {
            cerr << "Duplicate State" << endl;
            throw DuplicateState();
        }
    }

    states.insert_element(new_state);
    states.mark_modified();
}
```

LISTING 10-4.

```
void
Workflow_Specification::add(const d_Ref<Workflow_Transition>& tsn)
{
    if(frozen)
    {
        cerr << "Spec Already Frozen" << endl;
        throw SpecAlreadyFrozen();
    }

    transitions.insert_element(tsn);
    transitions.mark_modified();
}
```

LISTING 10-5.

```
void
Workflow_Specification::check_and_freeze()
{
    if(frozen)
    {
        throw SpecAlreadyFrozen();
    }

    // Make sure there is a path between starting and ending state.
    const char* s = starting_state;
    while(s = _next_possible_state(s))
    {
        if(ending_state == s)
        {
            break;
        }
    }
    if(s == 0)
    {
        throw InvalidSpecification();
    }

    // Make sure each state has non-null name & at least one task.
    d_Iterator<d_Ref<Workflow_State> > iter1 =
        states.create_iterator();
    d_Ref<Workflow_State> a_state;
    while(iter1.next(a_state))
    {
        if(a_state->name.length() == 0 ||
        (a_state->tasks.is_empty() && a_state->name!= ending_state))
        {
            throw InvalidState();
        }
        d_Iterator<d_String> iter2 =
            a_state->tasks.create_iterator();
        d_String a_task;
        while(iter2.next(a_task))
        {
            if(a_task.length() == 0)
            {
                throw InvalidState();
            }
        }
    }
}
```

LISTING 10-6.a.

```
// check_and_freeze - continued.

    // make sure each transition specifies a current_state
    // that exists in states & an ending_state that exists in states.
    d_Iterator<d_Ref<Workflow_Transition> > iter3
        = transitions.create_iterator();
    d_Ref<Workflow_Transition> a_transition;
    while(iter3.next(a_transition))
    {
        d_Ref<Workflow_State> c_state=
            _get_state(a_transition >current_state);

        // make sure transition event only involves
        // tasks that are legal for the current_state.
        d_Iterator<d_Ref<Workflow_Result> > iter4 =
        a_transition->event.create_iterator();
        d_Ref<Workflow_Result> r;
        d_Set<d_String> tasks;
        while(iter4.next(r))
        {
            tasks.insert_element(r->task);
        }
        if(!tasks.is_subset_of(c_state->tasks))
        {
            throw InvalidEvent();
        }
        // verifies that next state is legit.
        _get_state(a_transition->next_state);
    }

    frozen++;
    this->mark_modified();
}
```

LISTING 10-6.b.

```
const char*
Workflow_Specification::_next_possible_state(const d_String& s)
const
{
    const char* next_state = 0;
    d_Iterator<d_Ref<Workflow_Transition> > iter =
        transitions.create_iterator();
    d_Ref<Workflow_Transition> a_transition;
    while(iter.next(a_transition))
    {
        if(a_transition->current_state == s)
        {
            next_state = a_transition->next_state;
        }
    }
    return next_state;
}
```

LISTING 10-7.

```
d_Ref<Workflow_State>
Workflow_Specification::_get_state(const d_String& name) const
{
    d_Iterator<d_Ref<Workflow_State> > iter =
        states.create_iterator();
    d_Ref<Workflow_State> a_state;
    while(iter.next(a_state))
    {
        if(a_state->name == name)
        {
            return a_state;
        }
    }
    throw InvalidState();
    return a_state;// never gets here, but won't compile without
}
```

LISTING 10-8.

```
Workflow_Assignment::Workflow_Assignment() : done(0)
{
}

Workflow_Order::Workflow_Order(const d_String& i,int u) :
id(i), urgent(u)
{
    when_created = d_Timestamp::current();
    last_state_change = when_created;
}

Workflow_Manager::Workflow_Manager(const d_String& d, int m,
  const char* n) : database_name(d), manager_driven(m)
{
    if(n)
    {
        notifier = n;
    }
    database = new d_Database;
    database->open(database_name);
}
```

LISTING 10-9.

```
void
Workflow_Manager::process_order(const d_String& order_id,
              int urgent)
{
    d_Transaction t;
    t.begin();
    d_Ref<Workflow_Manager> shadow = _get_shadow();
    d_Ref<Workflow_Order> order =
        new(database) Workflow_Order(order_id,urgent);
    order->current_state = shadow->spec->starting_state;
    d_Timestamp now = d_Timestamp::current();
    order->when_created = now;
    order->last_state_change = now;

    // make sure order id doesn't already exist
    for(int i = 0; i < shadow->all_orders.cardinality(); i++)
    {
        if(shadow->all_orders[i]->id == order_id)
        {
            throw DuplicateOrderId();
        }
    }

    if(urgent)
    {
        shadow->all_orders.insert_element_first(order);
    }
    else
    {
        shadow->all_orders.insert_element_last(order);
    }
    shadow->mark_modified;
    t.commit();
    _notify_observers();
}
```

LISTING 10-10.

```
d_Ref<Workflow_Manager>
Workflow_Manager::_get_shadow() const
{
    d_Transaction t;
    t.begin();
    d_Ref<Workflow_Manager> shadow;
    d_Ref<Workflow_Specification> spec_ref;
    if((shadow = database->lookup_object("Workflow_Manager"))
        == NULL)
    {
        shadow = new(database) Workflow_Manager;
        database->set_object_name((d_Ref_Any&)shadow,
            "Workflow_Manager");
        if(((spec_ref =
            database->lookup_object("Workflow_Specification"))
            == NULL) || !spec_ref->frozen)
        {
            throw NoWorkflowSpecification();
        }
        shadow->spec = spec_ref;
        shadow->mark_modified();
    }
    t.commit();
    return shadow;
}
```

LISTING 10-11.

```
void
Workflow_Manager::_notify_observers()
{
    if(notifier.length()
    {
    Subject_var subject = CORBA::ORB::string_to_object(notifier);
    subject->notify();
    }
}
```

LISTING 10-12.

```
char*
Workflow_Manager::get_new_worker_id(const d_String& task)
{
    char* new_id = _new_worker_id();
    d_Transaction t;
    t.begin();
    d_Ref<Workflow_Manager> shadow = _get_shadow();
    shadow->worker_ids.insert_element_last(new_id);
    shadow->tasks.insert_element_last(task);
    t.commit();
    return new_id;
}
```

LISTING 10-13.

```
char*
Workflow_Manager::assign_order(const d_String& worker_id)
{
    char* order_id = new[bufSize];
    order_id[0] = '\0';
    d_Transaction t;
    t.begin();
    d_Ref<Workflow_Manager> shadow = _get_shadow();
    d_String task;
    _get_task(worker_id, shadow, task);
    for(int i = 0;i < shadow->all_orders.cardinality(); i++)
    {
        int j;
        if(shadow->all_orders[i]->current_state !=
            shadow->spec->ending_state &&
            (j=_get_open_assignment(task,shadow->all_orders[i]))!=-1)
        {
            shadow->all_orders[i]->current_assignments[j]->worker_id
             = worker_id;
            shadow->mark_modified();
            strncpy(order_id,shadow->all_orders[i]->id, bufSize);
            break;
        }
    }
    t.commit();
    return order_id;
}
```

LISTING 10-14.

```
void
Workflow_Manager::done_with_task(const d_String& order_id,
    const d_String& worker_id,const d_String& task,
    const d_String& result)
{
    d_String new_state;
    int notify_flag = 0;
    d_Transaction t;
    t.begin();
    d_Ref<Workflow_Manager> shadow = _get_shadow();
    for(int i = 0; i < shadow->all_orders.cardinality(); i++)
    {
      if(shadow->all_orders[i]->id == order_id)
      {
        int found_assignment = 0;
        int j = 0;
        d_Iterator<d_Ref<Workflow_Assignment> > iter1 =
        shadow->all_orders[i]->current_assignments.create_iterator();
        d_Ref<Workflow_Assignment> a;
        while(iter1.next(a))
        {
          if(a->worker_id == worker_id && a->task == task)
          {
            found_assignment++;
          shadow->all_orders[i]->current_assignments[j]->result =
                result;
            shadow->all_orders[i]->current_assignments[j]->done++;
            break;
          }
          j++;
        }
        if(found_assignment == 0)
        {
            throw AssignmentViolation();
        }
```

LISTING 10-15.a.

```
    // done_with_task - continued.

if(_is_state_complete(shadow->all_orders[i]))
{
  d_Iterator<d_Ref<Workflow_Transition> > iter2 =
     shadow->spec->transitions.create_iterator();
  d_Ref<Workflow_Transition> wt;
  while(iter2.next(wt))
  {
     // change state of order if the event conditions
     // have been satisfied for any transition specified
     // in spec.
    if((wt->current_state == shadow->all_orders[i]->current_state)
       && _event_satisfied(wt->event,
                       shadow->all_orders[i]->current_assignments))
    {
      shadow->all_orders[i]->current_state = wt->next_state;
      new_state = wt->next_state;
      shadow->all_orders[i]->last_state_change =
          d_Timestamp::current();
      shadow->all_orders[i]->current_assignments.remove_all();
      shadow->mark_modified();
      notify_flag++;
      break;
    }
  }
  if(!notify_flag)
  {
    throw OrderStuckInState();
  }
}
}
}
t.commit();
if(notify_flag)
{
  _state_changed(order_id,new_state);
  _notify_observers();
}
}
```

LISTING 10-15.b.

```
void
Workflow_Manager::_get_task(const d_String& worker_id,
  d_Ref<Workflow_Manager> shadow,d_String& task)
{
    for(int i = 0;i < shadow->worker_ids.cardinality(); i++)
    {
        if(worker_id == shadow->worker_ids[i])
        {
            task = shadow->tasks[i];
            return;
        }
    }
    throw IllegalWorkerId();
    return ;
}
```

LISTING 10-16.

```
int Workflow_Manager::_get_open_assignment(const d_String& task,
 const d_Ref<Workflow_Order>& order)
{
    if(_state_needs_task(order->current_state,task))
    {
        int current_index = 0;
        d_Iterator<d_Ref<Workflow_Assignment> > iter
            = order->current_assignments.create_iterator();
        d_Ref<Workflow_Assignment> a;
        while(iter.next(a))
        {
            if(a->task == task)
            {
                return -1;
            }
            else
            {
                current_index++;
            }
        }
        d_Ref<Workflow_Assignment> new_assignment =
            new(database) Workflow_Assignment;
        new_assignment->task = task;
      order->current_assignments.insert_element_last(new_assignment);
        return (order->current_assignments.cardinality()-1);
    }
    return -1;
}
```

LISTING 10-17.

```
int
Workflow_Manager::_state_needs_task(const d_String& state_name,
const d_String& task)
{
    d_Ref<Workflow_Manager> shadow = _get_shadow();
    d_Iterator<d_Ref<Workflow_State> > iter1 =
        shadow->spec->states.create_iterator();
    d_Ref<Workflow_State> s;
    while(iter1.next(s))
    {
        if(s->name == state_name)
        {
            d_Iterator<d_String> iter2 =
                s->tasks.create_iterator();
            d_String t;
            while(iter2.next(t))
            {
                if(t == task)
                {
                    return 1;
                }
            }
        }
    }
    return 0;
}
```

LISTING 10-18.

```
int
Workflow_Manager::_is_state_complete(const d_Ref<Workflow_Order>&
order)
{
    d_Ref<Workflow_Manager> shadow = _get_shadow();
    d_Ref<Workflow_State> state =
        shadow->spec->_get_state(order->current_state);
    if(order->current_assignments.cardinality() <
            state->tasks.cardinality())
    {
        return 0;
    }
    d_Iterator<d_Ref<Workflow_Assignment> > iter =
            order->current_assignments.create_iterator();
    d_Ref<Workflow_Assignment> a;
    while(iter.next(a))
    {
        if(!a->done)
        {
            return 0;
        }
    }
    return 1;
}
```

LISTING 10-19.

```
int
Workflow_Manager::_event_satisfied(const
d_List<d_Ref<Workflow_Result> >& transition_conditions,
const d_List<d_Ref<Workflow_Assignment> >& current_conditions)
{
    d_Iterator<d_Ref<Workflow_Result> > iter1 =
        transition_conditions.create_iterator();
    d_Iterator<d_Ref<Workflow_Assignment> > iter2 =
        current_conditions.create_iterator();
    d_Ref<Workflow_Result> r;
    d_Ref<Workflow_Assignment> a;
    int satisfied = 1;
    while(iter1.next(r))
    {
        satisfied = 0;
        while(iter2.next(a))
        {
            if(r->task == a->task && r->result == a->result)
            {
                satisfied++;
                break;
            }
        }
        if(!satisfied)
        {
            break; // A transition condition was not satisfied.
        }
    }
    return satisfied;
}
```

LISTING 10-20.

CHAPTER 11
A Framework for Monitoring Financial Risk

In this chapter, we are going to attack a very complex domain, starting with a domain analysis and evolving the analysis into a framework design. Not all of the design details, and little of the implementation, will be presented. Otherwise, this would end up being a book in itself. What I hope you get out of reading this chapter is a better understanding of how to partition a complex domain into a manageable set of facets and a vertical framework.

In layperson's terms, a *financial risk* is a possibility that something will happen that negatively affects certain investments. Risk monitoring systems are supposed to identify such risks before they become reality. If you are aware of an excessive risk in your investments, there are strategies for reducing or removing it.

Such systems have been around for years in large financial institutions, but they have been very localized to one trader's portfolio or positions in one type of instrument (e.g., stock). It is only recently that firms are attempting to normalize and aggregate different types of risk and calculate them at a firm-wide level.

Much publicized incidents of terrible risk management have prompted considerable interest in such capabilities, both from within the financial institutions incurring the risk and watchdog government agencies. Do you remember when Barings PLC, a very old and respected financial institution, went bankrupt? It was caused by one trader's highly risky investment activity that went undetected until it was too late. How about the Orange County California bankruptcy fiasco? Brokers recommended and sold very risky derivatives to the County. The treasurer did not have the background to see just how risky the investments were, and there was no automated way for him, or his superiors, to assess and monitor the risks. Quite a coincidence that this is Chapter 11, don't you think?

Having the ability to monitor risk at a firm-wide level, in real time, is the most desired state of operation. However, I don't know of any institution that is able to do this yet. One of the reasons is that most firms still use batch systems, so the current set of all investments that a firm has at a given instant is not in one system. Sometimes it takes days to collect all of the firm's position information into one place. Another reason that real-time risk monitoring is rare is because calculating risk can be very cpu intensive. Increasing cpu power and client/server architecture are reducing this second problem.

We are going to focus on the domain of monitoring risk, rather than the specific problem of how to actually calculate it. There is a very significant difference. Calculating risk can involve extremely complex calculations that can vary from firm to firm. The monitoring domain, on the other hand, is concerned with supporting the problem of calculating risk. Given that a firm has figured out the calculations that will be used to determine the risk of individual investments, the monitoring domain supports the goals of:

- Triggering recalculations when necessary
- Aggregating the risk associated with the investment positions comprising a firm's portfolio
- Being able to "drill down" into the risk numbers, looking at them from a variety of views

Let's start with the domain analysis. There is a significant amount of background discussion that I felt was necessary because of the domain's complexity. I wanted to make sure that you understand it well enough so that when I discuss the design, you will be able to see the rationale behind the design decisions made. This is such a rich example of how design patterns can be applied, I hope you enjoy it.

11.1 Domain Analysis: Financial Risk Monitoring

11.1.1 Background Discussion

Different Types of Financial Risk

Some financial risks are pretty easy to understand. For example, if I have 1000 shares of stock XYZ, and historical data suggests that it is not uncommon for the stock to drop by $1 per share in one day, I know I'm risking at least $1000 dollars.[1] I'm actually risking

---

1. I'm assuming that nothing catastrophic is going to happen to the stock and that I don't have a sell order pending.

more than that, because if I decided to sell it the day after it dropped $1 per share, the price may have dropped even further before I get my sell order in.

When you begin to consider the risk associated with a portfolio consisting of more than one stock, the risks are not nearly as straightforward. Now you have to take two things into consideration:

- The historical volatility of each stock's price
- The correlation in the price movements of each stock

The correlation in the price movements of stocks is the basis of modern portfolio theory, which suggests that you diversify your portfolio to reduce your risk. The whole idea here is that if you choose stocks whose prices are affected by different factors, or differently by the same factors, when the price of one of your stocks goes down, the price of another in your portfolio will probably hold its ground or even go up. One of the fundamental laws of risk is that when you reduce it, you should expect to make less money. In the case of a low-risk, diversified stock portfolio, you will never make a killing because when you make money in one of your stocks, you theoretically lose it in another.

When you are holding a portfolio of stocks and bonds, you can't lose more than you invest. Although losing everything you invest is a very uncomfortable feeling, one that I have personally experienced, many of new financial products called "derivatives" are designed such that you can lose much more than you originally invest (e.g., futures). The danger, and in some cases the reality, is that the worst possible outcome occurs and you don't have enough money to cover your losses (e.g., Barings PLC, Orange County). Determining the value you are risking with these types of investments can be extremely complicated, requiring calculations that take into consideration many factors.

Techniques for Monitoring Financial Risk

There are really two ways to monitor risk:

1. Set up an automated system that continuously reestimates the current levels of risk.
2. Create on-demand risk estimates based on a speculative risk scenario.

The first technique involves forecasting the probability distribution of the prices of instruments underlying the investments in your portfolio. Some feel that using historical data as a forecast of the future distribution is good enough for purposes of risk measurement. Others feel it is more accurate to develop a set of pricing models (e.g., Black-Scholes for options pricing) to calculate an expected distribution based on underlying market factors, forecast the movement of the market factors, and then calculate the distributions. The market factors themselves can be based on their own models or based on historical data. In summary, forecasting prices of instruments can be based strictly on historical data or on a combination of historical data and models (i.e., equations).

The other approach to monitoring risk is to speculate about the future movement of certain market factors and play out a scenario, involving a specific sequence of changes in such factors, to see what the potential loss could be if the scenario occurred. This technique most definitely depends on user-provided pricing models. A firm should probably employ both techniques when monitoring risk. This second technique fills a gap in the first one, because the first does not take into account aberrations in the financial markets.

Risk Factor Relationships

A risk factor is a variable that is used in a risk calculation. Systems that monitor risk must take into account the feedback relationships between risk factors, resulting in the nonlinear pricing models of many financial instruments. All risk monitoring systems must support feedback (see Figure 11-1).

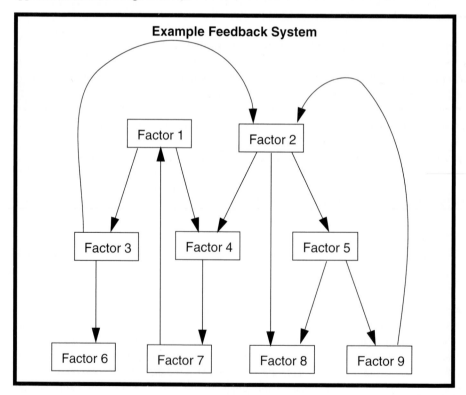

FIGURE 11-1.

Decomposition of Risk

When a risk manager is told the amount of risk that exists for a given portfolio, the first question he or she will ask is, "What factors contribute to this risk?" It seems logical to want to know what portion of the overall risk is attributed to each factor, so that appropriate risk reduction measures can be taken. A risk monitoring system must, therefore, provide a mechanism for determining the portion of a given risk that is attributable to each of the underlying causes (i.e., factors). This may involve at least two levels of correlation analysis. The first involves the historical correlation between the factors affecting the prices of the instruments in the portfolio. The second involves the historical correlation between the price movements of the instruments themselves. Obviously, the correlation between the underlying factors affects the correlation between the instrument prices themselves, but this does not translate in a straightforward way.

It is also assumed that if the value of one factor is modified, thereby changing the value of an investment position, the other factors affecting the value of that position may now have more or less influence over the value of that position. This is called derivative risk and complicates the process of determining how much risk should be attributed to each factor. It implies that the chronological order of factor changes affects the outcome of risk calculations and the portions of the risk that are attributed to each risk factor.

Because there are numerous methods for decomposing a risk into its component factors, a risk monitoring system must be flexible enough to easily allow users to plug in new ones. To illustrate why attribution of risk to causing factors is not straightforward, consider the following simple example. Assume that there is a position in an instrument currently valued by the formula $P(I,FX)$. The price risk associated with this instrument is attributable to two factors: interest rate I and a foreign exchange rate FX. Now assume that historical volatility predicts that there is a risk that I could change to I_{new}, FX could change to FX_{new}, and P could change to P_{new}. There are a number of problems that need to be dealt with. First, P_{new} will probably not equal $P(I_{new}, FX_{new})$, begging the question: Which is a realistic $Risk_{total}$? It is subjective, and therefore the risk monitoring system must be flexible enough to deal with either view.

Now, consider the following two inequalities:

$$P(I, FX_{new}) - P(I_{new}, FX_{new}) \neq P(I, FX) - P(I_{new}, FX)$$

$$P(I, FX) - P(I, FX_{new}) \neq P(I_{new}, FX) - P(I_{new}, FX_{new})$$

The first inequality shows potential values for $Risk_I$ (i.e., the risk associated with interest rate changes) and the second for $Risk_{FX}$. Which combination of the sides of the inequalities provide the best estimate of the risk attributable to each factor? One might choose the values on the left-hand side if it was felt that FX rate changes caused changes in I, the right-hand side values if it was felt that changes in I trigger changes in FX, and the upward sloping diagonal if they were deemed to be independent variables.

There is a third problem introduced by unexplained influences and the fact that risk factors are not perfectly correlated:

$$Risk_{total} \neq Risk_I + Risk_{FX}$$

How, then, does one properly decompose the total risk? One approach is to introduce two more terms, one to account for risk introduced by unknown factors ($Risk_{residual}$) and one that accounts for the fact that the risk factors are not perfectly correlated ($Risk_{unsystematic}$). Since total risk is reduced because I and FX are not perfectly correlated, $Risk_{unsystematic}$ is subtracted.

$$Risk_{total} = Risk_I + Risk_{FX} + Risk_{residual} - Risk_{unsystematic}$$

This may not be an acceptable view of a risk profile for some risk managers, especially if $Risk_{residual}$ is large. In this case, there are other options: add more factors until $Risk_{residual}$ becomes negligible; rationalize some division of $Risk_{residual}$ between the other two risk terms.

"Bucketing" Positions

There must be a way for management to determine the value of some arbitrary aggregation of positions. For example, it should be possible to request the firm's total exposure to Mexican securities, or floating rate cash flows to be received in the first quarter of next year, or the amount of money that is at risk for profit center X. It should then be possible for the user to iterate through this collection of positions.

When a risk manager is viewing an arbitrary aggregation of investment positions, we refer to these aggregations as *buckets*. A bucket is really the same thing as a portfolio that exists only for purposes of viewing risk by some arbitrary categorization.

Managing Large Numbers of Positions

Many types of instruments can comprise investment positions (350,000+). This creates two problems:

- It is very difficult to keep accurate time-series data for all such instruments.
- The models become far too complex.

To solve both problems, the real-life characteristics of positions will need to be transformed into a simpler model. The real-life set of positions is modeled as an equivalent set of "surrogate" positions in more general instruments. We take what is in reality a large number of instrument types, each with a few corresponding position instances, and transform that into a smaller number of instrument types, each with a larger number of position instances. Because there are fewer instruments, the number of required time series' is reduced.

A position can be transformed into one or more new positions. A case where it would be a one-to-one transformation would be when an equity is transformed into a Standard and Poors 500 equivalent. Also, it should be possible to trace back transformed positions to their original form; otherwise, risk managers will not know how to reduce specific exposures.

An example of the transformation process is converting a large number of bonds with similar characteristics into cash flows that can then be aggregated into buckets. Each bucket would contain the cash flows occurring within a specified time period. It also means that the risk manager can identify risk in a small number of buckets, as opposed to many individual bonds. Of course, after a bucket has been identified as a major source of risk, it should be possible to drill down to the underlying investments (i.e., bonds themselves).

Managing the Evolving Nature of Instruments

The price of an instrument may behave more like that of another instrument as time goes by. Consequently, the volatility of instruments may change over time. For example, a 15-year bond that is 13 years old will have a price that behaves like a 2-year bond. For purposes of risk measurement, it makes sense to use the historical volatility of 2-year bonds to calculate the risk of the 15-year bond that is 13 years old, rather than the historical volatility of 15-year bonds.

This must be accommodated in a risk monitoring system and will be done by employing the approach discussed in the previous section. Only now, the transformations are performed to account for natural evolution of an instrument.

Dealing with Incomplete Time-Series Data

More than one risk calculation methodology relies on the price history of instruments. What do you do if the methodology for determining the risk of a portfolio relies on the existence of one year of daily pricing history, and one of the instruments in the portfolio is only one week old? You have no choice but to use the history of a similar instrument that has been around for at least a year.

Summary of Background Discussion

There are numerous sources of information on how to measure, monitor, and manage financial risk. I've touched on a number of the more significant issues in this section. If you are interested in studying the topic further, I would recommend reading [RISK_METRICS95]. You can download it from JPMorgan's Web site (http://www.jpmorgan.com).

11.1.2 Glossary: Financial Risk Monitoring Domain

correlation – measure of the observed degree of similarity in the movement of two variables, calculated from two time series starting and ending at the same time.

instrument – a contractual agreement granting rights to the purchaser.

portfolio – a position that is an aggregation of one or more positions.

position – investor's ownership stake in something with an expected rate of return (i.e., an investment).

position value – present value of all expected future cash flows to be received by the holder of a position.

risk – a non-zero probability that a scenario will occur, the realization of which may negatively affect the expected returns of one or more positions (e.g., 5 percent chance that interest rates will rise by half a percentage point).

risk factor – abstraction with a numeric value. The value of one factor may depend on or affect the value of other factors.

scenario – a sequence of specific changes in the values of a set of factors.

time series – a sample of values, collected at a fixed interval over some period of time.

value at risk (VAR) – given a position that is subject to a specific risk, the position value that would be lost over a specified holding period, assuming that the risk is fully realized throughout this period.

volatility – measure of the amount of variability of a value over some time horizon.

11.1.3 Financial Risk Monitoring: Characteristics

1. Such systems shall support real-time monitoring of financial risk but shall work for non-real-time monitoring also.

2. There could be different types of financial instruments in a firm's portfolio. Positions could be frequently taken, modified, and liquidated.

3. The values of factors affecting the level of risk associated with positions could be constantly changing. The financial markets driving the risk calculations are feedback systems. To prevent infinite feedback loops, recalculation of risk shall be based on thresholding. In other words, recalculation shall not be triggered unless a particular factor affecting the calculation has changed by more than a prespecified amount.

4. New types of financial instruments could emerge and shall be easily introduced into the risk monitoring system. It shall be easy to "plug in" new equations for calculating risk.

5. Such systems shall be able to monitor the risk associated with any arbitrary aggregation of positions.

6. Such systems shall allow users to perform "what if" scenarios to determine the value at risk if a given scenario was to occur. The scenario could be of any duration. The result of playing out a risk scenario could result in a) a value at risk, b) no value at risk but lower than expected returns, c) higher than expected returns.

7. Some risk factors shall be independent and some shall be calculated, based on other risk factors.

8. When viewing the risk associated with a portfolio, it could be that you are only interested in some positions in that portfolio. In fact, you may only be interested in drilling down on one type of instrument.

9. Time-series data shall be critical to value at risk calculations.

10. In order for a risk manager to adjust a portfolio to reduce risk, he or she must know how to decompose a value at risk into the percentage that is attributed to each risk factor contributing to its calculation. Determining this is not straightforward and varies according to how the risk manager models the risk profile. A risk monitoring system shall provide a mechanism for determining the portion of a given risk that is attributable to each of the underlying causes (i.e., factors).

11. Such systems shall work for any level of risk monitoring, from the risk of holding a position in one stock to global risk, which is concerned with measuring the aggregate risk associated with all positions currently held by a firm.

12. The monitoring system itself shall not be responsible for the pricing models (i.e., equations), but shall be responsible for calling them either to recalculate a forecast of future price distributions or to play out a user-specified scenario.

13. A risk monitoring system shall allow for a portfolio consisting of many different types of instruments to be transformed into an estimated portfolio consisting of positions in a few instrument types. It shall also be possible to trace back transformed positions to their original form; otherwise, risk managers will not know how to reduce specific exposures.

14. The current date shall be available, as shall a mechanism that will trigger certain risk calculations on certain days.

15. There could be events that can force a change in risk. For example, "Bond XYZ Called" is an event that forces you to change your investment to cash, thereby changing your risk. Other examples of events are "War," "Election," "7/2/99," and "Sell."

16. There shall be a mechanism whereby risk factor entities can easily find other risk factor entities by name.

17. There shall be a mechanism to initialize a risk monitoring system and reinitialize it should one or more failures occur.

18. There shall be a mechanism to create a simulated environment by copying some of the real environment. This enables scenarios to be run.

19. If it is determined that the price of one instrument is highly correlated with the price of another, it could be taken as a surrogate for purposes of calculating value at risk, thereby reducing both the amount of data that needs to be stored and the amount of time required to recalculate value at risk. In fact, due to the enormous number of instrument types, this "data multiplexing" shall be necessary in order to achieve satisfactory performance.

20. Missing data and outliers shall be dealt with in the statistics associated with a time series.

21. The correlation between two time series (e.g., instrument prices) shall be taken into consideration when calculating the risk associated with a portfolio.

22. Many standard statistical equations are used in risk calculations. Although the risk monitoring system shall not be directly responsible for implementations of risk calculations, it shall provide the basic algorithms generally used in such calculations, such as covariance and standard deviation.

Facets

I have identified a number of facets but am not going to engage in a detailed analysis of each. Below are the initially discovered characteristics of each new facet. I also offer some suggestions for possible implementations.

- **Time**

  1. There shall be a mechanism that allows the user to register an interest in being notified when a particular date/time occurs, and that mechanism shall provide the current date.

Implementation suggestion: If the CORBA Time service [RFP3] is not available, you can simply employ the OBSERVER pattern with THRESHOLDING, where the Subject state is the current date. This would make a nice little component. You will probably also want to employ the PERSISTENT DATA MANAGER pattern to store currently attached Observers and the specification of when they want to be notified.

- **Event Notification**

Implementation suggestion: Event notification can be implemented by applying the OBSERVER pattern.

- **Naming**

  1. There shall be a mechanism whereby entities in the system can easily find other entities in the system by name.

Implementation Suggestion: Look into using an implementation of the CORBA Naming Service [COSS94].

- **Life Cycle**

  1. There shall be a mechanism to initialize a distributed object system (i.e., instantiate objects), and reinitialize it should one or more failures occur.
  2. There shall be a mechanism to copy distributed objects.

Implementation suggestion: Look into using an implementation of the CORBA Life Cycle Service [COSS94]. The problem that must be addressed by this facet, for this particular problem domain, is how to manage a distributed environment with positions being constantly created and deleted and the ever-changing set of financial instruments that must be monitored for risk. It is also important to be able to make deep copies of positions to create an environment in which risk scenarios can be simulated.

- **Data Translation**

  1. There shall be a mechanism to facilitate the translation of data from one form into another.

Implementation suggestion: The INTERPRETER pattern is very useful for solving this type of problem.

- **Statistics**

  1. There shall be a set of algorithms for well-known statistical calculations, such as covariance and standard deviation.

Implementation suggestion: Use the GENERIC ALGORITHM pattern for all algorithms identified. See example for standard deviation presented in Chapter 2.

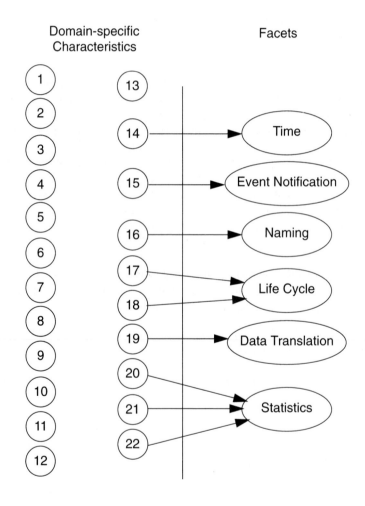

11.2 Design of the Risk Monitoring Framework

The framework will be designed to enable the organization to measure, in real time, the risks associated with any aggregation of positions, regardless of the underlying instruments. The framework shall be designed to do this in a way that is independent of the type of risk factors and the risk calculations. In other words, the framework does not predefine specific risks, calculations, or specific instrument types. Instead, the framework can be extended to suit evolving business needs.

With all the facets factored out, we now have a more reasonably sized problem to tackle. Our goal is to provide the domain-specific piece of the risk monitoring problem into the design of this framework.

I decided that there will be no management of persistent data performed by this framework. Most of the data that would be persistent relates to positions. This type of data management is normally associated with "back office" systems that handle the bookkeeping, rather than the type of systems in which this framework would be used, which are "front office" and deal more with the decision making that leads to the establishment of a certain set of positions. Position information will be cached in the objects of framework classes. The onus will be put upon the application programmer to write the code that reports updates in position information to these objects. In other words, that programmer will write the code that "glues" the back-office, position-management systems to the front-office, risk monitoring system, by reading their databases and then translating data into a form that is understood by the framework.

Initialization and disaster recovery are largely dependent on the applications and are not the responsibility of the framework, although support for each is provided in part by the Life Cycle Facet.

Framework Name Financial Risk Monitoring

Framework Type Vertical

Requirements Please refer to section 11.1.3.

Structure

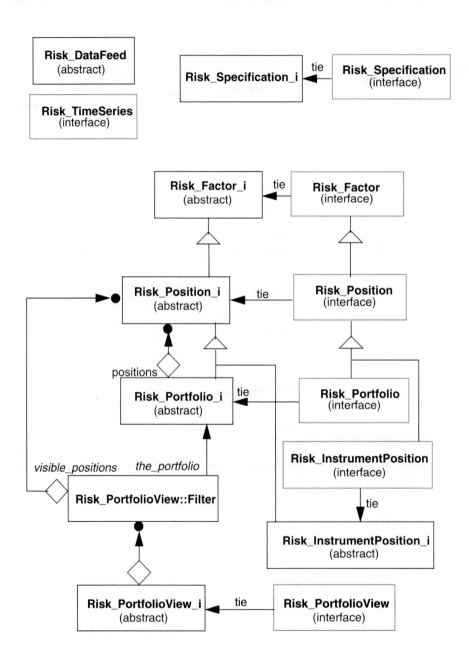

Typical Object Configuration

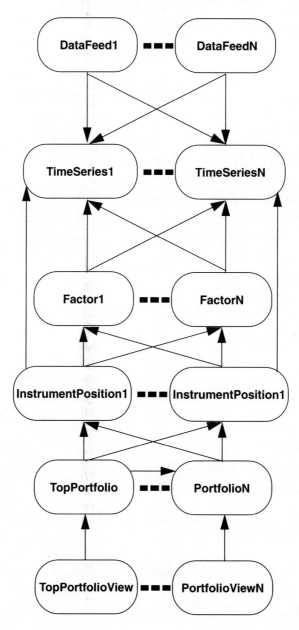

Pattern Used	Role	Role Played By
BLACKBOARD	*Subject*	Risk_TimeSeries
BLACKBOARD	*Blackboard*	provided by framework user
BLACKBOARD	*DataAnalyzer*	Risk_Factor_i
BLACKBOARD	*Data*	map<string,float>
COMPOSITE[a]	*Component*	Risk_Position
COMPOSITE	*Leaf*	Risk_InstrumentPosition
COMPOSITE	*Composite*	Risk_Portfolio
CORBA-FRIENDLY CLASS	*Server*	Risk_Factor
CORBA-FRIENDLY CLASS	*Server_i*	Risk_Factor_i
CORBA-FRIENDLY CLASS	*Server*	Risk_Position
CORBA-FRIENDLY CLASS	*Server_i*	Risk_Position_i
CORBA-FRIENDLY CLASS	*Server*	Risk_Portfolio
CORBA-FRIENDLY CLASS	*Server_i*	Risk_Portfolio_i
CORBA-FRIENDLY CLASS	*Server*	Risk_InstrumentPosition
CORBA-FRIENDLY CLASS	*Server_i*	Risk_InstrumentPosition_i
CORBA-FRIENDLY CLASS	*Server*	Risk_Specification
CORBA-FRIENDLY CLASS	*Server_i*	Risk_Specification_i
OBSERVER	*Subject*	Risk_Specification
OBSERVER	*Subject_i*	Risk_Specification_i
OBSERVER	*Observer*	Risk_Factor
OBSERVER	*Observer_i*	Risk_Factor_i
OBSERVER	*Subject*	Risk_Portfolio
OBSERVER	*Subject_i*	Risk_Portfolio_i
OBSERVER	*Observer*	Risk_PortfolioView
OBSERVER	*Observer_i*	Risk_PortfolioView_i
SPECIFICATION-ENGINE	*Specification*	Risk_Specification
SPECIFICATION-ENGINE	*Engine*	all concrete classes derived from Risk_Factor_i
DETAIL FILTERING	*DataManager*	Risk_Portfolio
DETAIL FILTERING	*Data*	Risk_Position
DETAIL FILTERING	*DataFilter*	Risk_PortfolioView::Filter
DETAIL FILTERING	*DataView*	Risk_PortfolioView
THRESHOLDING	*Thresholder*	Risk_Factor

Pattern Used	Role	Role Played By
THRESHOLDING	*ValueObserver*	Risk_Factor
THRESHOLDING	*Thresholder_i*	Risk_Factor_i
THRESHOLDING	*ValueObserver_i*	Risk_Factor_i

a. pattern from [PATTERNS95]

Participants

- `Risk_DataFeed`
  - Each class derived from this class will likely have one instance, responsible for reading data from a data feed and forwarding it to one `Risk_TimeSeries` interface for storage.
  - Each piece of data is assumed to be a single numeric value with a timestamp.

- `Risk_TimeSeries`
  - Interface used for storing simple numeric time-series data, such as instrument prices or interest rates.
  - The implementation may store the data transiently, or persistently using: a PERSISTENT DATA MANAGER that is CORBA-FRIENDLY, a flat file or a legacy database wrapper. It all depends on the nature of the data being stored and the application in which the framework is being used.

- `Risk_Factor`
  - Interface to `Risk_Factor_i` class. May be used as the interface to a wide variety of risk factor implementations.

- `Risk_Factor_i`
  - Abstract class for risk factors.
  - Intended to capture one time-stamped numeric value that depends on other risk factors or time-series data.
  - Derived class provides implementation that calculates or sets the value of the factor.
  - Enables other risk factors (i.e., Observers), to be updated when its value has changed by an amount specified by the Observer in a threshold specification string assumed to conform to the following grammar:

```
Trigger  ::=   Expr [or Expr]
Expr     ::=   increased | decreased To | By
To       ::=   to Number
By       ::=   by Number[%] [from original]
Value    :=    Number[%]
Number   ::=   [0-9]*[\.[0-9]*]
```

- When created, an object of this class should attach to the `Risk_Factors` and `Risk_TimeSeries` that are needed to determine its value. It should then initialize its value.

- `Risk_Factor_i` objects that require the values of other `Risk_Factor_i` and `Risk_TimeSeries` objects should create the ones they need but that don't yet exist.

- When a `Risk_Factor_i` object has received a `detach()` from all its Observers, it should remove itself. Its destructor should detach itself from all Subjects that it is observing (i.e., `Risk_Factor` and `Risk_TimeSeries` interfaces).

• `Risk_Specification`

- Interface for `Risk_Specification_i`.

• `Risk_Specification_i`

- One object per *runtime namespace* (runtime namespace is explained in the description of the object naming convention to follow).

- Concrete class that contains two variables that must be used in all risk calculations in a given context: probability and time horizon.

- An object of this class must be created before any `Risk_Position` in the same runtime namespace.

• `Risk_Position`

- Interface for `Risk_Position_i`, derived from `Risk_Factor`.

• `Risk_Position_i`

- Abstract class.

- One `Risk_Position_i` object represents one position taken by the firm monitoring its risk.

- Every `Risk_Position` object has a value (inherited from `Risk_Factor_i`), a value at risk (VAR), and a decomposition of VAR into the amount that can be attributed to each relevant risk factor. All three of these are initialized at construction and recalculated with each update.

- All `Risk_Position_i` objects are required to attach to a `Risk_Specification`, because all will calculate risk, which requires the variables that can be obtained through such an interface. This normalizes risk values across a position hierarchy.

• `Risk_InstrumentPosition`

- Interface for `Risk_InstrumentPosition_i`.

- `Risk_InstrumentPosition_i`
  - Type of `Risk_Position_i` representing a firm's position in one type of instrument (e.g., IBM stock).
  - Defined by the quantity of instrument units being held (e.g., 1000 shares).

- `Risk_Portfolio`
  - Interface for `Risk_Portfolio_i`.

- `Risk_Portfolio_i`
  - Type of `Risk_Position_i` representing an aggregation of other positions.
  - Positions in a portfolio can be either positions in individual instruments or smaller portfolios.
  - Relies on an external Position Management System to add and remove positions.
  - A portfolio value is calculated in a straightforward manner by adding up the values of the constituent positions.

- `Risk_PortfolioView`
  - Interface for `Risk_PortfolioView_i`.

- `Risk_PortfolioView_i`
  - Abstract class.
  - A class derived from this is intended to provide the risk manager's view(s) into the current risk profile of the firm.
  - The derived class implementation "hooks" into the GUI (i.e., this would be the *View* in the Model-*View*-Controller model often used by GUI toolkits).
  - Through a portfolio view, a user can view all risk associated with a particular portfolio or just that associated with certain instrument types.
  - Attaches to its associated `Risk_Portfolio`; this is its only attachment. When it attaches, it should specify a threshold of 0, because you can't conclude anything about the relevance of the size of a change in a portfolio to its view.
  - When a `Risk_PortfolioView_i` object is constructed, the full portfolio is visible.
  - Used for "bucketing" positions.

- `Risk_PortfolioView_i::Filter`
  - Used by `Risk_PortfolioView_i` to allow the user to view the risk associated with only certain instrument types.

Collaborations

I am now going to present three primary usage scenarios. You can assume that they occur chronologically.

Adding an InstrumentPosition to a Portfolio[1]

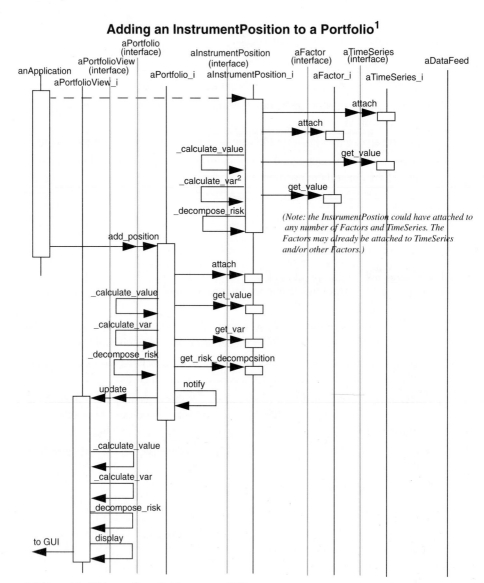

(Note: the InstrumentPostion could have attached to any number of Factors and TimeSeries. The Factors may already be attached to TimeSeries and/or other Factors.)

---

1. I dropped the Risk_ prefix so that the names will fit.
2. May involve getting multiple `Risk_Factor` values and will definitely require retrieving probability and time horizon requirements from the `Risk_Specification` object in the same runtime namespace.

Recalculating the Portfolio's Risk[1]

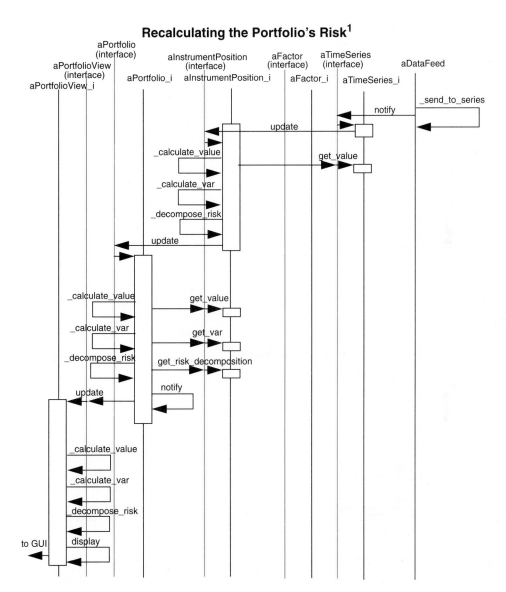

1. Risk needs to be recalculated if 1) a position is added, 2) a position is removed, 3) a position is changed, 4) a risk factor affecting one or more instruments in a portfolio changes, or 5) a new price quote for an instrument in the portfolio is received from a data feed. For this scenario, we will assume the trigger condition is 5.

Removing an InstrumentPosition from the Portfolio

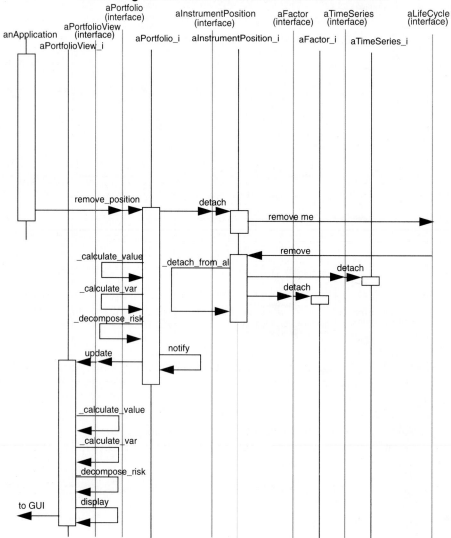

Object Naming Convention

Related to collaborations is the object naming convention used in the framework, which enables objects in the framework to find each other in a CORBA environment. There must be a convention for uniquely naming each object participating in the risk monitoring application. What we will do is start by defining the following IDL types, which closely match those defined for the CORBA Naming Service [COSS94]. This will make it very easy to use an implementation of the Naming Service, but does not make the framework dependent on it. The types are as follows:

```
typedef string Risk_NameComponent;
typedef sequence <Risk_NameComponent> Risk_Name;
```

Risk_Name allows you to express a name as a hierarchy of components, much like a set of filenames in a file system (e.g., "/home/rogers/project/src/Foo.C"). Now that we have this type, I will explain how it shall be used by the framework classes and application code added by the framework user. An object name shall be specified in a Risk_Name consisting of at least two Risk_NameComponents:

- Its runtime namespace
- Its most derived framework interface name (e.g., "Risk_Factor," "Risk_Portfolio").

These components should be sequenced in this order. If there is only one instance of a given interface, then no other components are required. If there are many, then at least a third component will be required to uniquely identify each.

An object's *runtime namespace* is just a string used to partition objects engaging in the same type of behavior into different groups.[2] In general, objects should only interact with other objects in the same runtime namespace. The reason that a runtime namespace is so important to this framework is because of the desire to run scenarios. In order to run a scenario, we need to be able to copy an entire web of interconnected Risk_Factor objects and artificially propagate changes in the variables that affect risk. A reasonable way to accomplish this is to define a new runtime namespace and have all the copied objects attach to each other in this new namespace.

Consider a Risk_Factor that keeps the standard deviation of the daily price changes of AT&T stock for the past year. When this object registers itself with a naming service, it may uniquely identify itself with six naming components: "Primary", "Risk_Factor", "StandardDeviation", "Daily", "NYSE", and "ATT". As you can see, the naming convention can be extended. For example, it may be desirable to keep two Risk_TimeSeries objects for each stock, one for end of day (i.e., closing) prices and the other for real-time intra-day pricing. So, the lower components of the name would have to distinguish the two (e.g., "CLOSE", "NYSE", "IBM", and "LIVE", "NYSE", "IBM"). Only the application will understand this level of semantics and which types of Risk_TimeSeries implementations should be used in a given circumstance.

---

2. This is different from a C++ namespace. Sorry if this causes confusion, but I couldn't think of better term to describe it.

Design Details

```
class Risk_DataFeed
{
  public:
    Risk_DataFeed(const Risk_Name&);
  protected:

      // the following will be called by the implementation of the
      // class derived from Risk_DataFeed (e.g., ReutersFeed).
    _send_to_series(const Risk_Name& series_name, float value,
                const string& the_date);

    const Risk_Name name;
};
```

LISTING 11-1.

```
struct Risk_DVPair {
    string the_date;
    float value;
};

typedef sequence<Risk_DVPair> Risk_Series;

interface Risk_TimeSeries
{
    void attach(in Risk_Factor f);
    void detach(in Risk_Factor f);

        // The notify function is generally called by a Risk_DataFeed
        // object when a new piece of data has been retrieved.
        // Observers shall be updated when notify is called.
    void notify(in float value,in string the_date);
    Risk_Series get_series(in string start_date, in string end_date);
    float get_value(in string the_date);
};
```

LISTING 11-2.

```
interface Risk_Factor {

    void attach(in Risk_Factor f, in string threshold_spec);
    void detach(in Risk_Factor f);
    void update(in string the_date, in Risk_Name name, in float value)
    float get_value();
    Risk_Name get_name();
};
```

LISTING 11-3.

```
class Risk_Factor_i {
  public:
    Risk_Factor_i(const Risk_Name&);
    virtual ~Risk_Factor_i()    {_detach_from_all();}
   virtual void attach(Risk_Factor_var, const char* threshold_spec,
                        CORBA_Environment&);
    virtual void detach(Risk_Factor_var, CORBA_Environment&);
    virtual void update(const char* the_date, const Risk_Name& name,
                   float value, CORBA_Environment &) = 0;
    float get_value(CORBA_Environment&);
    Risk_Name* get_name(CORBA_Environment&);
  protected:

      // will attach to combination of TimeSeries and Risk_Factors.
    void _attach_to(const Risk_Name&);
    void _detach_from_all();
    virtual void notify();

    Risk_Name name;
    float value;
};
```

LISTING 11-4.

```
interface Risk_Specification {
    void attach(in Risk_Factor f);
    void detach(in Risk_Factor f);
    attribute float probability;
    attribute short time_horizon;
};
```

LISTING 11-5.

```
class Risk_Specification_i {
  public:
    Risk_Specification_i(const Risk_Name&);
    void attach(Risk_Factor_var, CORBA_Environment&);
    void detach(Risk_Factor_var, CORBA_Environment&);
    void probability(float, CORBA_Environment&);
    float probability(CORBA_Environment&) const;
    void time_horizon(short days, CORBA_Environment&);
    short time_horizon(CORBA_Environment&) const;
  protected:
        // name is either "probability" or "time horizon".
    void notify(const string& name, float value);
    float the_probability;
    short the_time_horizon;
};
```

LISTING 11-6.

```
struct Risk_NVPair {
    string risk_type;
    string amount;
};

typedef sequence<Risk_NVPair> Risk_Set;

interface Risk_Position : Risk_Factor {
    float get_value_at_risk();
    Risk_Set  get_risk_decomposition();

};
```

LISTING 11-7.

```
class Risk_Position_i : public Risk_Factor_i {
  public:
      Risk_Position_i(const Risk_Name&,
                         const string& parent_portfolio_name);

          // following updates position value, var and determines
          // breakdown of risk.
      virtual void update(const char* the_date,
                            const Risk_Name&, float value,
                            CORBA_Environment &);
      float get_value_at_risk(CORBA_Environment&) const;
      Risk Set* get_risk_decomposition(CORBA_Environment&);

  protected:
      virtual void _calculate_value(char* the_date,
                         const Risk_Name&, float value) = 0;
      virtual void _calculate_var(char* the_date,
                         const Risk_Name&, float value) = 0;
      virtual void _decompose_risk(char* the_date,
                         const Risk_Name&, float value) = 0;
      float var;
      map<string,float, less<string> > risks;
      const string parent_portfolio_name;
};
```

LISTING 11-8.

```
interface Risk_InstrumentPosition : Risk_Position {
      attribute float quantity;
};
```

LISTING 11-9.

```
class Risk_InstrumentPosition_i : public Risk_Position_i {
  public:
      Risk_InstrumentPosition_i(const Risk_Name&,
                              const string& parent_portfolio_name);
      void quantity(float, CORBA_Environment&);  // calls update()
      float quantity(CORBA_Environment&);
  protected:
      float the_quantity;
};
```

LISTING 11-10.

```
typedef sequence<Risk_Position> Risk_PositionSet;
interface Risk_Portfolio :  Risk_Position {
     void attach1(in Risk_PortfolioView pv);
     void add_position(in Risk InstrumentPosition p);
     void remove_position(in Risk InstrumentPosition p);
     Risk_PositionSet get_positions();
  };
```

LISTING 11-11.

```
class Risk_Portfolio_i : public Risk_Position_i {
  public:
    Risk_Portfolio_i(const Risk Name&,
                    const string& parent_portfolio_name);
    void attach1(Risk_PortfolioView_var, CORBA_Environment&);
    void add_position(Risk_InstrumentPosition_var,
                    CORBA_Environment&);
    void remove_position(Risk InstrumentPosition_var,
                     CORBA_Environment&);
    Risk_PositionSet* get_positions(CORBA_Environment&) const;
  protected:
    void _calculate_value(char* the_date,const Risk_Name&,float val);
    void notify(); // must update PortfolioViews and Risk_Factors
    vector<Risk_Position_var> positions;
};
```

LISTING 11-12.

```
enum Risk_ChangeType {added, modified, removed};

interface Risk_PortfolioView
{
    void view_only(in string instrument_name);
    void add_to_view(in string instrument_name);
    void remove_from_view(in string instrument_name);
    void update(in Risk_Position changed_position,
                in Risk_ChangeType type);
};
```

LISTING 11-13.

```
class Risk_Filter {
        Risk_Portfolio_var the_portfolio;
        vector<Risk_Position_var> visible_positions;
        float value;
        float var;
        map<string,float,less<string> > risks;
};

class Risk_PortfolioView_i
{
  public:
    Risk_PortfolioView_i(const Risk_Name& portfolio_name);

            // each of the following will explore the current
            // portfolio profile and set up the filters accordingly.
    void view_only(const string& instr_name, CORBA_Environment&);
    void add_to_view(const string& instr_name,CORBA_Environment&);
    void remove_from_view(const string& instr_name,
                          CORBA_Environment&);
    virtual void update(Risk_Position_var changed_position,
                        Risk_ChangeType, CORBA_Environment &);
  protected:
    void _calculate_value(Risk_Position_var changed);
    virtual void _calculate_var(Risk_Position_var changed) = 0
    virtual void _decompose_risk(Risk_Position_var changed) = 0;
    virtual void display() = 0;

    const Risk_Name portfolio_name;
    vector<Risk_Filter> filters;
};
```

LISTING 11-14.

Requirements Verification

	Risk monitoring characteristic	How the framework supports characteristic
1	Such systems shall support real-time monitoring of financial risk but shall work for non-real-time monitoring also.	Extensive use of the OBSERVER pattern or a variation of it.
2	There could be different types of financial instruments in a firm's portfolio. Positions could be frequently taken, modified, and liquidated.	The `Risk_Portfolio` interface supports adding and removing positions. The `InstrumentPosition` interface allows modifying quantity.
3	The values of factors affecting the level of risk associated with positions could be constantly changing. The financial markets driving the risk calculations are feedback systems. To prevent infinite feedback loops, recalculation of risk shall be based on thresholding. In other words, recalculation shall not be triggered unless a particular factor affecting the calculation has changed by more than a prespecified amount.	The THRESHOLDING pattern is used in the design of `Risk_Factor_i`.
4	New types of financial instruments could emerge and shall be easily introduced into the risk monitoring system. It shall be easy to "plug in" new equations for calculating risk.	`Risk_InstrumentPosition_i` is abstract. The functions for calculating risk are pure virtual.
5	Such systems shall be able to monitor the risk associated with any arbitrary aggregation of positions.	The COMPOSITE pattern [PATTERNS95] is applied to accomplish this.
6	Such systems shall allow users to perform "what if" scenarios to determine the value at risk if a given scenario was to occur. The scenario could be of any duration. The result of playing out a risk scenario could result in a) a value at risk, b) no value at risk but lower than expected returns, c) higher than expected returns.	The naming convention is such that separate risk worlds can be created with the help of the Life Cycle facet. The scenarios can be run with fake data feeds and cloned copies of portfolios.
7	Some risk factors shall be independent and some shall be calculated, based on other risk factors.	Implementations of the `Risk_TimeSeries` interface will contain externally acquired values, which are essentially the independent factors. `Risk_Factor_i` objects contain the dependent ones.

	Risk monitoring characteristic	How the framework supports characteristic
8	When viewing the risk associated with a portfolio, it could be that you are only interested in some positions in that portfolio. In fact, you may only be interested in drilling down on one type of instrument.	The DETAIL FILTERING pattern is applied through the `Risk_PortfolioView_i` class.
9	Time-series data shall be critical to value at risk calculations.	The `Risk_TimeSeries` interface is used by the `Risk_Factor_i` objects, which perform the risk calculations.
10	In order for a risk manager to adjust a portfolio to reduce risk, he or she must know how to decompose a value at risk into the percentage that is attributed to each risk factor contributing to its calculation. Determining this is not straightforward and varies according to how the risk manager models the risk profile. A risk monitoring system shall provide a mechanism for determining the portion of a given risk that is attributable to each of the underlying causes (i.e., factors).	`Risk_Position_i::_decompose_risk ()` is a pure virtual function that the framework guarantees will be called at appropriate times.
11	Such systems shall work for any level of risk monitoring, from the risk of holding a position in one stock to global risk, which is concerned with measuring the aggregate risk associated with all positions currently held by a firm.	The combination of COMPOSITE and OBSERVER are the two biggest influences in supporting this.
12	The monitoring system itself shall not be responsible for the pricing models (i.e., equations), but shall be responsible for calling them either to recalculate a forecast of future price distributions or to play out a user-specified scenario.	THRESHOLDING is used to propagate recalculation of risk numbers.

	Risk monitoring characteristic	How the framework supports characteristic
13	A risk monitoring system shall allow for a portfolio consisting of many different types of instruments to be transformed into an estimated portfolio consisting of positions in a few instrument types. It shall also be possible to trace back transformed positions to their original form; otherwise, risk managers will not know how to reduce specific exposures.	Supported by the Data Translation facet.
14	The current date shall be available, as shall a mechanism that will trigger certain risk calculations on certain days.	Supported by the Time facet.
15	There could be events that can force a change in risk. For example, "Bond XYZ Called" is an event that forces you to change your investment to cash, thereby changing your risk. Other examples of events are "War," "Election," "7/2/99," and "Sell."	Supported by the Event Notification facet.
16	There shall be a mechanism whereby risk factor entities can easily find other risk factor entities by name.	Supported by the Naming facet.
17	There shall be a mechanism to initialize a risk monitoring system and reinitialize it should one or more failures occur.	Supported by the Life Cycle facet.
18	There shall be a mechanism to create a simulated environment by copying some of the real environment. This enables scenarios to be run.	Supported by the Life Cycle facet.
19	If it is determined that the price of one instrument is highly correlated with the price of another, it could be taken as a surrogate for purposes of calculating value at risk, thereby reducing both the amount of data that needs to be stored and the amount of time required to recalculate value at risk. In fact, due to the enormous number of instrument types, this "data multiplexing" shall be necessary in order to achieve satisfactory performance.	Supported by a combination of the Data Translation facet and the design and implementation of classes derived from `Risk_Factor_i`.

	Risk monitoring characteristic	How the framework supports characteristic
20	Missing data and outliers shall be dealt with in the statistics associated with a time series.	Supported by algorithms in the Statistics facet.
21	The correlation between two time series (e.g., instrument prices) shall be taken into consideration when calculating the risk associated with a portfolio.	Supported by the covariance algorithm provided with the Statistics facet.
22	Many standard statistical equations are used in risk calculations. Although the risk monitoring system shall not be directly responsible for implementations of risk calculations, it shall provide the basic algorithms generally used in such calculations, such as covariance and standard deviation.	Supported by the Statistics facet.

Sample Code and Usage

All of the framework classes, with the exception of Risk_Specification_i, are abstract. All of the abstract classes are intended to be derived from. The derived classes are all expected to add value by providing implementations of one or more pure virtual member functions. An inheritance hierarchy in an application using this framework might look like the one shown on the next page. There will typically be one class derived from Risk_Portfolio_i and one from Risk_PortfolioView_i, because these derived classes are where you put the logic that normalizes the view of risk throughout the firm. The user of the framework must provide implementations of derived classes, using the assets provided for each of the facets. The facets become important to the application developer primarily when it comes to implementing risk calculations. The facets provide basic components for implementing the calculation algorithms, without dictating the details of how to calculate the risk.

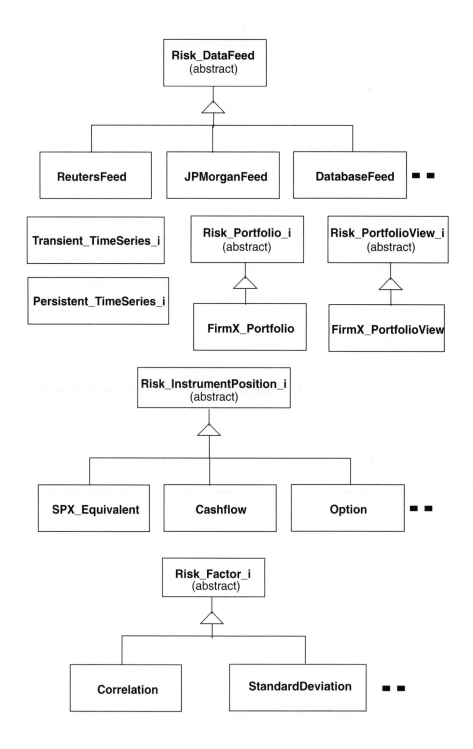

The following are some additional usage recommendations:

- Regarding the origin of raw data used in risk calculations: there is a lot of public data available for such things as the volatility of instrument prices and market indexes, and correlation between them. The most widely known source is the RiskMetrics™ Datasets available daily from JPMorgan's Web site (http://www.jpmorgan.com/ RiskMetrics/RiskMetrics.html). But, every firm must decide how much faith to put in one dataset, primarily because its availability is out of the firm's control, and also because it is free and could at some point either be charged for or discontinued. In addition, when many millions of dollars are at stake, it is prudent to confirm the data from a second source, which might mean calculating the statistics yourself from a data source with raw data that you have scrubbed to your firm's standards. There may also be time series data of risk factors that no one else tracks but that are vital to a firm's proprietary models.

- Application developers must use good judgement when deciding what to attach to what, and the size of the thresholds. Otherwise, there may be an excessive amount of recalculation or race conditions from feedback loops. To appreciate the sensitivity to this, consider the following. A `Risk_Portfolio_i` object attaches to three `Risk_Factors`: 1) InstrumentPosition A, 2) InstrumentPosition B, and 3) Correlation A-B. When either A's or B's price changes, the value, VAR, and decomposition of the portfolio's risk might be recalculated, depending on the thresholds set for each instrument price change. The price changes may affect the correlation value between their price movements to the point where a third recalculation is performed. This third calculation should not be much of a problem, however, since correlation values are probably only updated once a day, when markets close.

- It may make sense to design your `update` function to be smarter than the default implementation, which always recalculates everything. For example, if you know that all Correlations are recalculated after the market closes, you can attach to each Correlation that affects the Portfolio, setting the threshold to 0, which will cause the Correlation object to update the Portfolio object after it is recalculated, regardless of whether or not the value changes. When the `update` is received for the first Correlation value affecting your portfolio, don't recalculate until you receive updates from all the others that also affect your portfolio. This way, you recalculate once at the end of the day, instead of potentially multiple times.

- Your single, best, performance-tuning mechanism is the thresholding of updates. You should provide a way to control the thresholds of `Risk_Factors` at runtime, if for no other reason than to deal with calculation meltdown when the financial markets go into a frenzy. They shut down programmed trading on Wall Street for similar reasons.

The following Perl program will "lint"[1] C++ programs that use STL. Two types of mistakes are checked for. One type of mistake is not detectable by the compiler. It is the passing of a combination of illogical arguments to the STL template functions for algorithms. The other type of mistake will actually cause compiler errors, but because they are template related, the errors will not remotely indicate the actual problem.

The first type of mistake is less likely to occur, but if it does, who knows what the consequences will be? Most of the template functions for algorithms operate on a collection of objects kept in a container and require a start iterator and end iterator as the first two input arguments. The potential mistake is that the iterators passed are for different containers. Running this script as part of the build process is an alternative to introducing "helper" classes as a technique to try to prevent this mistake. A helper class wraps the algorithm by taking one container argument and then calling the algorithm with the begin and end iterators for that container. The problem with helper classes is that people can still forget to, or choose not to, use the helper classes and end up making the mistake. If this program is used as a screen during builds, on the other hand, the mistake will never be overlooked. You also don't have to confuse the programmer with another layer of classes.

The second type of mistake occurs when a container template is instantiated to contain a type that doesn't have the minimum required member functions. This script will collect a list of all types to be kept in containers, by scanning all the .C and .H files in both the

---

1. `lint` is a program that we used to run on C source code to point out potential flaws.

source and header directories. It will then search the header file directory for class declarations corresponding to these types. When it finds one, it will check to see if the class contains 1) a copy constructor, 2) a default constructor, 3) operator=, 4) operator==, and 5) operator<. If any of these are missing, either an error or a warning is printed. Both the copy constructor and assignment operator are required for all types of containers, so if either of these is missing, it is definitely an error. The equivalence operator and less than operator are sometimes required, so a warning is reported if either of these is missing. It is also a good idea to provide a default constructor with all classes, so a warning is printed if one is not explicitly provided.

To use this script, simply specify the source and header file directories as input arguments, respectively. The script will scan all `.C` and `.H` files for violations. Consider the two UNIX files: `/home/gfr/include/FooFum.H` and `/home/gfr/source/main.C`, shown in Panel A-1 and Panel A-2. Assuming that these are the only two files in their respective directories, invoking `stl_lint.pl` on these files results in the output shown in Panel A-3.

The source code for `stl_lint.pl` is shown in Panel A-4. Be warned that I'm not exactly a Perl wizard. Although I did test this script, I can't guarantee the accuracy of the results. I should also mention that this program can be enhanced by the ambitious. For example, I always print warnings when a class is missing any of the five member functions mentioned above. You could make it smarter by only printing an error for not having `operator<` if objects of the class are kept in a container that required ordering.

Panel A-1
FooFum.H

```
class Foo {
    public:
        Foo();
        Foo(const Foo&);
        operator=(const Foo&);
        operator==(const Foo&);
        operator<(const Foo&);
};

class Fum {
    public:
        Fum();
        Fum( const Fum& );
};
```

Panel A-2
main.C

```
    :
sort(v1.begin(),v1.end());
copy(v1.begin(),v2.end(),v3); // this is line 11.
sort(v1.begin());             // compiler will nail this.
copy(v1->begin(),v1->end(),v3);
sort(v1->begin(),v2->end());  // this is line 14.

vector<Foo>  v4;
vector<int>  v5;
vector<Fum>  v6;
    :
```

Panel A-3
stl_lint output

```
$stl_lint.pl /home/gfr/source /home/gfr/include
source directory: /home/gfr/source
include directory: /home/gfr/include
/home/gfr/source/main.C, line 11:,arg 1 and 2 inconsistent for copy
/home/gfr/source/main.C, line 14:,arg 1 and 2 inconsistent for sort
The following types are kept in containers:
Foo
int
Fum
Now verifying class declarations for completeness
Checking Foo
Checking Fum
Error:   Fum has no operator=(const Fum&)
Warning: Fum has no operator==(const Fum&)
Warning: Fum has no operator<(const Fum&)
$
```

Panel A-4
stl_lint.pl source listing (page 1)

```perl
#!/usr/local/bin/perl -w
###########################################################################
# Script Name: stl_lint.pl                                                #
###########################################################################
&main();

sub main
{
    $#ARGV == 1 || die "usage: stl_lint sourcedir includedir";
    print "source directory: $ARGV[0]\n";
    print "include directory: $ARGV[1]\n";
    $LS = "ls $ARGV[0]/*.C $ARGV[1]/*.H  |";
    if(open(LS, "$LS"))
    {
        while ($nextfile = <LS>)
        {
            chop $nextfile;
            if(open(CURRENTFILE,$nextfile))
            {
                while(<CURRENTFILE>)
                {
                    &check_all_algorithms();
                    &collect_class_names();
                    close(CURRENTFILE);
                }
            }
            else
            {
                die "can't open file: $nextfile, error: $!";
            }
        }
    }
    else
    {
        die "can't list files\n";
    }
    @keys = keys %cnames;
    local($key);
    print "The following types are kept in containers:\n";
    foreach $key (@keys)
    {
        print "$key\n";
        $ccnt++;
    }
    {
        print "Now verifying class declarations for completeness\n";
        &check_class_declarations();
    }
}
```

Panel A-4 (continued)
`stl_lint.pl` source listing (page 2)

```perl
#####################################################################
#    The following function verifies that the first two arguments   #
#    of all relevant STL algorithms refer to the same object.       #
#####################################################################
sub check_all_algorithms
{
    &check_alg_args("accumulate");
    &check_alg_args("adjacent_difference");
    &check_alg_args("adjacent_find");
    &check_alg_args("binary_search");
    &check_alg_args("copy");
    &check_alg_args("copy_backward");
    &check_alg_args("count");
    &check_alg_args("count_if");
    &check_alg_args("equal");
    &check_alg_args("equal_range");
    &check_alg_args("fill");
    &check_alg_args("fill_n");
    &check_alg_args("find");
    &check_alg_args("find_if");
    &check_alg_args("for_each");
    &check_alg_args("generate");
    &check_alg_args("generate_n");
    &check_alg_args("includes");
    &check_alg_args("inner_product");
    &check_alg_args("inplace_merge");
    &check_alg_args("itoa");
    &check_alg_args("iter_swap");
    &check_alg_args("lexicographical_compare");
    &check_alg_args("lower_bound");
    &check_alg_args("make_heap");
    &check_alg_args("max_element");
    &check_alg_args("merge");
    &check_alg_args("min_element");
    &check_alg_args("mismatch");
    &check_alg_args("nth_element");
    &check_alg_args("partial_sort");
    &check_alg_args("partial_sort_copy");
    &check_alg_args("partial_sum");
    &check_alg_args("partition");
    &check_alg_args("pop_heap");
    &check_alg_args("prev_permutation");
    &check_alg_args("push_heap");
    &check_alg_args("random_shuffle");
    &check_alg_args("release");
    &check_alg_args("remove");
    &check_alg_args("remove_copy");
```

Panel A-4 (continued)
`stl_lint.pl` source listing (page 3)

```perl
    &check_alg_args("remove_copy_if");
    &check_alg_args("remove_if");
    &check_alg_args("replace");
    &check_alg_args("replace_copy_if");
    &check_alg_args("replace_if");
    &check_alg_args("reverse");
    &check_alg_args("reverse_copy");
    &check_alg_args("rotate");
    &check_alg_args("rotate_copy");
    &check_alg_args("search");
    &check_alg_args("set_difference");
    &check_alg_args("set_intersection");
    &check_alg_args("set_symmetric_difference");
    &check_alg_args("set_union");
    &check_alg_args("sort");
    &check_alg_args("sort_heap");
    &check_alg_args("stable_partition");
    &check_alg_args("stable_sort");
    &check_alg_args("transform");
    &check_alg_args("unique");
    &check_alg_args("unique_copy");
    &check_alg_args("upper_bound");
}

#########################################################################
#    The following function collects names of classes that have        #
#    been instantiated in some kind of container. They are kept         #
#    in the associative array "cnames". The key is the class name       #
#    and the value is set to 1.                                         #
#########################################################################

sub collect_class_names
{
    while(/\svector\<(.+)\>/g)         {$cnames{$1}=1;}
    while(/\sbit_vector\<(.+)\>/g)     {$cnames{$1}=1;}
    while(/\sdeque\<(.+)\>/g)          {$cnames{$1}=1;}
    while(/\slist\<(.+)\>/g)           {$cnames{$1}=1;}
    while(/\smultiset\<(.+)\>/g)       {$cnames{$1}=1;}
    while(/\sset\<(.+)\>/g)            {$cnames{$1}=1;}
    while(/\smultimap\<(.+)\>/g)       {$cnames{$1}=1;}
    while(/\smap\<(.+)\>/g)            {$cnames{$1}=1;}
    while(/\sstack\<(.+)\>/g)          {$cnames{$1}=1;}
    while(/\squeue\<(.+)\>/g)          {$cnames{$1}=1;}
    while(/\spriority_queue\<(.+)\>/g) {$cnames{$1}=1;}
}
```

Panel A-4 (continued)
stl_lint.pl source listing (page 4)

```
############################################################################
#    The following function checks the arguments passed to an             #
#    algorithm function. It checks to see if the objects specified        #
#    as the first and second argument are the same. If they are           #
#    not, a warning is printed. The reason is that the first two          #
#    arguments represent beginning and end iterators. If they             #
#    are not for the same object, this is illogical.                      #
############################################################################
sub check_alg_args
{
    local($alg_fcn) = @_;
    while(/\s$alg_fcn\((.+)(\.|->)(.+),(.+)(\.|->)(.+)/g)
    {
        if($1 ne $4)
        {
            print("$nextfile, line $.:");
            print(",arg 1 and 2 inconsistent for $alg_fcn\n");
        }
    }
}
############################################################################
#    The following function verifies that the declarations of the        #
#    classes, whose names are the keys in the cnames associative          #
#    array, contain the minimum required member functions to be           #
#    kept in an STL cotainer.NOTE:Doesn't handle nested classes.          #
############################################################################
sub check_class_declarations
{
  $LS1 = "ls $ARGV[1]/*.H  |";
  if(open(LS1, "$LS1"))
  {
    while ($nextfile = <LS1>)
    {
      chop $nextfile;
      if(open(CURRENTFILE,$nextfile))
      {
        while(<CURRENTFILE>)
        {
          $cpy_constructor= 0; # required
          $dft_constructor= 0; # good idea
          $assignment_op= 0;   # required
          $equivalence_op= 0;  # sometimes required
          $lessthan_op= 0;     # sometimes required
          $c = NULL;
```

Panel A-4 (continued)
`stl_lint.pl` source listing (page 5)

```perl
        if(/^class\s(\w+)\s/)
        {
          if($cnames{$1} == 1)
          {
            &check_next_class();
            if($cpy_constructor == 0)
            {
              print "Error:   $c has no $c(const $c&)\n";
            }
            if($assignment_op == 0)
            {
              print "Error:   $c has no operator=(const $c&)\n";
            }
            if($equivalence_op == 0)
            {
              print "Warning: $c has no operator==(const $c&)\n";
            }
            if($lessthan_op == 0)
            {
              print "Warning: $c has no operator<(const $c&)\n";
            }
            if($dft_constructor == 0)
            {
              print "Warning: $c has no $c()\n";
            }
          }
        }
      }
    }
  }
}
```

Panel A-4 (continued)
stl_lint.pl source listing (page 6)

```perl
###########################################################################
#    This function assumes that we have just entered a class              #
#    declaration. It checks the declaration for a copy constructor,       #
#    default constructor, operator=, operator==, and operator<.           #
#    For those that are present, a flag will be set.                      #
###########################################################################

sub check_next_class
{
    print "Checking $1\n";
    $c = $1;
    $rcnt = 0;
    $lcnt = 0;
    while(/{/g)
    {
        $lcnt++;
        $inbody = 1;
    }
    while(/}/g)
    {
        $rcnt++;
    }

    while(<CURRENTFILE>)
    {
        while(/{/g) {$lcnt++; $inbody = 1;}
        while(/}/g) {$rcnt++;}
        if($inbody == 1 && $lcnt>$rcnt)
        {
          if(/^\s*$c\(\s*const\s$c&.*\)/)        {$cpy_constructor++:}
           if(/^\s*$c\(\s*\)/)                   {$dft_constructor++;}
            if(/^\s*operator=\(\s*const\s$c&.*\)/) {$assignment_op++;}
             if(/^\s*operator==\(\s*const\s$c&.*\)/){$equivalence_op++;}
              if(/^\s*operator<\(\s*const\s$c&.*\)/) { $lessthan_op++;}
        }
        elsif($inbody == 1 && $lcnt==$rcnt)
        {
            return;
        }
    }
}
```

APPENDIX B
Notation

I am not a purist when it comes to OO modeling. I believe that if you know your implementation constraints during the design phase, you shouldn't pretend that you don't. The modeling notation that is used in this book reflects this philosophy by going a little beyond what is typically viewed as pure modeling notation. It contains implementation-specific implications, for example, whether the class is persistent. Implementation constraints may become vaguely apparent even in domain analysis but become obvious very early on in a design.

Class Diagram Legend

The legend for graphical symbols used in this book are shown in the following table. It is a mixture of OMT, the notation used in [PATTERNS95], and additions that I made to represent things that just weren't captured in either of these. All words in italics will be replaced with words that are specific to that which is being modelled.

Notation	Meaning
(*ObjectName*)	Represents an object.
[*ClassName*]	Represents a class without showing any members.
ClassName *fcn1()* *fcn2()*	Represents a class, showing only member functions. Each function is shown as a subset of a legal C++ function signature. If a return code is not shown, then it is unspecified. Not all arguments are necessarily shown either, only those that are known at the time. If the type of an argument is not known, its name may be shown alone.
ClassName *fcn1()* *fcn2()* *attr1* *attr2*	Represents a class, showing member functions and attributes. Attributes may be specified in C++ declaration syntax or just have their names specified if the type is not known.
InterfaceName (interface)	Represents a CORBA class. You can use the same syntax as a class box for functions and attributes.
ClassName (persistent)	Represents a persistent class. You can use the same syntax as a class box in all other respects.
ClassName (abstract)	Represents an abstract class. Same syntax as class box in all other respects.
[*Foo*] —ref→ [*Bar*]	A *Foo* object references exactly one *Bar* object. *ref* is the name of the data member in a Foo object that keeps the reference to the *Bar* object.

Notation	Meaning
	A *Foo* object references exactly one *Bar* object, but a *Bar* object can be referenced by zero or more *Foo* objects.
	A *Foo* object references zero or more *Bar* objects, and a *Bar* object is referenced by exactly one *Foo* object.
	A *Bar* object is a part of a *Foo* object.
	A *Foo* object is an aggregation of zero or more *Bar* objects. *bars* is the name of the collection in a *Foo* object that keeps the references to the *Bar* objects that are a part of it.
	A *Foo* object instantiates a *Bar* object.
	A *Bar* is derived from *Foo*.
	An arrow should be drawn from an interface box to each class that provides an implementation of that interface. The arrow should be labeled with the word "tie" to indicate that it is possible for a tie object (not shown) to delegate calls received by a CORBA object to an object of the class pointed to. Please note that the only arrows that will ever leave an interface box will be those labeled "tie."
	This is how to show an object referencing another object. The arrow depicting the reference originates next to the attribute that stores the reference (NOTE: the dot on the originating end has nothing to do with cardinality).

Notation	Meaning
  aFoo *collection* ● ↓ ● *aBar* 	This shows an object (*aFoo*) with a *collection* element that contains references to *Bar* objects.
⟶	In a pattern description, if a reference is drawn lightly, this indicates a reference from a class that is not actually participating in the pattern.
▪ ▪ ▪	This indicates repeat. If you see this between two class boxes, this means that there are many similar classes. If you see it between two objects, this indicates many similar objects.
aBar *aFoo_i* *aFoo* (interface) *aClient* fcn fcn new	This is an Object Interaction Diagram (OID), which shows objects as vertical lines, and a call to a function depicted as an arrow from the caller to the callee. The function names appear on the arrow, with or without arguments. Object names appear above the vertical lines. The convention for naming an object is to prefix the associated class name with "a". Time increases as you descend the diagram. When an object's member function is called, the period of activation is shown as a rectangle. Return indications are not shown. An instantiation is shown as a dotted arrow. Before an object is instantiated, it is shown as a dotted vertical line. CORBA objects will appear with "(interface)" under their names. In addition, the vertical line representing a CORBA object will be a lighter shade than that of a regular object. Last, because the CORBA objects are simply a conduit, activation time is never indicated for a CORBA object.
PATTERN	An entire pattern may be shown as a box with a lightly shaded border and the name of the pattern (all caps) in the upper part of the box. The classes participating in the pattern may be shown within the border of the box.

Notation	Meaning
	This shows an object named *aFoo* in a database.
	This shows an object named *aFoo* in an executing process.
	State Transition Diagram syntax is taken from OMT [OMT92]. Unfortunately, states are represented by essentially the same shape as objects, so don't let this confuse you.

Bibliography

[ANNOTC++92] Stroustrup, Bjarne and Ellis, Margaret A. *The Annotated C++ Reference Manual*. Addison-Wesley, 1990.

[ANSIC++96] American National Standards Institute (ANSI), Working Paper for Draft Proposed International Standard for Information Systems-Programming Language C++. January 26, 1996.

[COPLIEN92] Coplien, James O. *Advanced C++ Programming Styles and Idioms*. Addison-Wesley, 1992.

[CORBA95] The Object Management Group. *The Common Object Request Broker: Architecture and Specification*. Rev 2.0, July 1995.

[CORBA_GUIDE95] Ben-Natan, Ron. *CORBA - A Guide to Common Object Request Broker Architecture*. McGraw-Hill, 1995.

[COSS94] *Common Object Services Specification*, V. I, Object Management Group, March 1, 1994.

[DICTIONARY85] *The American Heritage Dictionary*. Houghton Mifflin Company, Boston. 1985.

[ELLEMTEL92] Henricson, Mats, and Erik Nyquist. *Programming in C++—Rules and Recommendations*. Ellemtel Telecommunication Systems Laboratories, April 1992.

[FINANCE90] Pinches, George E. *Essentials of Financial Management*. 3rd Ed. HarperCollins. 1990.

[INFOWORLD96] "Object spec wakes up Web," *INFO WORLD*, August 26, 1996.

[JODA93] Holibaugh, Robert. Joint Integrated Avionics Working Group (JIAWG) *Object-Oriented Domain Analysis Method (JODA)* .Ver. 1.3, Nov. 1993, Software Engineering Institute, Carnegie Mellon University, Publication Number CMU/SEI-92-SR-3.

[JONES91] Jones, Capers. *Applied Software Measurement - Assuring Productivity and Quality*. McGraw-Hill, Inc., 1991.

[0295] *ODMG C++ Binding Guide*. O2 Technology, Inc., 1995.

[OBJECTSPACE95] *STL<Toolkit> (TM) User Guide*. ObjectSpace, Inc.,1995.

[ODMG93] *The Object Database Management Group. ODMG-93*. Ver. 1.2, Morgan Kaufmann Publishers, 1995.

[OMT92] Rumbaugh, James, Michael Blaha, William Premerlani, Frederick Eddy, and William Lorensen. *Object Oriented Modeling and Design*. Prentice-Hall, 1991.

[ORBIX95] *Orbix 2 Programming Guide*. Iona Technologies Ltd., 1995.

[OSA95] *Object Services Architecture*, Rev. 8.1, Object Management Group, January 12, 1995.

[PATTERNS95] Gamma, Erich Richard Helm, Ralph Johnson, and John Vlissides. *Design Patterns Elements of Reusable Object-Oriented Software*. Addison-Wesley, 1995.

[PRIETO91] Prieto-Diaz, R. "Reuse Library Process Model." Technical Report AD-B157091, IBM CDRL 03041-002, STARS, July 1991.

[STL95] Stepanov, Alex, and Meng Lee. *The Standard Template Library*. Hewlett-Packard Laboratories, 1995.

[STYLE79] Strunk, William, Jr., and E.B. White. *The Elements of Style*. MacMillan Publishing Co. 1979.

[RISK_METRICS95] Guldimann, Till M. RiskMetrics ™ — Technical Document, 3rd Ed. JPMorgan, May 26, 1995.

[STALLINGS93] Stallings, William. *Networking Standards - A Guide to OSI, ISDN, LAN and MAN Standards*. Addison-Wesley. 1993.

Index

Boldface page reference numbers designate pages of principal discussion.